ARCHAEOLOGY AND ORAL
TRADITION IN MALAWI

ARCHAEOLOGY AND ORAL TRADITION IN MALAWI

Origins and early
history of the Chewa

Yusuf M. Juwayeyi

UCT
PRESS

JC JAMES CURREY

Archaeology and oral tradition in Malawi: Origins and early history of the Chewa

First published in South Africa 2020
by UCT Press, an imprint of
Juta and Company (Pty) Ltd
PO Box 14373, Lansdowne 7779, Cape Town, South Africa
www.uctpress.co.za

First published in hardback
and Africa-only paperback edition (excluding South Africa) 2020
by James Currey, an imprint of Boydell & Brewer Ltd
PO Box 9, Woodbridge, Suffolk IP12 3DF, UK
and of Boydell & Brewer Inc.
668 Mt. Hope Avenue, Rochester NY 14620-2731, USA
website: www.boydellandbrewer.com

© 2020 UCT Press

ISBN 978 1 77582 249 3 (UCT Press paperback)
ISBN 978 1 77582 250 9 (UCT Press Web PDF)
ISBN 978 1 84701 253 1 (James Currey hardback)
ISBN 978 1 84701 254 8 (James Currey Africa-only paperback)

The publisher has no responsibility for the continued existence or accuracy of URLs for external or third-party internet websites referred to in this book, and does not guarantee that any content on such websites is, or will remain, accurate or appropriate

This book has been independently peer-reviewed by academics who are experts in the field.

A CIP record for this title is available from the British Library

For my wife Elsie Lexa Namulauzi
and in memory of my parents
McDadlly Juwayeyi and Edina Juwayeyi

CONTENTS

PREFACE

This book is a comprehensive account of the origins and early history of the Chewa who began to refer to themselves as 'A Malawi' (the Malawi) at some point after they arrived in the southern Lake Malawi area. Seventeenth-century Portuguese explorers and traders recorded the term as 'Maravi' whereas modern scholars use 'Maravi' interchangeably with the term 'Chewa'.

Some readers will undoubtedly be surprised that an archaeologist rather than a historian has written this book. They should bear in mind though that archaeology is the only tool available for unearthing (literally) history and culture before any written records. Archaeologists call that time the pre-historic period and that is where the narration of the origins and early history of the Chewa begins. It ends about two decades before the imposition of colonial rule by the British in 1891.

Before delving into the narration, here is a synopsis of the intellectual journey that has brought me to this point. During the first few decades of the colonial period, the British attempted to record the oral traditions of the various indigenous groups in the country, perhaps with a view towards understanding their history. They published nothing from the exercise and any history taught in the country's schools was the history of the British themselves. In primary school, the favourite topics included Dr David Livingstone's exploration of the country and of other parts of southern Africa. Pupils also learned about the efforts of early Scottish missionaries to establish mission stations and schools, and about the arrival in Malawi of early British traders and settlers. The traders established the African Lakes Company, a trading company that locally assumed the name Mandala, meaning 'spectacles' (a fascination to the local people), worn by one of the joint managers, John Moir.[1]

In secondary school, students came face to face with the history of the British Empire and the Commonwealth. Teachers drilled them in this history so well that some of those students still vividly recall important events in British colonial history. Perhaps what is unfortunate is that they can intelligently discuss events such as the Boston Tea Party, the Black Hole of Calcutta incident, the Anglo-Boer war and others better than they can the arrival of the Chewa at Mankhamba, or of the Tumbuka, Yao or Ngoni in various parts of the country.

Not long after Malawi became independent of colonial rule, the book *Mbiri ya Achewa* (*The History of the Chewa*), written by Samuel Josia Ntara, was introduced as required reading in secondary schools.[2] It is now out of print, but it is the only book that

---

1   Kalinga OJM & Crosby CA. 2001. *Historical Dictionary of Malawi*. Lanham, MD: The Scarecrow Press: 234.
2   Richard Grey Kankondo, the author's secondary school Chichewa teacher, personal communication, 7 January 2019.

has ever been published on the history of the Chewa. Still, the fact that teachers used the book not in a history class, but in a Chichewa language class, is indicative of how education authorities regarded it. They viewed it as a Chichewa literature book and not as a history textbook. Perhaps the intention of the authorities was to make students appreciate Chichewa as spoken in central Malawi. Ntara was a Chewa from that region, as was the president at the time, Hastings Kamuzu Banda. Four years after Malawi became an independent country, the president made Chichewa the country's national language. The school I attended was located in southern Malawi, where the common language is Chinyanja. The majority of the students were not used to Chichewa and, consequently, did not enjoy reading the book. However, as a budding archaeologist I enjoyed reading it and it was in this book that I first learned that a place called Mankhamba was said to be the original settlement site of the Chewa.

Ntara's book was based on oral traditions. This is also true regarding almost everything that is available on the history and culture of the Chewa. Scholars simply arranged to interview people in various Chewa villages after which they analysed the information and disseminated the results. Unfortunately, the most comprehensive of those studies resulted in unpublished doctoral theses, none of which is available for general reading.

When I went to study at at the University of Malawi's Chancellor College, I found that nothing much seemed to have changed regarding the kind of history offered to students. The only difference was that this time it was not by design. There were simply no resources available to enable even the most enthusiastic lecturers to create a good course on the history of Malawi before the colonial period. Instead, they taught students about the history of Portuguese settlement and the colonisation of Mozambique, American history, the slave trade, and the conflict between the British and the Dutch in South Africa. When it came to Malawi, they taught only the well-documented story of John Chilembwe's 1915 uprising against colonial rule and other topics related to the colonial period. Nevertheless, I graduated, majoring in History (albeit not Malawi's) and Sociology. Subsequently, I joined the Malawi Department of Antiquities which is where I had my first contact with archaeology.

Unlike historians, archaeologists are unlikely to record oral traditions, unless they are convinced that the traditions will significantly clarify some aspects of their archaeological data. Success in archaeology depends on locating suitable archaeological sites. I needed to locate either the site of Mankhamba or any suitable sites in the various areas where the Chewa had settled. In fact, I would have been perfectly satisfied with any settlement site of the early Chewa, but God in the heavenly skies was smiling on me. I located the site of Mankhamba itself. I excavated it and recovered a wide range of material remains, including imported material such as glass beads, Chinese porcelain and objects made of copper.

The material remains that archaeologists recover are objects that people made or acquired, used and then discarded or abandoned after use. In other words, the objects had become garbage, as the people no longer needed them. Producing garbage has been an aspect of human behavior throughout history and archaeologists are in the business of looking for places where the ancient people lived or threw away their garbage. When they find such places, they dig them up in a systematic manner. To the archaeologist, the objects recovered in the excavations are no longer garbage but important material remains. After recovering them, the next step is to make the remains 'speak' or tell their story. This is achieved by the careful study and analysis of the material remains so that their story is brought to a level that is discernible even to non-archaeologists. That is exactly what I did with the material remains that I excavated at Mankhamba. Among other things, they show that the Chewa lived a good and prosperous life and that their way of life made them economically, politically and militarily powerful. As a result, they were able to expand their area of influence so widely that Portuguese settlers of the early seventeenth century were compelled to refer to their king as the Emperor of the 'empire of Maravi'.[3]

What to expect

Realising that many readers may not have sufficient knowledge regarding the history of research into Malawi's past, how archaeologists do their work, and the environment of the research area, I have provided that information in Chapter 1 and in Chapters 5–7.

Chapter 1 discusses the efforts of early European explorers, missionaries and settlers in recording Malawi's history. The chapter begins by listing Malawi's major ethnic groups and the initial attempts to record their oral traditions and some aspects of indigenous life. When the country became a British colony, colonial district administrators did the same in their respective districts. The later part of the colonial period witnessed the emergence of indigenous scholars. Some of them recorded the oral traditions of their respective ethnic groups and proceeded to write books about their histories. Ntara was one of them.

Soon after Malawi became an independent country in 1964, the newly established University of Malawi and the Malawi government initiated efforts to develop professional cultural heritage personnel. They identified young Malawian college graduates and sent them abroad to study History, Archaeology or Museum Management. Some of them acquired doctoral degrees and on returning home, they embarked on various research projects in history and archaeology.

Chapter 5 is about the practice of archaeology itself, but this is discussed in a non-technical way. Readers with little or no knowledge of archaeology will find this chapter enlightening, as — among other things — it discusses how archaeologists locate and

---

3   Barretto M. 1964. Report upon the State and Conquest of the Rivers of Cuama. In *Records of South-Eastern Africa*. Vol. 3. GM Theal (ed). Cape Town: Struik: 480.

excavate sites, and analyse the material they recover. There is also a section in which I discuss some of the dating methods, such as carbon-14 (C-14) dating. This chapter will give readers enough archaeological knowledge to enable them to appreciate and enjoy the chapters that follow.

Chapter 6 discusses the archaeological research that various researchers carried out in the southern Lake Malawi area before the discovery and excavation of the Mankhamba site. All the sites they investigated were Iron Age sites, which led me to discuss the importance of pottery in Iron Age archaeological research. It is pertinent to point out that details about the Iron Age archaeology of the southern Lake Malawi area have been published extensively and so archaeologists are familiar with this. The area has an unbroken Iron Age pottery sequence dating from the early third century to the nineteenth century, when the current modern pottery began to emerge.

In Chapter 7, I discuss the environment of the Mankhamba area, which migrants like the Chewa found attractive for settlement. Also discussed in that chapter is the archaeological survey that led to the discovery of the Mankhamba site and the excavation itself. The results of the analysis and the interpretation of the material remains are the central foci of the rest of the book.

LIST OF MAPS, PLATES, FIGURES AND TABLES

MAPS

PLATES

FIGURES

TABLES

ACKNOWLEDGEMENTS

I would not have accomplished this work on my own. I relied on the assistance of professional and technical staff from the Malawi Department of Antiquities, colleagues in various local and international organisations, and my family. I wholeheartedly acknowledge their assistance and I would like them to be proud that their support has resulted in this book.

I thank Alfred Topeka for being a reliable lead technician during my fieldwork. He was the lead technician in both the field and the laboratory. Alfred not only supervised other technicians in my absence, he also handled various administrative responsibilities and hence ensured that the research progressed uninterrupted. Special recognition goes to the Director of Museums and Monuments, Elizabeth Gomani-Chindebvu, for the initial mapping of the site. I am also indebted to Chrissy Chiumia, head of the Malawi Department of Antiquities, for sorting out various administrative details that contributed to the smooth running of my research. I appreciate too the assistance of the following present and past staff of the Department of Antiquities: Medson Makuru, Martin Chikonda, Mathias Zalinga Phiri, Adriana Lizi, CG Chapotera and posthumously, Kamwadi Moyo, Simon Chikapa, Selino Mithi, Stanley Mphaya, Beston Kayira and Chalakwa Mwenda.

I would like to thank two members of staff of the Malawi Department of Surveys, Mkondo Moyo and Felix Tembo, for mapping the site using GPS technology and drawing the figures in Chapter 7, and Herbert Chihana, then a college student, for his participation in the project.

I must extend my special gratitude to the following colleagues whose expertise in their respective fields gave a deeper insight into my research. I thank Owen Kalinga for his encouragement and prompt responses to my various queries. Spana Davison, thank you for your helpful comments on Mawudzu pottery and some of the iron objects, and for drawing the figures in Chapters 8–10. Bennet Bronson, I also thank you for both identifying the Chinese porcelain and for your comments regarding their age and area of origin in China. Marilee Wood, I greatly appreciate your work in identifying and analysing the glass beads. David Killick, thank you for identifying the sole object made of lead. Karin Scott and Ina Plug, you agreed to work on a large faunal assemblage. Thank you.

I thank Alisa Yalan-Murphy, Stuart Alleyne and Puja Shah of Long Island University (LIU), Brooklyn New York, for helping me with computer-related tasks. Alisa and Puja, your patience was commendable. Although the task of revising figures appeared endless, you maintained exceptional professionalism. I thank Hyacinth Reneau, also of LIU, Brooklyn, for typing some of the tables in Chapters 8–10.

I am grateful to Fr Claude Boucher, of Kungoni Centre of Culture and Art at Mua Catholic Mission, for taking Alfred Topeka and me to Mpando wa Nyangu — Mankhamba's ritual water pool — and for the full-board accommodation at the Centre. I also thank Group Village Headman Kafulama of the Mtakataka-Mua area for welcoming us to his village. His support made our interaction with the local people easy.

Some members of my family provided various forms of assistance and I am grateful to all of them. I thank my mother-in-law Phyllis Chipendo who, besides providing accommodation, always made me packed lunches whenever I went out to the field. I appreciate the cheerful and warm welcome of my sister-in-law, Philadelphia Ambali, and her husband George who hosted me in their house for many days. I thank my sister, Phyllis Neniwa, and her husband Anthony for letting me use their truck to travel to my laboratory at Nguludi, and my brother, Daudi Juwayeyi, for shedding light on various ethnographic questions. I am grateful to my daughter, Atuweni-tupochile, and her husband Kabass Agbermodji for putting their car and their guest room at my disposal, and their children — my grandchildren Talia Chipo and Azariah Pambone — for the pleasure they have always given me whenever I am in their home. I thank my sons, Murendehle Mulheva and Kalole Kamasile, for their encouragement. Murendehle, you read the entire book and some chapters twice. I truly appreciate your editorial skills. Kalole, thank for your computer expertise. You rescued me several times when I was stuck.

Finally, yet importantly, I thank my wife Elsie Lexa Namulauzi for her understanding. I was absent from home for many months, but she was patient and encouraging. Since she studied history, she was eager to see the history of the Chewa written.

Financial Support

I am grateful to various organisations and individuals for their financial support. Besides procuring camp, excavation and laboratory equipment, the Malawi Department of Antiquities also provided transport and paid wages to locally hired assistants. The British Institute in East Africa, through the Department of History at Chancellor College, provided funding for initial field investigations and, later, for faunal identification and analysis. The Vine Group through its president, Henry Akintunde, provided additional funds to finalise faunal analysis and for an air ticket to Malawi and South Africa. Hildi Hendrickson, former chairperson of the Department of Sociology and Anthropology, and David Cohen, former Dean of Conolly College at LIU, Brooklyn, approved funds for carbon-14 dates. Last, but not at all least, my colleague, Timothy Bromage, of the College of Dentistry at New York University, and my friend, Gary Allen, president of the Christian Mission for the United Nations Community, gave generous financial support for one of my trips to Malawi. This project would not have been accomplished without this support. I am truly grateful.

Figures, Maps and Plates

Acknowledgement is extended to the following for permission to reproduce figures, maps and plates. Figures 6.1, 6.2a, 6.3, 6.4, 6.5, 6.6 and Map 6.1, Plates 6.1 and 12.1: Malawi Department of Antiquities; Figures 7.1, 7.2; 8.1, 8.2, 8.3, 8.4, 8.5, 8.6, 9.1, 9.2, 10.1; Plates 8.1, 8.2, 9.1; Tables 7.1, 7.2, 8.1, 8.2, 9.1, 9.2: Taylor & Francis; Tables 10.2, 10.3: Ditsong National Museum of Natural History.

CHAPTER 1

Introduction

In this book, archaeological evidence has been used to re-examine the origins and early history of the Chewa, Malawi's largest ethnic group. Much of the evidence has come from the archaeological site of Mankhamba, located in the southern Lake Malawi area.[1] Until now, scholars have documented the history of the Chewa largely through using oral traditions.[2] Many sources of the traditions agree that Mankhamba was the place where the king of the Chewa, whose title was Kalonga, established his major settlement many centuries ago. The author was fortunate to discover this site, the excavation of which has helped clarify the early history of the Chewa and has shed some light on other aspects of their way of life.

The earliest of the written documents on Malawi go back to the sixteenth century.[3] Some adventurous Portuguese explorers and traders who periodically passed through central and southern Malawi as they sought minerals and other resources in the interior of the region wrote these documents. In their reports home, they sometimes mentioned the places they had passed through and described some of the people they had seen or met.[4] It is from such accounts that historians first read about the 'Maravi' people. The term 'Maravi' was the Portuguese rendering of the term 'Malawi', by which the Chewa referred to themselves.[5] It is also from such records that historians were able to crosscheck the accuracy of oral traditions about Kalonga and other Maravi kings

---

1   Juwayeyi YM. 2010a. Archaeological excavations at Mankhamba, Malawi: An early settlement site of the Maravi. *Azania: Archaeological Research in Africa*. 45 (2): 175–202.

2   Rangeley WHJ. 1952. Two Nyasaland rain shrines. *The Nyasaland Journal*. 5(2); Marwick MG. 1963. History and Tradition in East Central Africa through the Eyes of the Northern Rhodesian Cewa. *The Journal of African History*, 4; Hamilton RA. 1955. Oral tradition: central Africa. In *History and Archaeology in Africa*. RA Hamilton (ed). London: School of Oriental and African Studies; Ntara SJ. 1973. *The History of the Chewa (Mbiri ya Achewa)*. Translated by WS Kamphandira Jere. Wiesbaden: Franz Steiner Verlag GMBH; Langworthy HW. 1969. A history of Undi's kingdom to 1890: aspects of Chewa history in east central Africa. PhD thesis. Boston University; Langworthy H. 1973. Introduction and chapter comments. In *The History of the Chewa*. SJ Ntara. Translated by WS Kamphandira Jere. Wiesbaden: Franz Steiner Verlag GMBH; Phiri KM. 1975. Chewa history in central Malawi and the use of oral tradition, 1600–1920. PhD thesis. University of Wisconsin, Madison; Schoffeleers, JM. 1973. Towards the identification of a proto-Chewa culture: a preliminary contribution. *Journal of Social Science*. 2; Schoffeleers JM. 1978. Nyau symbols in rock paintings. In *Rock Art and Nyau Symbolism in Malawi*. NE Lindgren & JM Schoffeleers. (Department of Antiquities publication no. 18) Limbe, Malawi: Montfort Press; Schoffeleers JM. 1992. *River of Blood: The Genesis of a Martyr Cult in Southern Malawi, c. A.D. 1600*. Madison, WI: University of Wisconsin Press; McFarren WE. 1986. History in the land of flames: the Maravi states of pre-colonial Malawi. PhD thesis. University of California, Berkeley.

3   Theal GM. 1964. *Records of South-Eastern Africa*. Vol 3. Cape Town: Struik.

4   Bocarro A. 1964. Of the performance of the Portuguese in east Africa. In *Records of South-Eastern Africa*. Vol 3. GM Theal (ed). Cape Town: Struik. Barretto 1964.

5   Ntara 1973: 15.

such as Lundu. Some of the Portuguese also described the nature of local villages and towns[6] but very little else.

Because there was not much in these documents to enable historians to reconstruct the history of the Chewa or of any other ethnic group, they resorted to recording oral traditions. Of the more than a dozen ethnic groups in Malawi, historians mostly recorded the oral traditions of the Chewa. This was probably because the Chewa or the 'Maravi' were the most mentioned of Malawi's ethnic groups in the Portuguese documents and this gave historians a good starting point for understanding them and their history.

Malawi's major ethnic groups

The 2018 Malawi Population and Housing Census Main Report[7] shows that Malawi has 12 major ethnic groups and several smaller ones (see Map 1.1). Out of a national population of about 17.5 million people, the Chewa totalled a little over 6 million or 34.4 per cent, thus over one third of the total population. The next four most populous ethnic groups were the Lhomwe at 18.9 per cent, the Yao at 13.3 per cent, the Ngoni at 10.4 per cent, and the Tumbuka at 9.2 per cent. Seven other ethnic groups had fewer than one million people each. They are, in descending order based on their population, the Sena, Mang'anja, Nyanja, Tonga, Nkhonde, Lambya and Sukwa.

The separation of the Chewa, Nyanja and Mang'anja from one another in the census main report is interesting because they all speak dialects of Chinyanja, the language of the Nyanja. The dialectical variation among them is, however, so minor that foreigners, and even some local people, fail to distinguish the three languages. In Malawi, when the name of an ethnic group or tribe is preceded by the letters 'Chi,' it denotes the language spoken by that ethnic group. It follows that the Chewa speak Chichewa; the Nyanja, Chinyanja; the Tumbuka, Chitumbuka and so on. This attribute is evidenced in some other Bantu languages, as in Kenya, through the use of 'ki': the language of the Kamba is Kikamba.

The dialectical differences emerged due to the geographical isolation of the three ethnic groups, which has been in place for a long time. The Chewa are the major ethnic group in the central region of the country and the Nyanja live on the Shire Highlands in southern Malawi, specifically the districts of Thyolo, Blantyre, Chiradzulu and Zomba. They were the dominant ethnic group in those districts before the arrival of the Yao and the Lhomwe. The Mang'anja on the other hand live in the Lower Shire River Valley. Newitt[8] and Schoffeleers[9] referred to sixteenth-century Portuguese sources that suggest

---

6   Bocarro, 1964: 416.

7   National Statistical Office (NSO). 2018 Malawi population and housing census. www.nsomalawi.mw (accessed 31 May 2019).

8   Newitt MDD. 1982. The Early History of the Maravi. *The Journal of African History*. 23.

9   Schoffeleers JM. 1987. The Zimba and the Lundu state in the late sixteenth and early seventeenth centuries. *The Journal of African History*. 28: 337.

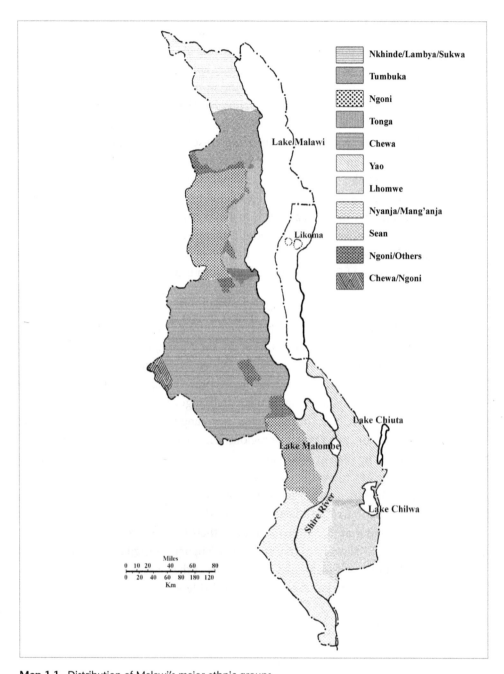

Map 1.1. Distribution of Malawi's major ethnic groups.

Source: Adapted from Pachai B. 1972a. History and settlement. In Malawi in Maps. *S Agnew & M Stubbs (eds). London: University of London Press: 43.*

3

the ancestors of the Mang'anja were already in the area by then. Since the Sena in the Lower Shire Valley now outnumber the Mang'anja, maps tend to depict the entire area as a Sena area.[10] Although the Lower Shire Valley is less than 24 kilometres from the southern edge of the Shire Highlands, it is, in the words of one scholar, 'a single unit in space, distinct from other regions like the Tchiri Highlands and the Lower Zambezi'.[11] Mandala[12] calls it Tchiri. There is a big difference in the elevation of the Lower Shire Valley and the Shire Highlands and that is the reason for the dialectical differences between the Mang'anja and the Nyanja. The elevation of the Lower Shire Valley ranges from 36 to 107 metres above sea level whereas that of the Shire Highlands ranges from 610 to 1981 metres above sea level.[13] The steep climb from the Lower Shire Valley to the Shire Highlands was and still is an almost insurmountable obstacle to pedestrian-based communication. Consequently, the two ethnic groups remained largely isolated from each other until the twentieth century. Now that the Sena outnumber the Mang'anja, an interesting slow mixing of Chimang'anja and Chisena is in progress in the Lower Shire Valley.

Meanwhile, the dialects of Chichewa and Chinyanja have been adopted or are in the process of being adopted by at least three major ethnic groups which have lost, or are slowly losing, their respective languages. They are the Ngoni, the Yao and the Lhomwe. However, the Ngoni, who came from South Africa and began to settle in Malawi permanently from the 1850s onwards,[14] no longer speak Chingoni. Those who settled in central Malawi now speak Chichewa as their first language and those who settled in northern Malawi speak Chitumbuka as their first language. Both languages are the major vernaculars of the two respective regions. The Ngoni lost their language within the relatively short time span of less than 150 years. One of the reasons for losing their language so quickly was the existence of unrestricted social mixing, including intra-ethnic marriage. The Ngoni came in as military conquerors[15] and they often gained subjects in their tribal wars.[16] In Malawi, they lived close to or within the land of the conquered people and that forced them to speak their language more than their own. The Ngoni in central Malawi lost more than their language. Originally patrilocal, they eventually adopted the matrilocal rules of residence of the Chewa. Patrilocal traditions require the groom's family to pay the bride's family bride wealth, or *lobola*, as people call

10 Pachai B. 1972a: 43.
11 Mandala EC. 2005. *The End of Chidyerano: a History of Food and Everyday Life in Malawi, 1860–2004.* Portsmouth, NH: Heinemann. 3.
12 Ibid.
13 Stobbs AR & Young A. 1972. Natural regions. In *Malawi in Maps.* S Agnew & M Stubbs (eds). London: London University Press: 40.
14 Omer-Cooper JD. 1969. *The Zulu Aftermath: A Nineteenth-Century Revolution in Bantu Africa.* London: Longmans.
15 Ibid.
16 Langworthy 1973; Pachai B. 1974. *Malawi: the history of the nation.* London: Longman.

it in Malawi and elsewhere in southern Africa (see Huffman[17] regarding the origins of *lobola*). Traditionally, the bride wealth is in the form of cattle, but sometimes a cash amount based on the going price for cattle is accepted after which the wife takes up residence with the husband's relatives in his village. The husband's family help to raise the children and they remain part of his family forever. Matrilocal traditions of the Chewa, called *chikamwini* in Chichewa, are the exact opposite of patrilocal traditions. No bride wealth is payable and the man goes to reside with the wife's relatives in her village to provide labour for his wife and her family.[18] The wife's family raises his children but they remain part of her family forever. Besides the Chewa, the Nyanja, Yao and Lhomwe also practise *chikamwini*.

Both the Yao and the Lhomwe migrated into Malawi from Mozambique.[19] By the mid-nineteenth century, the Yao had established settlements in some parts of southern Malawi[20] whereas the Lhomwe began to settle in the same region towards the end of that century.[21] They both settled among the Nyanja who had been in the area for centuries. Although the population of each respective ethnic group now outnumbers that of the Nyanja, originally the Nyanja were the majority, which meant therefore that it was unavoidable for the new arrivals to use Chinyanja as their public language. Many of their descendants now use it as their first language and for some, it is their only vernacular language.

Unable to distinguish the minor dialectical differences between Chichewa, Chinyanja and Chimang'anja, early British colonial administrators simply assumed that Chinyanja was the language spoken by most of the people in southern and central Malawi and that a high percentage of the remaining people understood it. Four years after Malawi became an independent country, the new political leadership made Chinyanja the country's sole national language but changed the name to Chichewa.[22] It became the only vernacular language on Malawi's publicly funded national radio station and the only one taught in all schools in the country.[23] As a result, it remains the most widely used vernacular language in Malawi. People in eastern Zambia also speak the language but they still call it Chinyanja.

---

17 Huffman TN. 1998. Presidential address: the antiquity of lobola. *The South African Archaeological Bulletin*. 53 (168).

18 Colson E & Gluckman M. 1951. *Seven tribes of British Central Africa*. London: Oxford University Press.

19 Abdallah YB. 1973. *The Yaos*. London: Frank Cass: 7; Pachai 1974; Soka LD. 1982. *Mbiri ya Alomwe*. London: Macmillan Education Limited.

20 Pachai 1974: 52.

21 Soka 1982: 1; Pachai 1974.

22 Kishindo PJ. 1994. The impact of a national language on minority languages. *Journal of Contemporary African Studies*. 12(2); Chirwa WC. 1998. Democracy, ethnicity and regionalism: the Malawian experience, 1992–1996. In *Democratization in Malawi: a stocktaking*. KM Phiri & KR Ross (eds). Blantyre, Malawi: CLAIM.

23 Chirwa 1998: 62.

Recording history and culture before the colonial period

Originally called British Central Africa (BCA) and later Nyasaland, Malawi was brought to the attention of the British people by the Scottish missionary and explorer, Dr David Livingstone, whose exploration of the country began towards the end of the 1850s.[24] He called for western civilisation to be introduced through Christianity and commerce.[25] His call was so well received in Britain that during the fifteen-year period between 1860 and 1875, three different Christian missionary teams and some commercial settlers arrived in the country.[26] The Europeans, who took time to observe the people's behaviour and other aspects of their way of life, asked pertinent questions and carefully recorded the responses. The most successful of them published books, with two of the earliest authors being John Buchanan and Reverend Duff Macdonald. Buchanan arrived together with the pioneer Church of Scotland party that established its first mission station at Blantyre in southern Malawi in October 1875.[27] The mission authorities hired him to work as an agriculturist[28] whereas Macdonald came to head the mission in 1878. By 1881, however, both had been dismissed[29] with their superiors in Scotland having accused them of indiscipline and unacceptable abuses of the local people.[30] In 1882, Macdonald published a book entitled *Africana: Or the Heart of Heathen Africa*. It was a two-volume book and it discussed among other things the early history of the Scottish Mission and the customs, beliefs and technology of the African people.

Buchanan was more adventurous. When he lost his job, he went solo to Zomba district to grow coffee and was, in fact, the person who introduced that crop in the country.[31] In 1885, he became an acting British vice-consul and, upon receiving instructions, declared the country a British Protectorate in 1891.[32] He published a book in 1885 entitled *The Shirè Highlands*, in which he included chapters on chiefs and tribes, and on the customs and beliefs of the local people.

Other than publications put out by earlier explorers and missionaries, such as Livingstone and the Reverend Henry Rowley, the books written by Macdonald and Buchanan marked the beginning of publications by missionaries, settlers and colonial administrators in Malawi. Besides history and culture, they also studied the fauna and

---

24 Livingstone D & Livingstone C. 1866. *Narrative of an Expedition to the Zambesi and its Tributaries: And of the Discovery of the Lakes Shirwa and Nyassa, 1858–1864*. New York: Harper & Brothers.

25 McCracken J. 2013. *A History of Malawi, 1859–1966*. Woodbridge: James Currey: 38.

26 Ross AC. 1972. Scottish missionary concern 1874–1914: A golden era? *The Scottish Historical Review*. 60; McCracken 2013: 45.

27 McCracken 2013: 45; Buchanan J. 1982. *The Shirè Highlands*. Blantyre, Malawi: Blantyre Printing and Publishing Co; Kalinga & Crosby 2001.

28 Kalinga & Crosby 2001: 47; McCracken 2013.

29 Macdonald D. 1882. *Africana; Or, the Heart of Heathen Africa*. London: Simpkin Marshall & Co. viii; Kalinga & Crosby 2001; McCracken 2013: 50.

30 Kalinga & Crosby 2001: 47.

31 Kalinga & Crosby 2001: 47; McCracken 2013: 77

32 Kalinga & Crosby 2001: 47; McCracken 2013: 1.

flora of the country. Perhaps the best known of these early publications was Harry Johnston's 1898 book entitled *British Central Africa*.

Recording history during the colonial period

When the British government declared Malawi a British protectorate, it appointed Harry Johnston to be its first Commissioner and Consul General.[33] Johnston, who immediately proceeded to establish the administrative machinery of the new protectorate, divided the territory into administrative districts. At first, he created four districts, and two years later, he re-divided the territory into twelve districts in each of which he placed an individual in charge.[34] Today there are 28 districts (see Map 1.2). These individuals were officially entitled 'collectors' because they were expected to collect taxes even though they were essentially administrators. They also had judicial responsibilities and carried out public works.[35]

Unpublished archival records show that British colonial administrators and settlers, as well as early Malawian scholars, recorded oral traditions on the history and culture of various ethnic groups in the country. The original recordings of the colonial administrators are in the Malawi National Archives headquarters in Zomba.

The settlers published their research findings as journal articles whereas the Malawian scholars wrote books. The collective efforts of these people set the foundation on which subsequent university-trained scholars built their own research projects.

Colonial government administrators

Some of the details that colonial administrators wanted to know and record were the origins of the various ethnic groups and their intra-ethnic relatedness; how long they had lived in their respective areas; their customs, traditions, beliefs and other aspects of their culture. They hoped such knowledge would lead to the formulation of culturally appropriate government regulations and policies. To achieve their goal, they collected data directly from the people by interviewing them. In an age without tape recorders, they recorded the information in longhand in books labelled 'district notebooks' which were eventually deposited at the National Archives, where they have been intensively consulted by many scholars and other interested individuals.

Because the district administrators had no specific research question, the thoroughness with which some of them recorded the traditions depended on the interest and diligence of these individuals and their preconceived notions about Africans. It

---

33   McCracken 2013: 57.
34   Baker CA. 1972. Administration: 1891–6 districts and government stations. In *Malawi in Maps*. S Agnew & M Stubbs (eds). London: University of London Press: 44.
35   Ibid: 44.

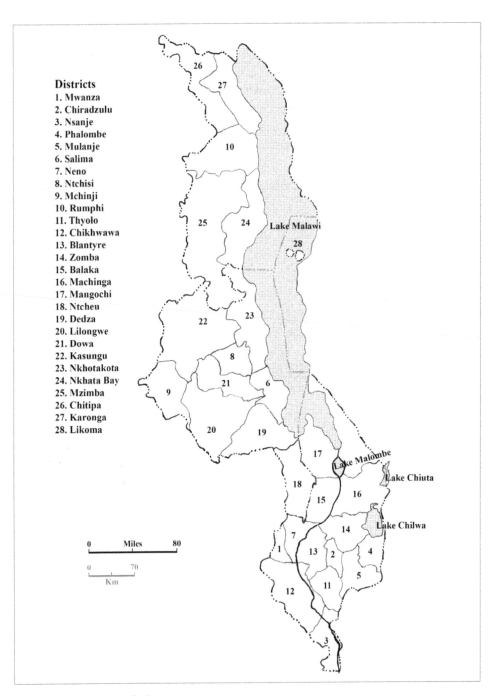

Districts
1. Mwanza
2. Chiradzulu
3. Nsanje
4. Phalombe
5. Mulanje
6. Salima
7. Neno
8. Ntchisi
9. Mchinji
10. Rumphi
11. Thyolo
12. Chikhwawa
13. Blantyre
14. Zomba
15. Balaka
16. Machinga
17. Mangochi
18. Ntcheu
19. Dedza
20. Lilongwe
21. Dowa
22. Kasungu
23. Nkhotakota
24. Nkhata Bay
25. Mzimba
26. Chitipa
27. Karonga
28. Likoma

Map 1.2: Administrative districts.
Source: Adapted from Baker 1972: 47.

should be borne in mind that some of the early colonialists, including missionaries, believed that Africans, or in this case Malawians, were inferior beings.[36] One anonymous traveller made this view clear[37] and the notes in some of the district notebooks suggest that some district administrators were in accord. The district administrators did their work half-heartedly, only so that they could have something to present to their superiors.[38] Others, however, were diligent — they took the work seriously and did it not only to please their superiors but to learn something from it as well. Some of the well-recorded traditions included those done by Gordon Cummings in Dedza district and Eric Smith in Nkhotakota district.[39] In the 1930s, MC Hole, then District Commissioner for Lilongwe, recorded traditions 'on the history and territorial claims of Chewa chieftainships in Lilongwe district'.[40] Unlike earlier administrators, Hole had a specific topic to deal with and he was therefore very focused in the manner in which he recorded the traditions.

One exceptionally diligent and enthusiastic government administrator who came on the scene later was WHJ Rangeley, born in Zambia in 1910 where his parents were pioneer settlers.[41] Years later, he studied at Oxford University in England where he obtained a diploma in Social Anthropology.[42] Initially hired as a district commissioner, he rose in rank to become a provincial commissioner,[43] and in the 1940s and 1950s he carried out field research in many districts of the country as well as archival research.[44] He published several papers in a local historical and scientific journal called *The Nyasaland Journal*, which was renamed *The Society of Malawi Journal* when Malawi became an independent country and changed its name from Nyasaland to Malawi. His reports show that he was the only administrator of his time who 'came close to meeting the requirements of modern historical scholarship'.[45] The material he gathered and his other documents are preserved by the Society of Malawi library in Blantyre as the Rangeley Papers, which are accessible to researchers upon obtaining special permission from the library authorities.

---

36   Chiphangwi, SD. 1971–1972. The development of African participation in the Blantyre Mission. History seminar paper. Chancellor College, University of Malawi.
37   First impressions of African character. 1896. *The Central African planter.* 1(8).
38   Phiri 1975: 15.
39   Ibid: 16.
40   Ibid: 16.
41   McCracken 2013: 217.
42   Kalinga & Crosby 2001: 348.
43   Ibid: 348.
44   Phiri 1975: 20.
45   Phiri 1975: 17.

Early African historians

Years before Rangeley began to publish his work, some indigenous scholars who were curious about their ethnic history had already recorded oral traditions and published books on the history and culture of their respective ethnic groups. They were Yohanna Barnaba Abdallah, a Yao; Yesaya Mlonyeni Chibambo, a Ngoni; and Samuel Josia Ntara, a Chewa. These three were some of the many Africans who took advantage of western education once European missionaries had introduced it in southern and eastern Africa. They pursued it to the highest level possible.

Abdallah was not a Malawian and, apparently, historians are not in agreement regarding his nationality. Alpers[46] says he was a stepson of Barnaba Matuka from Mtwara region of southern Tanzania, whereas others maintain he was born in northern Mozambique.[47] Since Abdallah was educated in Tanzania, he was most likely a Tanzanian and he had access to good education because his father was also educated. His father attended St. Andrew's College, at Kiungani, described as 'the prestigious and influential U.M.C.A. secondary school on Zanzibar Island'.[48] Professionally, Abdallah was a clergyman but he was also a historian and a scholar of the Greek language and of the Bible.[49] In 1898, he was ordained an Anglican priest at Likoma Cathedral on Likoma Island in Malawi[50] and seven years later in 1905, his life's major ambition was realised when he travelled to the Holy Land — Israel.[51] Those accomplishments notwithstanding, it was his book *Chiikala cha Wayao* (*The Yaos*), published in 1919, that made Abdallah well known among scholars. Edward Alpers wrote an introduction to the second edition published in 1973. It was the first book on the Yao that had been made available in Malawi, hence his inclusion as a historian in this book along with Malawian historians. Scholars of Yao history and culture have consulted *Chiikala cha Wayao* intensively over the years.

Chibambo, who was from northern Malawi, attended Scottish mission schools at Ekwendeni and Livingstonia located in that region.[52] In 1920, the mission authorities awarded him the 'honours schoolmaster's certificate',[53] resulting in his becoming the first alumnus to achieve that distinction. Besides being a teacher, he was also a historian and an ordained clergyman of the Free Church of Scotland. That alone made him a well-known personality, particularly among the Ngoni and the Tumbuka in northern Malawi.

---

46   Alpers EA. 1973. Introduction to second edition. In *The Yaos*. Abdallah YB. London: Frank Cass: vii.
47   Kalinga & Crosby 2001: 1
48   Alpers 1973: viii.
49   Kalinga & Crosby 2001.
50   Alpers 1973: x.
51   Ibid.
52   Kalinga & Crosby 2001: 60.
53   Ibid.

In the period from 1932 to 1942, he wrote two books: *Makani gha baNgoni (The Story of the Ngoni)* and *My Ngoni of Nyasaland.*[54]

Ntara, from central Malawi, attended a school at Mvera in Dowa district run by Dutch Reformed Church missionaries from South Africa. He later qualified as a teacher at Nkhoma mission, another Dutch Reformed Church institution in central Malawi.[55] Besides being an educator, he was also an author of both fiction and history. In his early writings, Ntara's middle name was spelled in the vernacular, that is 'Yosia'. In later writings, he anglicised this to 'Josia' to which he sometimes added the letter 'h' at the end as in 'Josiah'. Among the several books he wrote were *Nthondo* and *Msyamboza*. In a literary competition organised in London by the International Institute of African Languages and Cultures in 1932, *Nthondo* won the biography division of the competition.[56] The Scottish missionary, Reverend Thomas Cullen Young, translated *Nthondo* into English and The Bible and Tract Society published the book as *Man of Africa* the following year. Young also translated *Msyamboza* which was published in 1949 as *Headman's Enterprise: An unexpected page in Central African History.*

Impressive as these achievements sound, Ntara is in fact well known in Malawi and among various scholars elsewhere for his book *Mbiri ya Achewa*, first published by Nkhoma Press either in 1944 or 1945.[57] In 1973, WS Kamphandira Jere translated the book's 1965 edition into English as *The History of the Chewa*. As a required textbook in the country's secondary schools, *Mbiri ya Achewa* was the most widely read of any of the publications by indigenous authors.

Other African historians who published their books later were W Chafulumira, who in 1948 published *Mbiri ya Amang'anja (History of the Mang'anja)*, and LD Soka, who published *Mbiri ya Alomwe (History of the Lomwe)* in 1953. We must make an exception, though, and include the Reverend Thomas Cullen Young, a Scottish missionary who trained in accountancy first and theology later. He came to Malawi in 1904 to work at Livingstonia Mission in northern Malawi. Besides translating and helping with the publication of some of Ntara and Chibambo's books, he also promoted 'studies in the languages, cultures and history of the Lake Malawi people'.[58] He wrote and published widely, and one of his well-known books, which was published in 1932, was about the Tumbuka-Kamanga people: *Notes on the History of the Tumbuka-Kamanga peoples in the northern province of Nyasaland.*

---

54   Ibid.
55   Pachai B. 1968. Samuel Josiah Ntara: writer and historian. *The Society of Malawi Journal.* 26(2).
56   Kalinga & Crosby 2001: 312.
57   Langworthy 1973: vii.
58   Kalinga & Crosby 2001: 406.

European settlers

Unlike colonial administrators and early African scholars, European settlers were interested more in archaeology than in recording the oral traditions of the people. By the 1950s, they had located several rock shelter archaeological sites in all the three regions of the country and at least one open archaeological site in the southern Lake Malawi area. A rock shelter is a cavity or a hollow naturally formed in what is otherwise a near vertical rock face. The resulting overhang protects the area underneath from rain and sometimes running water (see Plate 1.1). Rock shelters, which were natural habitation places for Stone Age people, were also used by Iron Age people on a temporary basis. Archaeologists find evidence of human use of rock shelters on the floor or during excavations, which includes tools made from stones, bones and wood, as well as pottery and metal objects. In addition, the early inhabitants sometimes painted the rock faces, and some of the paintings, which include geometric and zoomorphic figures, have survived. Geometric depictions consisted of concentric circles, line patterns, sun outbursts and other designs (see Plate 1.2) whereas zoomorphic depictions involved animals or animal-like designs (see Plate 1.3). Use of rock shelters in recent times has been documented in Malawi. In the Dedza-Chongoni area for instance, anthropologists found costumes used by the Nyau secret society stored or hidden in some rock shelters.[59]

These discoveries encouraged the settlers to think of how best to study the sites and to preserve the country's cultural heritage. Their good intentions were, however, thwarted by the fact that unlike some of the neighbouring countries, Malawi had no qualified archaeologists and other cultural heritage specialists. Further, the country had neither a museum in which objects of cultural and natural heritage could be stored, exhibited and studied, nor a regular publication for disseminating information on history and cultural heritage in general. They resolved these problems initially by forming themselves into a society in 1946 called the Nyasaland Society which, when Malawi became independent, changed its name to the Society of Malawi. The society provided a forum for discussing many subjects of interest, including anthropology, natural sciences, history, literature and travel.[60] In order to accomplish archaeological research, they invited external archaeologists to carry out archaeological site surveys and excavations and they disseminated their activities by publishing research reports in *The Nyasaland Journal*. Later, the European settler community established a museum and a reference library in Blantyre.

---

59 Mgomezulu GGY. 1978. Food production: the beginnings in the Linthipe/Changoni area of Dedza district, Malawi. PhD thesis. University of California, Berkeley; Lindgren NE & Schoffeleers JM. 1978. *Rock Art and Nyau Symbolism in Malawi*. (Department of Antiquities publication no. 18). Limbe, Malawi: Montfort Press; Juwayeyi YM. 1997. Secrecy and Creativity: The Use of Rockshelters by the Nyau Secret Society in Malawi. In *The Human Use of Caves*. C Bonsall & C Tolan-Smith (eds). Oxford: Archaeopress.

60 Kalinga & Crosby 2001: 366.

Plate 1.1: Rock shelter on Mikolongwe Hill, southern Malawi.
Source: The author.

Plate 1.2: Geometric rock paintings from the Dedza-Chongoni area, central Malawi.[61]
Source: The author

Plate 1.3: Zoomorphic rock paintings from the Dedza-Chongoni area, central Malawi.
Source: The author

---

61   Anati, E. 1986. Malawi cultural heritage with reference to rock art sites: evaluation of rock art and training of specialists. A report to UNESCO and to the Government of Malawi (unpublished).

Between 1950 and 1967, they invited three archaeologists to undertake various archaeological projects in Malawi. J Desmond Clark and Ray Inskeep, based at the time at the Rhodes-Livingstone Museum in neighbouring Zambia, and Keith Robinson from Zimbabwe, carried out five archaeological projects during that period. The first, third and fifth projects were undertaken by Clark, who first came to Malawi in 1950. His project in that year involved excavating Later Stone Age rock shelter sites located on Mphunzi Hill in central Malawi[62] and Hora Hill in northern Malawi.[63] He returned later in 1965, 1966 and 1973. By then, he was Professor of Anthropology at the University of California, Berkeley, in the United States of America(USA). During the 1965 and 1966 seasons, he led an expedition of several scientists to northern Malawi.[64] They located several Middle Stone Age sites, of which the best known was an elephant butchery site at Mwanganda's village in Karonga district.[65] In 1973, Clark excavated a Late Stone Age rock shelter called Mwana wa Chencherere, located in Dedza district in central Malawi.[66] Ray Inskeep arrived in Malawi in 1958 to investigate a proto-historic burial site at Nkhudzi Bay in the southern Lake Malawi area. This was a salvage project intended, among other things, to quickly recover burials and burial goods that were eroding away from an old burial site due to rising lake water levels.[67] Robinson, who had been a team member of Clark's expedition to Karonga in 1965 and 1966, carried out the final project in 1967. This time, Beatrice Sandelowsky, one of Clark's graduate students, assisted him. The two surveyed and excavated several Later Stone Age and Iron Age sites from Nkhotakota to the Nyika plateau.[68] These archaeological projects had the effect of encouraging the settler community to intensify their work in cultural heritage awareness and preservation.

The last important undertaking by the European settler community before the end of colonial rule was the establishment of a museum in 1957.[69] Initially, they located it in temporary premises in Blantyre, which at the time was the country's largest urban centre, with a large population of European and Indian business people. A board of trustees ran the museum which exhibited 'small but important collections of ethnographic and archaeological material and ... some unique and valuable historic

62   Clark JD. 1956. Prehistory in Nyasaland. *The Nyasaland Journal*. 9: 101.
63   Ibid: 106.
64   Clark JD, Haynes CV, Mawby JE & Gautier A. 1970. Interim report on paleoanthropological investigations in the Lake Malawi Rift. *Quaternaria*. 13.
65   Clark JD & Haynes CV. 1970. An elephant butchery site at Mwanganda's Village, Karonga, Malawi, and its relevance for Paleolithic archaeology. *World Archaeology*. 1(3).
66   Clark JD. 1973. Archaeological investigations of a painted rockshelter at Mwana wa Chencherere, north of Dedza, central Malawi. *The Society of Malawi Journal*. 26.
67   Inskeep RR. 1965. *Preliminary investigation of a proto-historic cemetery at Nkudzi Bay, Malawi*. Livingstone, Zambia: The National Museums of Zambia: 1.
68   Robinson KR & Sandelowsky B. 1968. The Iron Age of northern Malawi: recent work. *Azania: Archaeological Research in Africa*. 3; Sandelowsky BH. 1972. Later stone age lithic assemblages from Malawi and their technologies. PhD thesis. University of California, Berkeley.
69   Clark JD. 1968. *Malawi antiquities programme*. Paris: UNESCO.

exhibits'.[70] It was a welcome addition to the country's educational, cultural and social needs.

Establishing the museum was a huge and commendable effort by the European settler community. The only problem was that there were no competent people in the country to manage it.[71] A lack of professional museum managers slowed or inhibited museum improvements. For instance, museum displays rarely changed, which tended to discourage people from visiting the museum regularly.[72] After a little more than two decades, the Malawi government decided to take over the operations of the museum: it dissolved the museum's board of trustees and set up its own management operation.[73] One immediate benefit of the government take-over was the recruitment of several recent Malawian university graduates who were sent abroad to train in various aspects of museum work. Within a few years, they all obtained graduate degrees at universities in Australia, South Africa and England.[74]

The postcolonial period

Political independence meant the end of colonial rule in the country and the establishment of a new government run by Malawians. The struggle for independence brought about a sense of patriotism among Malawians and local political leaders were quick to exploit this by actively promoting Malawi's history and culture. For instance, they changed the name of the country from 'Nyasaland' to 'Malawi'. Those who had read Ntara's *Mbiri ya Achewa* knew that 'Malawi' was the name of an area along Lake Malawi where a Chewa king and his people had settled a long time ago.[75] The new government moved quickly to establish structures that would have an impact on the country's cultural heritage and research into its history. In 1965, it passed a law called the Monuments Act[76] which was revised in 1991 as the Monuments and Relics Act.[77] It established the Department of Antiquities[78] in January 1967 while earlier, in 1965, the newly established University of Malawi had admitted its first class.[79] Its Department of History was to play an important role in researching the history of the country.

---

70 Ibid: 8.
71 Ibid; Juwayeyi YM. 2010b. Culture heritage conservation programs in Malawi and public responses. In *Heritage 2010: Heritage and sustainable development*. R Amoeda, S Lira & C Pinheiro (eds). Barcelos, Portugal: Green Lines Institute.
72 Juwayeyi 2010b.
73 Juwayeyi YM. 2011b. Excavating the History of Archaeology in Malawi. In *Comparative Archaeologies: A Sociological View of the Science of the Past*. L Lozny (ed). New York: Springer: 793.
74 Juwayeyi 2010b: 135.
75 Ntara 1973.
76 Monuments Act 44 of 1965. 1965. *Laws of Malawi*, Zomba, Malawi: Government Printer.
77 Monuments and Relics Act, Chapter 29: 01 of 1991. 1991. *Laws of Malawi*, Zomba, Malawi: Government Printer.
78 Clark 1968: 7.
79 Kalinga & Crosby 2001: 394.

The Monuments Act

The passing of the Monuments Act in 1965 was one of the new government's first actions that had to do with cultural heritage. The European settler community initiated and drafted that law just before the end of colonial rule. It compelled the government to protect objects of archaeological and historical interest, including structures erected in the late nineteenth century by the colonial government, missionaries and various European settlers. It also protected places of distinctive natural beauty.[80] Under that law, the government established a Monuments Advisory Council (MAC), which consisted of individuals appointed by the government minister responsible for national monuments. The council's functions included advising the government on matters related to the declaration and preservation of national monuments. It is perhaps noteworthy that the first chairperson of MAC was Ntara.[81] Further, the government sought the advice of the United Nations Educational, Scientific and Cultural Organization (UNESCO) on how best the country should manage its cultural heritage. The organisation responded in 1968 by sending Professor J Desmond Clark as a consultant to advise the government. His consultancy required him to advise the Malawi government on the country's archaeological programme and antiquities. In addition, the Museum of Malawi expected him to supervise ongoing archaeological excavations which amateur archaeologists were carrying out under its auspices.[82]

The Department of Antiquities

The Department of Antiquities was required to implement the provisions of the Monuments Act and to undertake the bulk of cultural heritage research. This included doing archaeological site surveys and excavations throughout the country and recording the oral traditions of all ethnic groups. The department was also expected to investigate and identify objects of historical interest, with the sole purpose of recording and recommending them to the MAC for protection as national monuments.[83] The most urgent of these activities, however, was the recording of oral traditions, as in the 1960s many people born in the previous century were still alive. There was therefore a hastiness in the department to interview as many of them as possible before they died. By then, tape recorders were available in Malawi and that made recording oral tradition easy and fast. Transcriptions of the interviews were placed in the National Archives of Malawi.

Archaeological research, however, proved to be difficult as the country had no locally based, qualified archaeologists. An expatriate official who was a historian, but

---

80   Juwayeyi 2010b.
81   Kalinga & Crosby 2001: 312.
82   Clark, 1968: 1
83   Juwayeyi 2010b.

who was interested in archaeology, managed the Department of Antiquities.[84] Unlike the Museum of Malawi when it first started, the Department of Antiquities moved quickly to train Malawian archaeologists. With the assistance of J Desmond Clark, Malawian students received training in archaeology at the University of California, Berkeley.

Gadi Mgomezulu was the first Malawian to go for training. He joined the Department of Antiquities soon after graduating from Chancellor College in 1972. Before he went to California in 1973, Mgomezulu had the opportunity to work with Clark at Mwana wa Chencherere rock shelter.[85] Later, Mgomezulu came back to the same area to carry out research for his doctoral thesis when he investigated the beginnings of food production in the area.[86] Yusuf Juwayeyi was the next person to receive training in archaeology. He also enrolled at the University of California, Berkeley, and like Mgomezulu he joined the Department of Antiquities soon after he graduated from Chancellor College in 1973. His major responsibility before he proceeded to the United States in 1975 was to record oral traditions of the Yao, Nyanja and Lhomwe in southern Malawi and of the Chewa in central Malawi. Three months before he left for the USA, Juwayeyi had an opportunity to be Robinson's assistant. At the time, Robinson was carrying out an archaeological investigation of the northern and eastern sides of Mulanje Mountain.[87] For his doctoral degree research, Juwayeyi decided to investigate the technology and economy of the Late Stone Age and Iron Age inhabitants of the Shire Highlands.[88] In subsequent years, the Department of Antiquities sent abroad four more of its newly recruited staff, including Zefe Kaufulu, the only one of the four to enroll at the University of California, Berkeley. His research interest was in the geological context of Early Stone Age sites and he studied sites in Karonga district and others in Tanzania and in Kenya.[89] Thereafter, he continued to work in Karonga and more or less continued from where Clark had stopped in 1966.[90] The three others were Willard Michala, Mapopa Chipeta and Elizabeth Gomani. Michala went to the University of Chicago in the United States where he studied Archaeozoology, which is the study of faunal remains from archaeological sites. Chipeta[91] pursued History at Dalhousie University in Canada,

---

84 Clark 1968: 7

85 Clark 1973: 29

86 Mgomezulu 1978.

87 Robinson KR. 1977. *Iron Age occupation north and east of the Mulanje plateau, Malawi*. (Department of Antiquities publication no. 17). Limbe, Malawi: Montfort Press.

88 Juwayeyi YM. 1981. The later prehistory of southern Malawi: a contribution to the study of technology and economy during the Later Stone Age and Iron Age periods. PhD thesis. University of California, Berkeley.

89 Kaufulu ZM. 1983. The geological context of some early archaeological sites in Kenya, Malawi and Tanzania: microstratigraphy, site formation and interpretation. PhD thesis. University of California, Berkeley.

90 Kaufulu ZM & Stern N. 1987. The first stone artefacts to be found *in situ* within the Plio-Pleistocene Chiwondo Beds in northern Malawi. *Journal of Human Evolution*. 16.

91 Chipeta MOJ 1986. Labour in colonial Malawi: a study of the Malawian working class c1890–1961. PhD thesis. Dalhousie University.

and Gomani[92] studied Paleontology, the study of fossils, at Southern Methodist University in Dallas, Texas. Further, with the sponsorship of various organisations, the Department of Antiquities sent several technicians for apprenticeship training with professional and technical staff at various institutions. Fidelis Morocco, Pharaoh Kamanga, Levant Mfune and Mathias Zalinga Phiri went to the National Museums of Kenya in Nairobi. Morocco and Zalinga Phiri also worked with the staff of Southern Methodist University in Dallas Texas, USA and Centro Camuno di Studi Preistorici (CCSP) in Capo di Ponte, Italy, respectively, whereas Harrison Simfukwe went to Darmstadt Museum in Germany. On their return, they became very helpful assistants to the department's professional staff.

The University of Malawi

The establishment of the University of Malawi in 1964[93] brought into the country academics from many parts of the world to teach and carry out research in various academic disciplines. One department that took full advantage of available research opportunities was the Department of History at Chancellor College whose founding head was Professor Bridglal Pachai.[94] He moved quickly to spearhead research into the history of various ethnic groups in the country. In order to cover as much ground as possible, the department came up with a programme that required final-year History students to undertake original research in history and write research papers, which the department referred to as seminar papers. Often, students chose research projects that led them to record oral traditions in their home areas. As a result, the Department of History amassed a large collection of student-authored seminar papers based on oral traditions on the history of almost all ethnic groups in Malawi. Currently unpublished, the seminar papers are available to readers in the Chancellor College library. Pachai himself proceeded to publish scholarly papers and books on the history of the country.[95] Further, the Department of History, like other departments at the university, embarked on a policy of assisting its brightest students to obtain scholarships for graduate studies abroad. The intention of the policy was to build up a pool of highly trained and well-qualified Malawians who would eventually take over teaching responsibilities from the expatriate faculty. The first two of the several students the department sent abroad were Owen Kalinga and Kings Phiri. After graduating from Chancellor College in 1969, Kalinga enrolled at the University of Birmingham in England to study for an MA degree, and then later moved to the University of London for his doctoral studies. He conducted part of the research for his doctoral dissertation among the Ngonde, located in northern

---

92 Gomani EM. 1999. Dinosaurs of the cretaceous sedimentary rocks of northern Malawi, Africa. PhD thesis. Southern Methodist University.
93 Kalinga & Crosby 2001: 394.
94 Ibid: 331.
95 Pachai 1974.

Malawi.[96] Having obtained his PhD degree, he returned to Malawi to join the Department of History at Chancellor College. Phiri on the other hand enrolled at the University of Wisconsin-Madison in the USA after his graduation from Chancellor College in 1971. He was interested in the history of the Chewa and that required him to spend many months in central Malawi recording their oral traditions as part of the research for his PhD degree.[97] After completing his doctoral studies, he too returned to Malawi to teach at Chancellor College.

By the mid-1980s, Malawi had a well-trained team of archaeologists, historians and museum curators. The country no longer needed to invite experts from abroad, but foreign-based researchers who wanted to work in Malawi could do so. One such researcher was David Killick, an archaeologist, born and raised in Malawi by English parents. He completed his graduate studies at Yale University and conducted his doctoral research among the Chewa in chief Chulu's area in Kasungu district. His research interest was in indigenous bloomery iron-smelting technology, during the relatively recent past 97. He is Professor of Anthropology at the University of Arizona, Tucson.[98]

Intensive research on the history and culture of the Chewa

While the training of Malawians was happening, foreign and locally based scholars pursued various research projects among the Chewa. Between 1969 and 1986, universities in the USA awarded at least three doctoral degrees on various aspects of Chewa history to individuals who had carried out research among the Chewa of Malawi and Zambia. One of these was Kings Phiri, whose research among the Chewa of central Malawi has already been mentioned, and the other two were Harry Langworthy and William McFarren.

Langworthy was a great-grandson of Joseph Booth,[99] a well-known former missionary to eastern and southern Africa. He is remembered for being a critic of the colonial government and an activist for African rights,[100] and also for mentoring the Reverend John Chilembwe, the country's first nationalist and revolutionary or freedom fighter.[101] Despite his great-grandfather's involvement with Malawi, Langworthy, as a

---

96 Kalinga OJM. 1974. The Ngonde kingdom of northern Malawi c1600–1895. PhD thesis. University of London.

97 Phiri 1975.

98 Killick DJ. 1990. Technology in its social setting: bloomery iron smelting at Kasungu, Malawi, 1860–1940. PhD thesis. Yale University.

99 Porter A. 1998. Review of 'Africa for the African': The Life of Joseph Booth by Harry Langworth. *The Journal of African History*. 39 (3).

100 Shepperson G & Price T. 1958. *Independent African: John Chilembwe and the origins, setting and significance of the Nyasaland native rising of 1915*. Edinburgh: Edinburgh University Press; Pachai 1974; Phiri DD. 1999. *Let us die for Africa: an African perspective on the life and death of John Chilembwe of Nyasaland/Malawi*. Blantyre, Malawi: Central Africana Limited.

101 Shepperson & Price 1958; Phiri 1999.

student at Boston University Graduate School, chose to do research among the Chewa of eastern Zambia. He was interested in the kingdom that a Chewa leader called Undi established there.[102] McFarren completed his doctoral studies at the University of California, Berkeley and like Phiri, he conducted his research in central Malawi in the 1980s. He investigated the history of the Chewa from the time of their arrival in the southern Lake Malawi area to the nineteenth century.[103] In addition to these historians, scholars in other disciplines developed an interest in the history and culture of the Chewa. Perhaps the most prominent of them was Fr Matthew Schoffeleers, a Catholic priest from Holland who came to Malawi after his ordination in 1955.[104] He worked in the Lower Shire Valley where, besides doing priestly work, he became involved with the local Mbona cult and the Nyau masked dance tradition practised by the Mang'anja people. His experiences there and his newly acquired knowledge of the culture of the Mang'anja may have influenced or encouraged him to pursue advanced studies in Anthropology. After obtaining the DPhil degree at Oxford University in 1968, he returned to Malawi where he taught at the Nguludi Roman Catholic seminary and later became the director at the Catechetical Training Centre at Likulezi in southern Malawi. In 1971, he joined Chancellor College as a senior lecturer.[105] Besides teaching, Schoffeleers conducted field research and published so much on religious cults that others described him as 'a leading Dutch anthropologist of Malawi and of African religion'.[106] While maintaining his interest in religious cults, Schoffeleers was quick to realise that his field data also held significant historical information, leading to his important contribution to the history and culture of the Chewa. He was the first scholar, for instance, to come up with a plausible chronological framework for the migration of the Chewa and their early settlement in central Malawi.[107]

As an archaeologist, I was encouraged by Schoffeleers' efforts to work out that chronology. The analysis of his work and that of the other scholars cited earlier convinced me that archaeological research was necessary to document the early history of the Chewa as it produced data which both archaeologists and historians can use. In brief, archaeology has helped clarify the early history of the Chewa, giving it a proper chronological perspective. It has also helped document many aspects of their way of life

---

102 Langworthy 1969.
103 McFarren. 1986.
104 Van Binsbergen WMJ. 2011. In memoriam: Matthew Schoffeleers (1928–2011) *Journal of Religion in Africa*. 41.
105 Ibid: 456.
106 Ibid: 455.
107 Schoffeleers 1973: 47.

that are entirely missing in the oral traditions. The result is a clear picture not only of their history of migrations and settlement, but also of their place in the history of southern and eastern Africa.

Summary

Constituting a little more than a third of the country's total population, the Chewa are the largest of the more than a dozen ethnic groups in Malawi. Other ethnic groups with more than a million people each are the Lhomwe, Yao, Ngoni and Tumbuka.

Some seventeenth-century adventurous Portuguese explorers and traders were the first to mention the 'Maravi' people in some of their written records. However, consistent writing about Malawi started with Dr David Livingstone and the missionaries and settlers who came after him. When the country became a colony in 1891, district administrators recorded oral traditions of the people under their jurisdiction. Scholars singled out one administrator, WHJ Rangeley, for the scholarly quality of his work. By the third decade of the twentieth century, some educated Africans published books after recording oral traditions of their respective ethnic groups. They were Yohanna Barnaba Abdallah, Yesaya Mlonyeni Chibambo and Samuel Josia Ntara.

However, European settlers were more interested in archaeology than in recording oral traditions and so after locating some sites, they invited archaeologists from Zambia and Zimbabwe to investigate them. The European settler community also came up with a journal in which they published research results and eventually, they established a museum in Blantyre.

Soon after Malawi became independent in 1964, the government established the University of Malawi. Its Department of History introduced a programme that led students to record oral traditions of their respective ethnic groups. The government also passed a law called the Monuments Act and established the Department of Antiquities to protect national monuments and to carry out cultural heritage research, including recording oral traditions and archaeology, among other things.

The Department of History at the university also sent some of its brightest students abroad for graduate training in history. The Department of Antiquities and the Museum of Malawi did the same with their newly recruited college-trained staff who were sent abroad to study Archaeology and Museum Management respectively. Meanwhile, locally based and foreign scholars embarked on research projects in archaeology, history and culture. They included J Desmond Clark who excavated Middle and Late Stone Age sites, R Inskeep and KR Robinson who excavated Iron Age sites, and Fr JM Schoffeleers whom others have described as the foremost expert on African religion. He carried out research among the Chewa and the Mang'anja.

CHAPTER 2

The Bantu origins of the Chewa

Ntara[1] was the first person to admit that it is very hard to identify the specific place of origin of the Chewa and to trace accurately their migration route into Malawi. He said that the old people whom he interviewed gave conflicting answers. They placed their home of origin as far north as Egypt with some saying it was Uganda and others mentioning Mombasa in Kenya. In 1970, Linden[2] interviewed a man whom he said was Ntara's principal source for the first few chapters of his book. The man mentioned Libya as the place of origin of the Chewa. A majority of the oral traditions of the Chewa, however, claim that they came from a place called Uluwa or Luba in the Shaba or Katanga area of the Democratic Republic of Congo (DRC).[3] This claim makes sense when one views the Chewa in the context of the general history of African people called the Bantu. The term Bantu does not refer to race, ethnic group or culture; rather, it is a linguistic term.[4] In many Bantu languages, the word-stem 'ntu' means 'person'. The prefix 'ba' indicates plural. Ba-ntu therefore means 'persons' or 'people'.[5] Linguists concluded that Bantu languages are part of one language family called the Niger-Congo language group.[6] The Bantu linguistic homeland is in the general area of eastern Nigeria and western Cameroon which is where the greatest diversity exists among modern Bantu dialects.[7]

1   Ntara 1973: 1.
2   Linden I. 1972. 'Mwali' and the Luba origins of the Chewa: Some tentative suggestions. *The Society of Malawi Journal.* 25(1): 13.
3   Ntara 1973; Bruwer J. 1950. Note on Maravi origin and migration. *African Studies.* 9 (1); Linden 1972; Langworthy 1969; 1973; Phiri 1975; Schoffeleers 1973.
4   Vansina J. 1990. *Paths in the Rainforests: Toward a History of Political Tradition in Equatorial Africa.* Madison, Wisconsin: University of Wisconsin Press.
5   Schneider HK. 1981. *The Africans: An Ethnological Account.* Upper Saddle River, New Jersey: Prentice Hall: 34; Shillington K. 1995. *History of Africa.* New York: St. Martin's Press: 49.
6   Greenberg JH. 1966. *The Languages of Africa.* Bloomington: Indiana University: 7; Guthrie M. 1967. *The Classification of the Bantu Languages.* London: International African Institute; Dalby D. 1975. The prehistorical implications of Guthrie's comparative Bantu: problems of internal relationship. *The Journal of African History.* 16.
7   Greenberg 1966; Vansina 1990; Vansina, J. 1995. New linguistic evidence and 'the Bantu Expansion'. *The Journal of African History.* 36 (2): 176; Bostoen, K. 2017. Historical linguistics. In *Field Manual for African Archaeology.* AL Smith, E Cornelissen, OP Gosselain & S MacEachern (eds). Tervuren: Royal Museum for Central Africa: 257.

Expansion of the Bantu

The expansion of the early Bantu, also referred to as the proto-Bantu,[8] led to the occupation of central, eastern and southern Africa by Bantu-speaking people. Today, there are nearly 900 Bantu language varieties[9] that show a remarkable level of relatedness.[10] They are spoken by more than 200 million people spread out over an area of more than 9 million square kilometres, from southern Somalia in the northeast to southern Africa.[11] Reasons for the Bantu dispersal and the directions or routes they took as they spread out to cover a disproportionately large part of Africa have been the subject of intensive research. The results have generated some disputes among linguists, archaeologists, historians and other scholars.[12] Since the research is ongoing, what is presented below is not the final word. It simply represents the current state of knowledge.

Linguistic studies[13] tend to discount the idea suggested by Phillipson[14] that population pressure due to the introduction of farming was one of the reasons for the dispersal of the proto-Bantu from their homeland. Currently, however, there are no plausible reasons, leading some scholars to speculate that the dispersal may have started by accident.[15] Further, archaeologists and linguists are not in full agreement as to whether the initial dispersal was a migration event[16] or discrete dispersals that were not continuous but occurred at different times.[17] There is one point of undisputed agreement, though, and it is that there was 'more than one dispersal scenario'.[18] Apparently, the proto-Bantu split and dispersed in two directions.[19] One group, referred to by scholars as the Western Stream, went south, crossing the equatorial rainforest to its southern edge and reached the vicinity of the DRC/Angola border. The other group, referred to as

---

8   Guthrie 1967; Dalby 1975; Ehret C. 2002. *The Civilizations of Africa: A History to 1800*. Charlottesville: University Press of Virginia.

9   Bostoen 2017: 258.

10 Vansina 1990: 49

11 Vansina 1990: 49; Phillipson, DW. 2000. *African Archaeology*. Cambridge: Cambridge University Press: 198.

12 Vansina 1995; Eggert M. 1996. Pots, farming and analogy: early ceramics in the equatorial rainforest. In *The Growth of Farming Communities in Africa from the Equator Southward*. JEG Sutton (ed). Nairobi: The British Institute in Eastern Africa: 332; Ehret 2002; Bostoen K. 2007. Pots, words and the Bantu problem: on lexical reconstruction and early African history. *The Journal of African History*. 48 (2):174; Phillipson, DW. 1977a. The Spread of the Bantu Language. *Scientific American*. 236(4). Phillipson 2000; Huffman, TN. 1989. *Iron Age Migrations*. Johannesburg: Witwatersrand University Press; Russell T, Silva F & Steele, J. 2014. Modelling the spread of farming in the Bantu-speaking regions of Africa: an archaeology-based phylogeography. *PLoS One*. 9(1); Skoglund, P, Thompson, JC, Prendergast, ME, Mittnik, A, Sirak, K, Hajdinjak, M, Salie, T, Rohland, N et al. 2017. Reconstructing prehistoric African population structure. *Cell*. 171.

13 Vansina 1990: 55; 1995: 173.

14 Phillipson 2000: 203.

15 Vansina 1995.

16 Phillipson 2000: 203.

17 Vansina 1990: 50, 1995: 190.

18 Russel, Silva & Steele 2014: 8

19 Vansina 1990; 1995; Phillipson 1977a; Phillipson DW. 1977b. *The Later Prehistory of Eastern and Southern Africa*. London: Heinemann.

the Eastern Stream, went east.[20] The languages spread by the two streams are referred to as Western Bantu and Eastern Bantu languages respectively.[21]

The Western Stream

Scholars have not been that successful in establishing a precise date for the dispersal or expansion of the two streams. Linguists such as Guthrie[22] noted only that the distinction between Western Bantu languages, spoken in central Africa, and Eastern Bantu languages, spoken in eastern and southern Africa, was such that the Western Stream and the Eastern Stream must have separated a long time ago. Further, linguists believe that by the time the Eastern Stream began to disperse from the Bantu homeland, the Western Stream had already spread out and settled in the equatorial rainforest.[23] Archaeologically, the site of Shum Laka in north-western Cameroon has yielded the oldest pottery ever found in an area occupied by Bantu speakers. It was dated to about 5000 BC.[24] Dates from other sites to the south of Shum Laka suggest that the expansion of the Western Stream started between that date and 3000 BC.[25] Some of the sites to the south of Shum Laka include Obobogo in south Cameroon, Denis 1 and 3 in Gabon, dated 3000–1000 BC, and Nzogobeyok, also in Gabon, dated 2800–2400 BC.[26] Relatively younger sites in Gabon include Okala, Kango, Lalala, Ndjolé and Lope, dated 800–300 BC.[27] The material remains at these sites show that the proto-Bantu were a Neolithic people, that is, people who used pottery, lived a settled village life, grew crops and raised livestock. This was while they were dependent on stone tools which included polished stone hoes and axes, grooved stones, and upper and lower grinding stones.[28] The proto-Bantu grew oil palm, 'nuts of the *Elaeis guineensis,* and the grains of the *Canarium schweinfurthii*[29] and even though there was no archaeological evidence of yams, it is possible that they grew them too.[30] They also had goats and guinea fowl and they may

---

20   Phillipson 1977b, 2000; Vansina 1990, 1995.

21   Guthrie 1967; Vansina 1995.

22   Guthrie 1967.

23   Vansina J. 1984. Western Bantu expansion. *The Journal of African History.* 25; Ehret C. 1982. Linguistic inferences about early Bantu history. In *The Archaeological and Linguistic Reconstruction of African History.* C Ehret & M Posnansky (eds). Berkeley, University of California Press.

24   Lavachery P. 2001. The Holocene archaeological sequence of Shum Laka Rock Shelter (Grassfields, Western Cameroon). *African Archaeological Review.* 18 (4): 224–225.

25   Clist B. 1989. Archaeology in Gabon, 1886–1988. *African Archaeological Review.* 7; Clist B. 1992. Interim report of the Oveng archaeological site 1991 excavations, Estuaire Province, Gabon. *Nsi*, 10/11.

26   Clist 1989.

27   Clist 1989; Oslisly R. 1996. The middle Ogooué Valley: cultural changes and palaeoclimatic implications of the last four millennia. In *The Growth of Farming Communities in Africa from the Equator Southward.* JEG Sutton (ed). Nairobi: The British Institute in Eastern Africa: 326; Vansina 1990.

28   Bostoen 2007; Clist 1989.

29   Vansina 1990; Bostoen 2007: 188.

30   Vansina 1990.

have been skilled at fishing, using boats which they built themselves.[31] Boat-building in Africa started long before the fourth millennium BC.[32] At the site of Dufuna in north-eastern Nigeria, archaeologists recovered a dugout canoe dated back to 8 000 years ago which makes it the oldest boat in Africa and 'one of the oldest in the world'.[33] The Bantu expansion must have occurred at a slow pace. The equatorial rainforest through which they passed was, and still is, an obstacle to pedestrian movement. The lack of iron tools that would have made clearing paths through the forest relatively easy made the situation difficult for them. The age of iron tools was more than two millennia into the future. Besides, within the forest were other obstacles such as swamps, marshes and mountains that slowed or hindered movement, forcing people to go around them.[34] Scholars have in fact suggested that instead of contending with the forest directly, they may have used the many rivers and streams that exist in the rainforest.[35] Using evidence from linguistics, Blench[36] suggested that some of them may also have used the sea to reach the southern edge of the rainforest.

The Eastern Stream

A dispersal model developed by Phillipson[37] suggested that the Eastern Stream spread directly eastwards from the Bantu homeland, skirting the northern fringes of the equatorial rainforest, and reached the Great Lakes region in East Africa. Other scholars, however, have disputed the idea of the people skirting along the fringes of the forest.[38] They believe that following rivers within the forest was how the people spread, and in this case, it was the Ubangi River,[39] a major tributary of the Congo. It flows directly westwards for hundreds of kilometres from the direction of the Great Lakes region, before it turns south to join the Congo River.

Within the Great Lakes region lived iron-using, non-Bantu-speaking people who also herded livestock, including cattle, and cultivated sorghum and millet.[40] Archaeologists call the pottery associated with them Urewe, after a site located in southwestern Kenya.[41] This pottery was originally called 'dimple-based ware' because of

---

31   Ehret. 2002: 111.
32   Connah G. 2009. *African Civilizations: An Archaeological Perspective*. Cambridge: Cambridge University Press.
33   Connah 2009: 135.
34   Vansina 1990.
35   Vansina 1995; Ciist 1989.
36   Blench R. 2012. Two Vanished African Maritime Traditions and a Parallel from South America. *African Archaeological Review*. 29.
37   Phillipson 1977a.
38   Vansina 1990.
39   Ibid
40   Phillipson 2000: 188.
41   Ibid.

a small concavity or 'dimple' made at the centre of the base[42] and first appeared in the area west of Lake Victoria around 500 BC.[43] The co-existence of Bantu speakers and the iron-using, non-Bantu speakers in that region led the Bantu speakers to adopt an Iron Age lifestyle.

Dispersal from the Great Lakes region

In reconstructing the expansion of the Eastern Stream from the Great Lakes region, Phillipson[44] indicated that the Bantu dispersed in two directions. One group spread southwards while another went westwards, south of the equatorial rainforest (see Map 2.1). The southward-bound group spread over eastern and southern Africa whereas the westward-bound group linked up with the Western Stream in the DRC/Angola border area.[45] These movements were in progress early in the first millennium AD.[46]

As the Bantu spread, they introduced an Iron Age lifestyle in the settlements they established, which entailed a settled village life; herding livestock, including cattle; cultivation of crops, of which the most important were cereals such as sorghum; and use of iron technology.[47] Since these elements were introduced together and so rapidly over a wide area, it suggests that there was physical movement of substantial numbers of people into the area.[48] The material culture of the Iron Age in eastern and southern Africa was so remarkably homogeneous that Phillipson[49] proceeded to give it a proper name. He called it the Chifumbaze complex, after the name of a site in Mozambique where the distinctive Early Iron Age pottery of this cultural complex was first excavated.

Pottery traditions

As discussed in Chapter 6, archaeologists pay great attention to the pottery they excavate because it preserves stylistic features that are culture specific[50] and vary in time and space, enabling them to establish, among other things, when movements of people and other events occurred. The Eastern Stream gave rise to two pottery traditions in eastern and southern Africa that archaeologists call Kwale and Nkope, both of which evolved from Urewe pottery.[51] The Western Stream on the other hand gave rise to Kalundu tradition and Bambata pottery. Archaeologists have used these pottery traditions, and

---

42 Leakey MD, Owen, WE & Leakey LSB. 1948. *Dimple-based Pottery from Central Kavirondo, Kenya Colony.* Nairobi; Phillipson 1977b: 105.

43 Phillipson 2000: 188; Huffman 1989: 65.

44 Phillipson 1977a; 1977b.

45 Phillipson 1977b; Nenquin J. 1959. Dimple-Based Pots from Kasai, Belgian Congo. *Man.* 59.

46 Phillipson 2000.

47 Ibid: 188.

48 Ibid.

49 Ibid.

50 Huffman TN. 1982. Archaeology and ethnohistory of the African Iron Age. *Annual Review of Anthropology.* 11:134.

51 Phillipson 1977b, 2000, Huffman 1982.

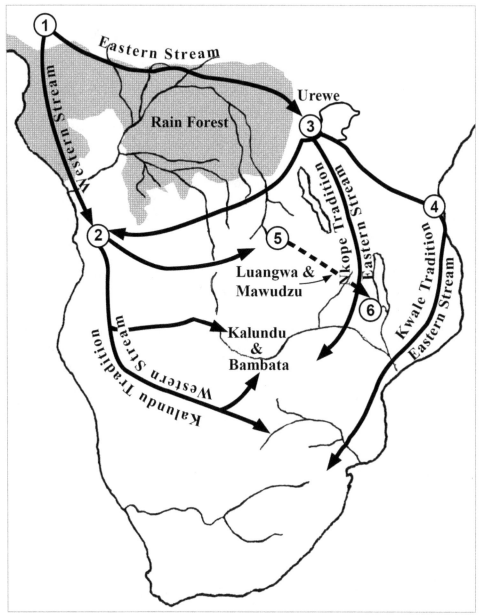

Map 2.1. The spread of the Bantu from their homeland to the southern half of Africa. (1) Primary dispersal area; (2) DRC/Angola border area; (3) The Great Lakes region; (4) Kwale site; (5) Shaba/Luba area; (6) Nkope site.

Source: Adapted from Phillipson 1977a; Huffman, TN. 2007. Handbook to the Iron Age: The Archaeology of Pre-colonial Farming Societies in Southern Africa. *Scottsville: University of KwaZulu-Natal Press.*

the various pottery types or facies that they eventually evolved into, to establish the geographical extent of the region's occupation by Early Iron Age people.

Kwale tradition

Kwale pottery is named after an archaeological site located south-west of Mombasa in Kenya.[52] This pottery has been found in well-watered places not far from Indian Ocean coastal areas and so it is referred to as the coastal or lowland facies of Eastern Stream pottery.[53] The distribution of sites containing Kwale pottery types in southern Africa suggests that the Bantu spread out widely and rapidly. By the end of the second century, they had reached the coastal areas of Mozambique and KwaZulu-Natal.[54]

Kwale pottery developed into three pottery facies.[55] The first is called Silver Leaves, named after a farm in the foothills of the Drakensberg in South Africa.[56] Silver Leaves pottery was also found at other sites located elsewhere in South Africa and in Swaziland and has been dated to AD 280–420,[57] dates which are not far removed from those of Kwale pottery at the Kwale site itself in East Africa.[58] The dates confirm the rapid southward movement of Early Iron Age communities. Klapwijk[59] suggested that boats might have been used to account for the rapid movement, and if not boats, perhaps that they 'at least moved south along the coast'.[60] The second pottery facies, called Mzonjani pottery,[61] was found at Mzonjani and at several other sites along the coastal belt of KwaZulu-Natal. At the Mzonjani site, the pottery has third- to fourth-century dates,[62] and elsewhere it is dated to the fifth and sixth century.[63] In recent times, researchers in Garonga Game Park in the north-eastern part of South Africa found pottery with some Kwale attributes[64] which they called Garonga pottery. This has not yet been dated but it is suspected that it dates to the early eighth and ninth centuries.[65]

---

52 Phillipson 2000: 190.
53 Phillipson 1977b, 2000; Huffman 1989.
54 Huffman 1982: 135.
55 Huffman. 2007.
56 Klapwijk M. 1974. A preliminary report on pottery from the north-eastern Transvaal, South Africa. *The South African Archaeological Bulletin.* 29(113/114):19.
57 Klapwijk M & Huffman TN. 1996. Excavations at Silver Leaves: a final report. *The South African Archaeological Bulletin.* 51: 91.
58 Klapwijk 1974: 22.
59 Ibid.
60 Klapwijk & Huffman 1996: 91.
61 Maggs T. 1980. Mzonjani and the beginning of the Iron Age in Natal. *Annals of the Natal Museum.* 24; Huffman 1998; 2007.
62 Maggs 1980: 71.
63 Huffman 1998; 2007: 343.
64 Burrett R. 2007. The Garonga ceramic assemblage. *Southern African Humanities.* 19.
65 Burrett 2007: 153; Huffman 2007: 131.

Nkope tradition

Nkope pottery, also referred to as the highland facies of the Eastern Stream,[66] was found at several sites on the highlands west of Lake Malawi and in eastern Zambia.[67] In the early third century, makers of Nkope pottery who had arrived in the southern Lake Malawi area[68] continued to spread southwards, crossing the Zambezi River into Zimbabwe by the beginning of the fourth century.[69] In Zimbabwe, Nkope pottery developed into several pottery facies, of which the most prominent were Ziwa and Gokomere pottery. The two were originally believed to be one facies called 'stamped-ware',[70] a name given by archaeologists because the most common decoration on the pottery consisted of stamp designs. These were made by stamping the vessels with either a single-toothed or a linear multi-toothed stamp while the pottery was still soft.[71] Stamped-ware pottery was first excavated at Great Zimbabwe,[72] and since then archaeologists have recovered it at many sites throughout the country. However, Ziwa pottery is common in the east and Gokomere pottery in the south of Zimbabwe.[73] Ziwa pottery came into being earlier than Gokomere pottery and has been dated 300–550.[74] Some of its attributes are so similar to those of Nkope that Huffman[75] views Ziwa pottery as Nkope's southern extension. Despite that, at some point Ziwa pottery was influenced by Western Stream Kalundu and Bambata pottery (discussed below) and, according to Huffman,[76] that mixing is what resulted in Gokomere pottery, dated 550–750.[77]

Kalundu tradition

The distribution of Kalundu pottery and its facies reflects the expansion of the Western Stream from the DRC/Angola border area easterly into Zambia, and southerly to the Angola/Namibia area. This pottery was found at Kalundu mound and at several other

---

66   Phillipson 1977b; Huffman 1982.

67   Robinson KR. 1970. *The Iron Age of the southern lake area of Malawi.* (Department of Antiquities publication no. 8). Zomba, Malawi: Government Press; Phillipson, DW. 1976. *The pre-history of eastern Zambia.* Nairobi: British Institute in Eastern Africa; Phillipson 1977b; Barham L & Jarman CL. 2005. New radiocarbon dates for the Early Iron Age in the Luangwa Valley, eastern Zambia. *Azania: Journal of British Institute in Eastern Africa.* 40(1): 118.

68   Robinson 1970.

69   Huffman 2007: 135.

70   Caton-Thompson G. 1931. *The Zimbabwe culture: ruins and reactions.* Oxford: Clarendon Press; Robinson, KR. 1961a. An early Iron Age site from the Chibi District, Southern Rhodesia. *The South African Archaeological Bulletin.* 16(63).

71   Phillipson 1976: 22.

72   Caton-Thompson 1931; Robinson 1961a.

73   Huffman, TN. 1971. A guide to the Iron Age of Mashonaland. *Occasional papers of the National Museums of Rhodesia: Elizabeth Goodall 1891–1971 commemorative issue.* A4(1):24.

74   Huffman 2007: 135

75   Huffman 1989: 65.

76   Huffman 2007: 335.

77   Ibid: 139.

sites in the southern province of Zambia, where it has been dated to the middle of the first millennium.[78] Archaeological evidence from the site of Benfica[79] in Angola yielded pottery ancestral to both Kalundu and Bambata pottery,[80] dated between the second and third centuries.[81] That pottery 'shares many Kalundu traits with the Early Iron Age pottery at Kaféle and Oveng'[82] in Gabon. The pottery at Oveng is dated between the first and third centuries AD.[83] Kalundu pottery also shares some traits with Urewe pottery,[84] confirming there was contact between the Eastern Bantu speakers who dispersed in a westerly direction from the Great Lakes region and Western Bantu speakers who were already in the vicinity of the DRC/Angola border area.[85] Other material remains associated with Kalundu tradition are consistent with mixed farming.[86] They include evidence of a settled village life, such as 'semi-permanent structures, storage facilities, a wide range of functional ceramic types ...'[87] and some bones of domestic animals.[88] These elements make Kalundu tradition a western expression of the Chifumbaze complex.[89]

Bambata pottery

Bambata pottery is so closely related to Kalundu pottery that Huffman[90] has referred to it as a sub-branch of that pottery. It was named after Bambata cave located on the Matopos Hills in Zimbabwe.[91] Besides the Benfica site mentioned earlier, Bambata pottery was also recovered on the Waterberg Plateau in Namibia,[92] Toteng in Botswana, Magaliesberg in South Africa, the Limpopo Valley in Zimbabwe, and at other sites.[93]

---

78 Huffman 1989: 65.
79 Dos Santos Jnr JR & Ervedosa CMN. 1970. A estação arqueológica de Benfica (Luanda-Angola). *Ciencias Biologicas* (Luanda). 1(1).
80 Huffman 1989: 74.
81 Ibid.
82 Huffman 2007: 359; see also Clist 1992.
83 Huffman 2007: 359.
84 Phillipson 1977b; Huffman 2007: 359.
85 Phillipson 1977b: 221; Nenquin 1959.
86 Huffman, 1989: 63.
87 Huffman 1989: 63.
88 Fagan BM. 1967. *Iron Age Cultures in Zambia*, Vol. 1. London: Chatto & Windus; Huffman 1989: 110.
89 Huffman 1989: 65.
90 Huffman 2007.
91 Robinson KR. 1966b. Bambata ware: its position in the Rhodesian Iron Age in the light of recent evidence. *The South African Archaeological Bulletin*. 21(82): 81; Huffman, TN. 1994. Toteng pottery and the origins of Bambata. *South African Field Archaeology*. 3.
92 Mitchell P & Whitelaw G. 2005. The archaeology of southernmost Africa from c. 2000 BP to the early 1800s: a review of recent research. *The Journal of African History*. 46(2).
93 Cooke CK. 1963. Report on excavations at Pomongwe and Tshangula Caves, Matopo Hills, Southern Rhodesia. *The South African Archaeological Bulletin*. 18; Robinson, KR. 1961b. Zimbabwe Pottery. *Occasional Papers of the National Museums of Southern Rhodesia*. 3A; Robinson KR. 1963. Further excavations in the Iron Age deposits at the Tunnel site, Gokomere Hill, Southern Rhodesia. *The South African Archaeological Bulletin* 18; Robinson 1966b; Denbow J & Campbell AC. 1980. National Museum of Botswana: archaeological research programme. *Nyame Akuma* November; Walker NJ. 1983. The significance of an early date for

The site distribution reflects the southeasterly dispersal of the Western Stream from the Angola–Namibia area to Botswana and the Transvaal, and later north into Zimbabwe, probably beginning from the second or third centuries AD.[94] An interesting characteristic of Bambata pottery is that it was represented by thin- and thick-walled pottery, with the thin type being common at sites occupied by hunter-gatherers.[95] Since the thin-walled pottery had no antecedents at those sites, it was unlikely that hunter-gatherers made it. Huffman[96] suggested that Early Iron Age Bantu farmers purposely made the thin-walled pottery for the purpose of trading with hunter-gatherers. Thin-walled pottery was lighter in weight than thick-walled pottery and so it suited the nomadic or mobile lifestyle of hunter-gatherers.[97]

Contact with hunter-gatherers

Contact between Iron Age farmers and hunter-gatherers, as demonstrated by the makers of Bambata pottery, was unavoidable since the farmers 'did not expand in *vacuo*':[98] they moved into areas where hunter-gatherers lived. In some areas of southern Africa, hunter-gatherers existed until relatively recent times.[99] As a result, archaeology,[100] ethnography and oral traditions[101] have provided evidence of the nature of their lifestyle, which in many respects was the exact opposite of that of the farmers. For instance, although Iron Age farmers used stone tools such as grinding stones to grind various food items, and pebbles for hammering, hunter-gatherers made and used stone tools all the time, as they had no knowledge of metallurgy. They also used bone and wooden tools, but they used stone tools to trim and shape them to desired sizes and shapes. Instead of farming, they subsisted by hunting wild animals and gathering plants,[102] hence the term 'hunter-gatherers'.

Hunting and gathering required them to be nomadic, often going to wherever wild food was in season. As a result, they did not live in villages, but they built temporary

---

pottery and sheep in Zimbabwe. *The South African Archaeological Bulletin.* 38; Walker NJ. 1994. The Late Stone Age of Botswana: some recent excavations. *Botswana notes and records.* 26; Huffman 1989, 1994; Huffman TN. 2005. The stylistic origin of Bambata and the spread of mixed farming in southern Africa. *Southern African Humanities.* 17: 65; Robbins LH. 1985. The Manyana rock paintings site. *Botswana notes and records* 17; Summers R. 1961. The southern Rhodesian Iron Age. *The Journal of African History.* 11:1–13.

94 Huffman 1989, 1994.
95 Huffman 1989, 2007.
96 Huffman 2005.
97 Ibid: 68.
98 Mitchell P. 2002. *The Archaeology of Southern Africa.* Cambridge: Cambridge University Press.
99 Lee RB. 1980. *The!Kung San: Men, Women, and Work in a Foraging Society.* Cambridge: Cambridge University Press.
100 Barham L & Mitchell P. 2008. *The First Africans: African Archaeology from the Earliest Toolmakers to Most Recent Foragers.* Cambridge: Cambridge University Press; Mitchell 2002; Kenyatta J. 1965. *Facing Mount Kenya: the tribal life of the Gikuyu.* New York: Vintage Books.
101 Lee 1980; Ntara 1973.
102 Lee 1980.

shelters[103] or occupied rock shelters and caves if any were available in their area. At some sites, archaeologists found material remains consistent with the lifestyle of hunter-gatherers and early farmers. For instance, they found pottery and iron implements at hunter-gatherer sites, and flaked stone tools, ostrich eggshell beads and bone points at early farmers' sites.[104] Archaeologists interpret this as evidence that some contact between them used to take place,[105] which was probably for the purpose of trade, as was the case with the makers of Bambata pottery,[106] and probably also for the purpose of procuring farm labour.[107]

Genetic studies[108] suggest that intermarriage was not common. In Malawi, for instance, genetic studies show that 'Present-day Malawian individuals are consistent with deriving all their ancestry from the Bantu expansion…'.[109] In other words, food producers almost totally replaced hunter-gatherers.[110] It is possible that in places like Malawi, the relationship between Early Iron Age farmers and hunter-gatherers was characterised by mutual avoidance or aloofness, as was observed elsewhere.[111]

By the second millennium, increased populations of Iron Age farmers and intensification of animal herding may have helped either to absorb or to displace hunter-gatherers.[112] Oral traditions suggest that, in some cases, their displacement was due to armed conflict.[113] In the end, the farmers pushed the hunter-gatherers to areas unsuitable for crop production.[114]

Whence the Chewa

The Chewa appear to be related to people who either made or had contact with the makers of a type of pottery called Naviundu, which is not part of the Chifumbaze complex.[115] This pottery had its origins somewhere in the equatorial rainforest.[116]

---

103 Ibid.
104 Mitchell 2002: 293.
105 Maggs T & Ward V. 1980. Driel Shelter: rescue at a Late Stone Age site on the Tugela River. *Annals of the Natal Museum*. 24(1): 61; Mazel AD. 1986. Mbabane Shelter and eSinhlonhlweni Shelter: the last two thousand years of hunter-gatherer settlement in the central Thukela Basin, Natal, South Africa. *Annals of the Natal Museum*. 27(2); Musonda F. 1987. The significance of pottery in Zambian Later Stone Age contexts. *The African Archaeological Review*. 5.
106 Huffman 1989, 1994.
107 Mitchell 2002: 293.
108 Skoglund et al 2017.
109 Ibid: 63.
110 Ibid.
111 Musonda 1987.
112 Phillipson 2000: 203.
113 Ntara 1973.
114 Phillipson 2000: 203.
115 Huffman 1989: 79.
116 Ibid: 85.

Archaeologists recovered the pottery at Naviundu near Lubumbashi,[117] in the Shaba area of the DRC, and at a site in the Kinshasa area.[118] At Naviundu, the pottery has been dated to the fourth century;[119] its attributes show that it is related to a ninth-century pottery type called Gundu[120] found in southern Zambia, and to an eleventh-century pottery type called Luangwa found in eastern Zambia.[121] Western Bantu speakers made both potteries.[122] Luangwa pottery on the other hand resembles Mawudzu pottery which, by the fourteenth century, was well established at some sites in Malawi including Mankhamba.[123] Some of the archaeologists who work or have worked in Malawi[124] believe that the Chewa, who are also Western Bantu speakers,[125] introduced Mawudzu pottery in the country. Other archaeologists[126] believe that makers of Luangwa pottery spread out from the Shaba area of the DRC at the beginning of the second millennium and replaced Eastern Bantu makers of Nkope pottery. The Chewa were probably part of that dispersal because in their oral traditions, they too claim to have originated from the same area.[127] To them we must now turn.

Summary

The Chewa are part of Bantu-speaking people who today are found over an area of some 9 million square kilometres from southern Somalia to central and southern Africa. The ancient ancestors of these people originated in western Cameroon and eastern Nigeria. The Bantu expansion, which started between 5000 and 3000 BC, spread in two directions but did not start at the same time. The first group spread southwards and reached the DRC/Angola border area. Scholars call this group the Western Stream, whereas the other group, called the Eastern Stream, spread easterly. These Bantu reached the Great Lakes region in East Africa where they found non-Bantu-speaking people who practised

---

117 Anciaux de Faveaux E & De Maret P. 1984. Premières datations pour la fonte du cuivre au Shaba (Zaire). *Bulletin de la Société Royale Belge d' Anthropologie et de Préhistoire*. 95; De Maret P. 1985. Recent archaeological research and dates from central Africa. *The Journal of African History*. 26: 138.

118 Mortelmans G. 1962. Archéologie des Grottes Dimba et Ngovo (Région de Thysville, Bas-Congo). *Annales du Musee Royal de l'Afrique Centrale*. Sciences Humaines Pre- et Protohistoire. 40(III): 407-426.

119 De Maret 1985: 138.

120 Huffman 1989: 78; 2007: 335.

121 Huffman 1989: 96.

122 Ibid: 110.

123 Robinson, KR. 1973. *The iron age of the upper and lower Shire Malawi*. (Department of Antiquities publication no. 13). Zomba, Malawi: Government Press; Mgomezulu 1978; Davison S. 1991. Namaso: a newly-defined cultural entity of the late first millennium AD, and its place in the Iron Age sequence of southern Malawi. *Azania: Archaeological Research in Africa*. 26; Davison, S. 1992. Namaso: a newly-discovered ceramic entity of the late first millennium AD, on the south-east arm of Lake Malawi. In *Occasional Papers of the Malawi Department of Antiquities* 1; Juwayeyi 2010a.

124 Robinson 1970; Mgomezulu 1978; Juwayeyi 1981; Juwayeyi 2010a.

125 Huffman 1989: 111; see also Vansina 1984; Skoglund et al 2017.

126 Phillipson 1977b: 230.

127 Ntara 1973; Linden 1972; Langworthy 1969, 1973; Phiri 1975; McFarren 1986; Schoffeleers 1973.

an Iron Age lifestyle. The elements of that lifestyle included practising mixed farming and making iron implements and pottery, called Urewe by archaeologists.

Early in the first millennium, these Bantu began to disperse southwards and westwards from the Great Lakes region, spreading their newly acquired Iron Age lifestyle. The southward-bound group gave rise to two pottery traditions called Kwale and Nkope, both of which evolved from Urewe pottery. Makers of Kwale pottery moved quickly along low-lying areas close to the Indian Ocean and reached KwaZulu-Natal, South Africa, by the second century. The distribution of Kwale pottery facies, such as Silver Leaves and Mzonjani pottery, shows that these people spread widely in what is now South Africa, whereas the makers of Nkope pottery moved along the highlands west of Lake Malawi. By the fourth century, they had crossed the Zambezi River into Zimbabwe where they continued to spread, as demonstrated by the distribution of facies of Nkope pottery, namely Ziwa and Gokomere pottery. The material culture of the Eastern Stream was so homogeneous that archaeologists gave it a proper name, the Chifumbaze complex.

The westward-bound group linked up with the Western Stream in the DRC/Angola border area, which gave rise to Kalundu and Bambata pottery. The distribution of those two pottery types shows that the Bantu spread eastwards, reaching southern Zambia, and south-east from the Angola/Namibia area to Botswana, the Gauteng area of South Africa, and later, north into Zimbabwe.

Archaeologists found another pottery type, which they called Naviundu pottery, at Naviundu near Lubumbashi and at a site in the Kinshasa area. Naviundu pottery, made by Western Bantu speakers, is related to Gundu pottery found in southern Zambia, and to Luangwa pottery found in eastern Zambia. Luangwa pottery, in turn, is related to Mawudzu pottery, also made by Western Bantu speakers, and recovered at Mankhamba and at other sites in central and southern Malawi.

CHAPTER 3

The origins and migrations of the Chewa according to their oral traditions

In Chapters 3 and 4, I have used both published and unpublished sources to summarise the current state of knowledge regarding the early history of the Chewa. Oral traditions were the basis of nearly all the consulted works, with the most prominent being *Mbiri ya Achewa*. All researchers investigating the history of the Chewa, following Ntara's publishing of his work, have consulted the book, which is considered seminal and the 'the fullest body of oral tradition'.[1] Ntara's work is of great value to researchers not only because it was the first authoritative study of the Chewa, but also because of the manner in which he presented his work. Ntara did not offer much analytical or interpretive detail, narrating instead the traditions in a summarised format. As a result, it afforded subsequent scholars the opportunity to use his work as if they were using unmodified oral traditions. They commented, analysed and interpreted it to suit the needs of their research. One researcher who made very elaborate comments was Langworthy[2] who, having written an introduction to the translated 1973 edition of the book, proceeded to provide general and interpretive comments to most of its chapters. While this has the disadvantage of making it unavoidable to view Ntara's work from Langworthy's perspective, it rendered the work readily comparable with other subsequent scholarly works on the history and culture of the Chewa. Besides the literature based on oral traditions, there are seventeenth-century documents written by the early Portuguese that refer to the Maravi.[3] The very mention of 'Maravi' in the documents is significant in that it confirms that the Maravi, as a distinct group of people, did indeed exist. Some of the documents have helped clarify oral traditions.

Oral traditions

Oral traditions are messages from the past that go beyond the present generation,[4] which are transmitted orally[5] and concern events that occurred beyond the lifetime of the informant. They are expressions of the past or what Vansina referred to as 'the

---

1   Linden 1972: 13.
2   Langworthy 1973.
3   Theal 1964.
4   Vansina J. 1985. *Oral Tradition as History*. Madison: University of Wisconsin Press: 27.
5   Schoenbrun D. 2017. Oral tradition. In *Field Manual for African Archaeology*. AL Smith, E Cornelissen, OP Gosselain & S MacEachern (eds). Tervuren: Royal Museum for Central Africa: 253.

representation of the past in the present'.[6] Often, oral traditions 'contain names, titles, or sayings with metaphorical content that also appears on material culture'.[7] Because of this, oral traditions can be useful to archaeologists if properly analysed and interpreted, although it is important not to confuse oral traditions with oral history, which involves messages or statements about the present generation. In sub-Saharan Africa, narrating or reciting oral traditions was how history was preserved, remembered and transmitted.

People tend to have stories of the origin of the world and of the creation of their respective ethnic group or community.[8] The stories often mention specific places of origin and how the people came to be in the places in which they are currently found. Sometimes they include details of wars they fought and won, famines that occurred due to locusts or other blights, names of settlements they established and abandoned, names of important people, and other aspects of their heritage. The long-term survival of the stories depended on the manner in which they were performed or presented. Recognised sages or state officials at royal courts or palaces, for instance, would recite stories about the people's past. They tended to have knowledge of issues such as origins of their clans and rulers, succession procedures, obligations and prerequisites of various offices, migration itineraries, conquests, and so on.[9] Sometimes their messages were crafted into poems or songs and therefore preserved through repetition. Although anthropologists call such stories myths,[10] they were functional in that they helped establish societal cohesion. The introduction of schools during the colonial period resulted in the writing down of some of the traditions[11] so that they became written accounts which were read rather than transmitted orally. Some are available to archaeologists in the national archives of various countries, university libraries and in private collections.

Archaeologists and other scholars, however, must exercise caution when using oral traditions in their research. They ought to bear in mind that informants had not been eyewitnesses to the information they provided. In many cases, the events they described occurred several centuries in the past and had been subjected to various forms of modification through time. Therefore, proper and patient evaluation of the reliability of oral traditions is essential. That, in fact, is how I handled the oral traditions of the Chewa. I did not, for instance, offhandedly reject or accept wholesale the story of the origins of the Chewa, subjecting it instead to some evaluation. For example, after reading in Ntara's[12] book that the Chewa king, Kalonga, established his settlement at

---

6   Vansina 1985: xii.
7   Schoenbrun 2017: 255.
8   Vansina 1985.
9   Vansina 1985; Schoenbrun 2017.
10   Vansina 1985.
11   Bostoen 2017.
12   Ntara 1973.

a place called Mankhamba along the Nadzipulu River, I interviewed the area's group village headman and others. I followed that up with an archaeological site survey of the Mankhamba area. The results of those activities were important in determining the next stage of the research. Further, I examined carefully the reasons that were presented for certain events that happened among the Chewa. For instance, Ntara[13] and other published oral traditions[14] said that at some point before Kalonga arrived at Mankhamba, two of his royal relatives called Kaphwiti and Lundu broke away from him. After he arrived at Mankhamba, another relative called Undi unilaterally abandoned the settlement. Today Kaphwiti is no longer heard of, but Lundu is a Mang'anja leader in the Lower Shire River Valley and Undi is a Chewa leader in eastern Zambia. Since there is linguistic and cultural homogeneity between the people of these two leaders and the Chewa in central Malawi, oral traditions claiming Lundu, Undi and Kalonga were related, and that they were together as the Chewa migrated from their ancestral homeland to Malawi, can be accepted. What cannot be accepted are the reasons for the conflicts that led them to break away from Kalonga because there are several different versions.

Chewa clan names and titles

Before proceeding with the story of the migration of the Chewa from Luba to Malawi, it is important to spell out at the outset some of the clan names and titles that the Chewa used and the terms that various scholars have adopted to refer to them. Ntara's oral traditions claim that the Chewa were so homogenous when they lived in Luba that they did not have clan names. In his opinion, they created them during their migration when they reached a place called Choma. But these traditions did not reflect reality. Ntara himself said, 'Nobody in Malawi is without a clan name. Everybody is proud to belong to a clan.'[15] This statement shows that the Chewa must have had clan names all along. What had disappeared from their memory was how the clan names came into being, causing them to come up with a legend to explain this. One legend recorded by Ntara[16] is worth quoting in full:

> One day two groups went about in search of arrowroots and some edible roots. They did not return home but slept in the bush. One group slept on a hill-top and the other at the foot of the hill. When morning came, those who slept on the hill-top were nicknamed Phiri ('of the hill') and those who slept at the foot of the hill and had to level or lay out the grass were called Banda ('those who tread the grass under their feet'). So it came to pass that the two clans were created in this way.

---

13 Ibid.
14 Rangeley WHJ. 1954. Bocarro's journey. *The Nyasaland Journal.* 7(2); Langworthy 1969; Phiri 1975.
15 Ntara 1973: 6.
16 Ntara 1973: 6.

> The advantage was that the creation of these clans made it possible for anyone from the Banda clan to marry into the Phiri clan and vice versa.

Other legends related to this state that at Choma some people decided to travel by way of the mountains and so they became 'Phiri' and those who chose to keep to the valleys referred to themselves as the Banda.[17] Legends, however, have functions in society and in this case they help to illuminate historical facts. This particular legend demonstrates that the two clans did not arrive in Malawi at the same time. However, the fact that the same legend created their clan names shows that there was a close relationship between them.

Ntara[18] also recorded the perpetual titles of various important Chewa personalities. As stated above, the king's title was 'Kalonga' which Ntara clarified when he said that the title was similar to that of 'king' or 'queen' as used by the British. Other Chewa royal people with titles were Kalonga's mother or sister, whose title was 'Nyangu', and Kalonga's principal wife, whose title was 'Mwali'.[19] Oral traditions are not clear regarding the relationship between Nyangu and Kalonga with some suggesting that she was not the mother but sister of the first Kalonga.[20] Coming from a matrilocal society, Nyangu was also the head or mother of the Phiri clan.[21] The other important title was that of 'Makewana', assumed by 'Mangadzi', the female priestess, rain-caller and leader of the Banda clan.[22] Makewana literally means 'the mother of children', but in this case the intention is to convey the belief that she was 'the mother of all people'.[23] They reserved the title for the female person responsible for ritual activities, the most important of which was rain-calling. The terms 'Makewana' and 'Mangadzi' are sometimes used interchangeably.[24]

In writing about the Chewa, it seems each of the primary scholars of Chewa history and culture adopted different terms to refer to the Banda and Phiri clans and this has not been helpful to readers. The literature shows the use of the terms 'proto-Chewa', 'proto-Malawi' and 'pre-Malawi' to refer to the Chewa of the Banda and to some of the small clans, such as the Mbewe and the Mwale.[25] Scholars believe that the Banda and some of the small clans arrived in Malawi before the Phiri clan[26] and they use the terms

---

17 Linden 1972: 14.
18 Ntara 1973: 4.
19 Ntara 1973:4; Langworthy 1973: 13.
20 Langworthy 1973: 11.
21 Ntara 1973: 12.
22 Langworthy, 1973: 10, Phiri. 1975: 46.
23 Rangeley 1952: 32.
24 Ibid.
25 Langworthy 1969; Schoffeleers 1973, 1992; Phiri, 1975.
26 Phiri 1975; Schoffeleers 1973, 1992; see also Hamilton 1955; Marwick 1963.

'Maravi' and sometimes 'Malawi' to refer to the Chewa of the Phiri clan.[27] The inconsistency is due to how people in the past used the term 'Malawi,' and how early Europeans spelled it when they first wrote it down. As an ordinary Chichewa word, *malawi* means 'flames of fire'.[28] In the ethnographic sense, however, Chewa oral traditions contain a myth that explains why the name Malawi came into use. Apparently, when the Chewa saw Lake Malawi for the first time from the surrounding highlands, it looked like a mirage or flames of fire.[29] This must have fascinated them and so they gave the term *malawi* both geographical and cultural identity. In the geographical sense, they began to refer to the land that stretches from Mangochi or Lake Malombe in the south to Linthipe River in the north as Malawi,[30] which is also the land referred to as the southern Lake Malawi area. Culturally, when they finally settled in that area, they referred to themselves as 'Amalawi', that is, Malawians.[31] The Portuguese of the seventeenth century referred to Chichewa-speaking people north of the Zambezi as the 'Maravi'.[32] Many scholars adopted this term rather than 'Malawi' for the Chewa of the Phiri clan, but they needed a term for the Banda clan. Since they came before the Maravi, Schoffeleers[33] called them the 'proto-Chewa'; Langworthy[34] named them the 'proto-Malawi'; and Phiri[35] used the term 'pre-Malawi'.

In this book, I have adopted the term 'pre-Maravi' in order to avoid confusion with the terms 'Malawi' for the country and 'Malawians' for the people. The term 'Maravi' on the other hand will be maintained but it will have dual usage. Depending on the context, it will be used to refer to the Phiri clan and to all the Chewa in general.

Abandoning Luba

Ntara[36] gives the impression that the Chewa moved out of Luba en masse which is most likely correct. When Phillipson[37] discussed the migration of Early Iron Age people from the Great Lakes region to eastern and southern Africa, he suggested it was probable that the migrations involved substantial numbers of people. During the sixteenth century, the early Portuguese in the Zambezi Valley witnessed slow-moving groups of people

27 Schoffeleers 1973: Langworthy 1969; Phiri 1975.
28 Schoffeleers JM 1972. The meaning and use of the name Malawi in oral traditions and precolonial documents. In *The Early History of Malawi*. B. Pachai (ed). London: Longman: 91.
29 Ntara 1973: 15.
30 Ntara 1973: 15; Schoffeleers 1972: 92.
31 Schoffeleers 1972
32 Barretto 1964.
33 Schoffeleers 1973: 47.
34 Langworthy 1969: VI.
35 Phiri 1975: 47.
36 Ntara 1973.
37 Phillipson 2000: 188.

that included women and children, who numbered in the thousands,[38] looking for a place to settle. The Portuguese referred to them as the 'Macabires' or 'Cabires'.[39] One scholar, Newitt,[40] saw a similarity between these two names and those of 'Kaphirintiwa' or 'Phiri'. If Newitt is correct, then these migrants were Kaphwiti and Lundu and their followers, the only Phiris who came that far south after they broke away from Kalonga, as discussed in the following chapter. A more recent example involving substantial numbers of people was the long-distance migration of the Maseko Ngoni from South Africa in the early nineteenth century. They passed through Mozambique, Malawi and reached Tanzania; and then turned back to southern Malawi, finally settling at Domwe in Mozambique and the adjacent areas of Dedza and Ntcheu in central Malawi.[41] As they went along, they attacked other ethnic groups in order to obtain food and to gain subjects.[42] What these examples demonstrate is that long-distance migrations involving large numbers of people used to occur in the region during the Late Iron Age and that the migrants were unlikely to have had a clear destination in mind. They settled wherever the physical environment met their needs. We must examine the migrations of the Chewa from that perspective.

Scholars who have carried out research among the Chewa[43] believe that the two clans migrated neither together, as a single group, nor at the same time. They claim that the Banda clan was the first to abandon Luba, and that it arrived in Malawi earlier than the Phiri clan. Schoffeleers[44] proposed that the Banda clan arrived between 1200 and 1400, referring to that time span as the proto-Chewa period. He said the period from 1400 to 1600 was when the Maravi arrived.

Scholars based the idea of separate migrations on the interesting observation that the Chewa have two contradictory stories of their origins, the first being a myth which is popular among them. It says that the Chewa were indigenous people who did not migrate from anywhere.[45] According to that myth, the Chewa and other creatures were created locally at Kaphirintiwa, a hill located on the Dzalanyama range along the western border of central Malawi and Mozambique.[46] This myth came about because of a geological feature on that hill. Wind- or water-related weathering of the granite rock has created a pattern that looks like the footprints of humans and animals.[47] As a result, the

---

38 De Couto D. 1964. Asia: of the deeds which the Portuguese performed in the conquest and discovery of the lands and seas of the east. In *Records of South-Eastern Africa*, Vol. 6. G.M. Theal (ed). Cape Town: Struik.

39 Ibid: 393.

40 Newitt 1982: 153.

41 Omer-Cooper 1969.

42 Langworthy 1973.

43 Langworthy 1969; Schoffeleers 1973; Phiri 1975.

44 Schoffeleers 1973: 1.

45 Hamilton 1955; Schoffeleers 1973.

46 Langworthy 1973: 9.

47 Langworthy 1973.

Chewa began to give the place religious veneration as the site of creation, believing that soon after God created the world and before it hardened, He also created humans and animals that walked on it,[48] imprinting their tracks for posterity. These kinds of geological features exist in many parts of central Africa, although they are not as dense as they are at Kaphirintiwa.[49] The second story is the exact opposite of this myth. It says simply that the Chewa are immigrants and that they originated from Uluwa or the Luba area in the southern Congo basin.[50] Scholars have tried to make sense of the two stories. The first scholar to attempt to solve this puzzle was Hamilton[51] who felt that the two stories could only have originated from two different groups of people with different stories of origin. He suggested that those Chewa who emphasise the creation myth must be those who were indigenous or who had arrived first. Those who emphasise migrations must have been later arrivals who probably came in as invaders. Marwick[52] supported Hamilton's suggestion by relating it to some important division of functions or responsibilities that existed between the Banda and the Phiri clans. He pointed out that, in Chewa society, the Banda were always responsible for ritual activities such as rain-calling, assuming that responsibility because as early arrivals they identified with the land. The Phiri, on the other hand, held secular authority,[53] a characteristic of invaders. Schoffeleers[54] agreed with the idea of interdependence of responsibilities of the two clans. He added that since the Phiri could not perform rituals to influence natural events such as rain, the prosperity of the entire Chewa community depended on the acceptance and respect of the ritual authority wielded by the Banda clan.

Migrations of the pre-Maravi

As demonstrated above, the archaeological evidence indicates that the pre-Maravi lived in a part of Luba that may not have been far from the Lubumbashi area. Although the migration of the Maseko Ngoni demonstrates that it is futile to determine routes of Iron Age long-distance migrations, the archaeological evidence shows that the pre-Maravi reached eastern Zambia and this suggests they took a southeasterly direction from Luba (see Map 3.1).

We are not aware of any significant events during their migration, but some of their cultural institutions have survived, including the Nyau secret society[55] which is an important cultural institution of the Chewa and the Mang'anja. Ethnographic

---

48 Ntara 1973: 8.
49 Langworthy 1973: 9.
50 Ntara 1973; Phiri 1975.
51 Hamilton 1955.
52 Marwick 1963.
53 Ibid.
54 Schoffeleers 1973: 49.
55 Schoffeleers JM. 1976. The Nyau societies: our present understanding. *The Society of Malawi Journal.* 29 (1): 59–68; 1992.

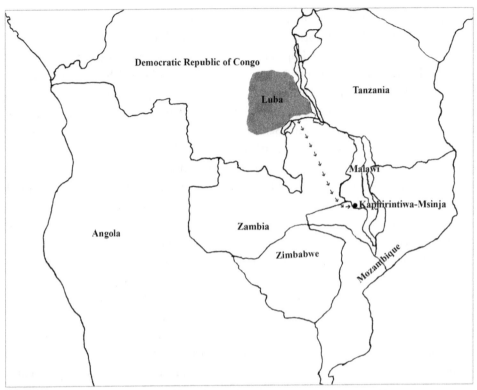

Map 3.1: South-easterly migration of the Chewa from Luba through eastern Zambia to Kaphirintiwa-Msinja.
Source: The author

evidence shows that the Nyau secret society is one institution that links them to Luba. For instance, the use of ceremonial masks by the Nyau is akin to the use of masks by the Bumbudye secret society in Luba.[56] Further, the people of Luba have an institution called Mwadi, which is similar to Mwali among the Chewa.[57] The Nyau secret society was well described by Schoffeleers[58] who said that it is perceived as a men's society even though women are also involved in its activities. Its members wear masks when they perform dances to disguise themselves as spirits and animals. Although as dancers the Nyau now perform at national events such as independence-day celebrations and other political rallies, traditionally they perform at special events or ceremonies in various villages.[59] For instance, they perform at final mourning rites 'which take place from a

---

56 Phiri KM. 1977. The Maravi state system and Chewa political development to c. 1840. Proceedings of a teachers' conference. Chancellor College, Zomba. Malawi: 3.

57 Linden 1972: 15.

58 Schoffeleers 1976, 1978, 1992.

59 Schoffeleers 1978, 1972.

few months to a year after a person's death, and at communal initiation ceremonies for girls'.[60] As a men's secret society, male membership used to be obligatory.[61] However, Christian mission influence has currently resulted in many non-initiates.[62] Although the public views members of the Nyau as entertainers, the Nyau see themselves as part of the spirit world. They call the dance *Gule Wamkulu* — the great dance — or *Pemphero Lalikulu*—the great prayer.[63] They prepare for events in secret, including the making of masks and other costumes, and they store their costumes 'in places which are sealed off from the intrusion of non-initiates by means of flags or other signs along pathways. Trespassers are severely punished and made to pay a heavy fine, and they may even be forcibly initiated'.[64]

Contact with local inhabitants

According to oral traditions, the pre-Maravi encountered two different groups of people on their arrival in central Malawi. The first comprised short-statured people, akin to the pygmies who still exist in the equatorial rainforest of central Africa[65] and the !Kung who thrived in the Kalahari Desert of southern Africa.[66] The Chewa and other ethnic groups in Malawi refer to these short-statured people variously as Akafula, Abatwa or Amwandionerakuti.[67] Oral traditions collected by Rangeley[68] contain some stories about the Akafula whose way of life was consistent with a hunter-gatherer existence. Although some legends exist that claim they lived in antbear holes,[69] it is likely that like the !Kung,[70] the Akafula constructed temporary shelters in which to live. Interaction between the Chewa and the Akafula seems to have been characterised by hostility, culminating in a battle near Mankhamba where legend has it that the Akafula were defeated and driven 'down the Shire valley and across the Zambezi River'.[71] This legend exists probably to explain why, in this part of the continent, we find short-statured people only south of the Zambezi River.

Oral traditions of other ethnic groups in East Africa, such as the Kikuyu of Kenya, also contain legends of their encounter with short-statured people, referred to by the Kikuyu as the Gumba.[72] Among the legends associated with them is one claiming that

---

60   Schoffeleers 1992: 34.
61   Ibid: 38.
62   Schoffeleers 1992.
63   Ibid: 38.
64   Schoffeleers 1978: 40.
65   Turnbull CM. 1961. *The Forest People*. New York: Simon & Schuster.
66   Lee 1980.
67   Rangeley WHJ. 1963. The earliest inhabitants of Nyasaland. *The Nyasaland Journal*. 16 (2): 36.
68   Ibid.
69   Ibid: 38.
70   Lee 1980.
71   Rangeley 1963: 39.
72   Kenyatta 1965: 24.

the Gumba dug tunnels underground where they lived, and another that says some relationship leading to intermarriage between them and the Kikuyu developed.[73] Intermarriage produced another group of people called Ndorobo or Aathi, whose stature was in between that of the Gumba and the Kikuyu,[74] a legend that helps explain why the Gumba do not exist in Kenya today.

The other group that the pre-Maravi met was the agriculturists, identified as the baKatanga, or baPule or baLenda[75] and about whom we know very little. Rangeley[76] offered three possible explanations for the use of the term 'baKatanga.' He said that it might be derived from the Tumbuka word 'kutanga', which in this case he understood to mean 'the first people'. Alternatively, it could have been derived from the name Katanga, a province of the DRC within which the Luba area is located. Last, he connected it to the Makaranga, who probably passed through Malawi on their way to Zimbabwe where they settled. Legends of this nature have a purpose, and in this case they help to show that there were people living in the area where the migrants passed through or settled. The fact that the owners of the traditions are the descendants of the pre-Maravi is important because it helps illustrate that their ancestors became the dominant group who took control of the land away from the original inhabitants.

Now let us examine the archaeological evidence. As discussed above, Early Iron Age farmers who made Nkope pottery began to settle in the southern Lake Malawi area early in the third century. The presence of Late Stone Age sites[77] suggests that the early farmers encountered Late Stone Age hunter-gatherers, some of whom may well have been the Akafula. Two other pottery types were introduced in the area between the eighth and the ninth century: Kapeni pottery, first excavated by Robinson[78] in the Bwanje River Valley south of the western arm of Lake Malawi; and Namaso pottery excavated at Namaso Bay by Davison.[79] These pottery types were in use until early in the second millennium. The presence of Nkope and the other potteries indicates that since the third century, Iron Age agriculturists had been in the area. When the pre-Maravi arrived, they encountered both the agriculturists and the Akafula. Oral traditions of the Chewa, however, only recall their encounter with the Akafula, perhaps because their physical appearance and their way of life were different. The pre-Maravi must have intermarried with their fellow agriculturists, and through time whatever each group remembered of its past became cloudy and, eventually, much of it forgotten.

---

73 Ibid.
74 Ibid:25.
75 Rangeley 1963: 40.
76 Ibid: 41.
77 Cole-King PA. 1973. *Kukumba mbiri mu Malaŵi: a summary of archaeological research to March 1973.* (Department of Antiquities publication no. 15). Zomba, Malawi: Government Press.
78 Robinson 1970.
79 Davison 1991, 1992.

The pre-Maravi at Kaphirintiwa-Msinja

Since the migration of the pre-Maravi had no predetermined destination, it is possible that they established and abandoned several settlements before they decided to settle permanently at Kaphirintiwa-Msinja. Though only a hill, Kaphirintiwa was better known than Msinja because it housed a *kachisi*, a rain-calling shrine.[80] The people lived and farmed at Msinja, a wide expanse of land below the Dzalanyama range extending southwards to the Diamphwe River and eastwards to Mitundu and Bunda Hill. The land is agriculturally rich, with good soils and abundant water. Judging by the thick vegetation on the Dzalanyama range, it is clear that Msinja also had a similar vegetation cover which has since been decimated by agricultural activities.

When the pre-Maravi first saw the geological feature on Kaphirintiwa Hill, it astounded them so much that they made the site the centre of their ritual activities. They established a shrine dedicated to the cult of Chisumphi, whom they considered their high god.[81] Makewana, the priestess, was assisted by the 'Matsano' or 'spirit wives' and a priesthood that consisted of members of the Mbewe clan.[82] The Matsano were a group of specially selected women of any age who lived a permanently celibate life.[83] With Makewana, they exercised ritual authority, including overseeing female initiation rites,[84] and acted as mediums who 'transmitted messages received in a state of ecstasis.'[85] The Mbewe priesthood, according to Rangeley,[86] had a cult object which was an imaginary snake called Thunga. A man named Kamundi, who was a senior member of the Mbewe clan, represented the imaginary snake. Among his functions was to be Makewana's consort, for both of them were supposed to be unmarried.[87] As a Thunga or snake, he would enter Makewana's hut on completion of girls' initiation ceremonies to perform ritual sexual intercourse.[88]

While Kamundi also had secular responsibilities, many scholars emphasise Makewana's ritual responsibilities but generally ignore the fact that she was also a chiefly figure[89] whose secular authority was inherent in her ritual position. A study of political traditions in central Africa by Vansina[90] among Western Bantu speakers shows that the pre-Maravi would fit the definition of a state. Vansina[91] demonstrated that statehood

80 Schoffeleers 1992.
81 Schoffeleers 1978.
82 Rangeley 1952; Schoffeleers 1973.
83 Rangeley 1952.
84 Schoffeleers 1992: 33.
85 Schoffeleers 1973: 52.
86 Rangeley 1952: 37.
87 Rangeley 1952; Schoffeleers 1992.
88 Rangeley 1952: 34; Schoffeleers 1992: 34
89 Schoffeleers JM 1979. The Chisumphi and Mbona cults in Malawi: a comparative history. In *Guardians of the Land*. JM Schoffeleers (ed). Gwelo, Zimbabwe, Mambo Press: 151.
90 Vansina J. 1989. Deep-down time: political tradition in central Africa. *History in Africa*. 16.
91 Ibid: 357.

evolved from humble beginnings and that a state was born when a single incumbent filled the highest rank. Going by that definition, one would conclude that the pre-Maravi, who were also Western Bantu speakers, achieved that level of political development. Some anthropologists may disagree with Vansina, though, because the anthropological definition of a state includes a high level of social stratification and 'a populace with substantial contrasts in occupation, wealth, prestige, and power'.[92] But judging by the manner in which Makewana controlled widely spread out rain-calling shrines, it is clear that she had significant secular authority. Some of the well-known satellite shrines were located at Chirenje near Nkhoma and at Mankhamba itself[93] in central Malawi. Others included the shrine of the Bimbi cult in the Upper Shire Valley[94] and the shrine on Thyolo Mountain in southern Malawi.[95] Makewana appointed the 'spirit wives' for these shrines and their positions also had inherent secular authority.[96] Thus, there was a hierarchical order of shrines, with Makewana and the Kaphirintiwa shrine at the top as the 'mother' of all shrines.[97] Someone, however, had to exercise the secular authority openly, and according to Schoffeleers[98] Kamundi was the de facto secular leader who was responsible for decisions generally attributed to Makewana.[99]

Another feature at Kaphirintiwa-Msinja and at each of the major shrines was the presence of a sacred pool[100] which played a role in rain-making ceremonies. According to legend, the process of calling rain required Makewana to disappear into the pool for three days at a time.[101] Only Makewana was allowed to drink or wash in the sacred pool at Kaphirintiwa-Msinja. When Makewana died, the Matsano took her body to the sacred pool at night, and after they tied stones to it they cast it into the pool.[102] At Mankhamba, the sacred pool was located about eight kilometres to the east of the settlement site. Today the local people call it Mpando wa Nyangu (Nyangu's Chair) because in the middle of the pool there are stones arranged to look like a high chair. Linden[103] used the term Mipando-a-Mwali, meaning Mwali's Chair(s). However, calling the pool by those names instead of Mpando wa Makewana (Makewana's Chair), or that of her representative at Mankhamba, is a misnomer. It suggests that either the people could no longer recall their traditions accurately or that future Kalongas became

---

92 Kottak CP. 2015. *Cultural anthropology: Appreciating Cultural Diversity.* New York: McGraw Hill. 317.
93 Schoffeleers 1979: 152, 180.
94 Amanze J. 2002. *African Traditional Religion in Malawi: the case of the Bimbi Cult.* Blantyre, Malawi: Christian Literature Association in Malawi: 157.
95 Schoffeleers 1992: 33.
96 Schoffeleers 1979: 153.
97 Schoffeleers 1953: 52.
98 Schoffeleers 1979: 182.
99 Ibid.
100 Rangeley 1952; Schoffeleers 1992.
101 Rangeley 1952: 34.
102 Ibid.
103 Linden 1972: 11.

so powerful that they could install either of the two senior women at Mankhamba to represent Makewana. Sacred pools contained water all year round, but these days silting causes some to be shallow during the dry season.

The ritual centre at Kaphirintiwa-Msinja had, and still has, an additional feature that researchers of Chewa history and culture often mention even though its significance is unclear — a sacred drum. According to tradition, it belonged to the Akafula.[104] The Chewa acquired it when the Akafula either left it behind or dropped it as they ran away from Chewa fighting forces.[105] The Chewa consecrated it and so made it sacred. It is a small drum, measuring no longer than 46 centimetres and no wider than 28 centimetres.[106] It is double-ended and cylindrical in shape, with tympanums of the skins of a monitor lizard (*Varanus* sp).[107] Called *mbiriwiri*,[108] it indeed looks old and it seems the only reason the drum was preserved was to use it to summon people to functions or to announce the death of an important person.[109] The drum was beaten by a specially selected person of the Mwale clan whose titular name was Tsang'oma[110] and it was due to its presence that the playing or beating of other drums at Kaphirintiwa-Msinja was prohibited. Ntara[111] says that was one of the reasons why the Maravi abandoned the area as they wanted to settle in a place where their children would have sufficient recreational facilities including playing drums. One wishes the oral traditions on prohibiting the playing of drums were clearer. It is hard to imagine how successful the prohibition was among the Nyau secret society, as playing drums is a significant part of Nyau performances.

The Chewa still venerate the drum, which they keep in a shrine (see Plate 3.1). It is one of only three portable relics of the early Chewa known to have survived to modern times. The other two are the iron stools of chiefs Kanyenda and Chulu of Nkhotakota and Kasungu districts respectively[112] which, according to oral traditions, were given to the first occupants of those chiefly offices by Kalonga himself as emblems of office.[113]

Migrations of the Maravi

Sources of oral traditions remember details of the migrations of the Maravi more than those of the pre-Maravi. This is understandable since the Maravi arrived later than the pre-Maravi, with a further reason being that the Maravi had secular leaders and history

---

104 Rangeley 1952: 39.
105 Ntara 1973: 40.
106 Rangeley 1952: 40.
107 Ibid.
108 Ntara 1973: 40.
109 Ntara 1973.
110 Ibid.
111 Ntara 1973: 10, 40.
112 Langworthy 1973: 69.
113 Phiri 1975: 61.

Plate 3.1: *Mbiriwiri,* the sacred drum of the Chewa. The current Tsang'oma is on the right.
Source: The author

revolves around such leaders. Their accomplishments tend to remain in the memory of their followers or subjects longer than those of ritual leaders unless the accomplishments were truly spectacular.

According to Ntara,[114] after the Maravi left Luba they stopped at many places, trying them out to see if they were suitable for permanent settlement. However, only those places where important events happened remained in their memory, and among them were Choma, Chewa Hill and Kaphirintiwa-Msinja.

Choma

Historians have yet to agree on which one of the several geographical features in central Africa called Choma was the Choma of the migrations of the Maravi. At least three different sites that go by that name have been identified. According to Phiri,[115] Choma was the most northerly one of the three, being a river flowing into Lake Mweru in

---

114 Ntara 1973: 4.
115 Phiri 1977: 3.

Zambia from the direction of Lake Tanganyika. Phiri[116] cited traditions that claim the first Maravi king called Chinkhole and his followers crossed that river.

The second Choma is a mountain by that name, which is located in Mzimba district in northern Malawi. It must be the same mountain that the Scottish missionary, Robert Laws,[117] passed by on his trip from Cape Maclear, in the southern Lake Malawi area, to northern Malawi in 1878. Rangeley[118] and Young[119] believe that the Maravi stopped at that Choma, with Young[120] citing traditions that suggest there is a burial site of a Kalonga in the area. The third Choma is located in the southern province of Zambia, and according to Langworthy[121] this must be the Choma mentioned by Ntara because its close proximity with the centre of Undi's kingdom made it memorable among the Chewa who live in adjacent areas. They have therefore come to believe that it is the Choma of their migrations.

The traditions of the Maravi remember Choma because, according to Ntara,[122] two important events occurred in the course of their stay at that site. They were the creation of clan names and the establishment of the very high office of king. Oral traditions say that, all along, the Maravi had no kings, but like the pre-Maravi before them, female ritual leaders led them. This situation would probably have continued had they not earlier on met an Arab trader called Hasan Bin Ali. According to Ntara,[123] when this man realised that the customs of the Maravi did not require them to have kings, he began to persuade them to ignore the customs and appoint him as their king. Hasan Bin Ali died before this could happen and his followers dispersed after his death. Perhaps it was the thought that divine intervention had prevented them from appointing a foreigner to be their king that made them appoint one of their own instead — a man called Chinkhole who was accorded the royal title of Kalonga.[124] With the appointment of a king, the importance of priestesses in the culture of the Maravi ended. Henceforth, the Maravi based their ritual or spiritual organisation on the veneration of deceased rulers, which made royal graves important cultic places.[125] Although the story of their meeting with Hasan Bin Ali sounds fantastic, it is of historical interest and it deserves a second look. Scholars of East African long-distance trade are familiar with the Hasan name. One such individual called al-Hassan ibn Suliman was the *wazir* of Kilwa who

---

116 Ibid.
117 Laws R. 1879. Journey along part of the western side of Lake Nyassa, in 1878. *Proceedings of the Royal Geographical Society and Monthly Record of Geography*. 1(5): 316.
118 Rangeley WHJ. 1963. The earliest inhabitants of Nyasaland. *The Nyasaland Journal*. 16(2): 39.
119 Young TC. 1970. *Notes on the history of the Tumbuka-Kamanga peoples*. London: Frank Cass.
120 Young 1970.
121 Langworthy 1969: 119; 1973: 5.
122 Ntara 1973: 4.
123 Ntara 1973.
124 Ntara 1973: 4.
125 Schoffeleers 1979: 155.

reigned twice between 1479 and 1490.[126] This was also the period when alternative routes to the rich gold-mining areas of the interior were opening up. It is therefore possible that he or his agents who spoke for him had contacts with the Maravi. Such contacts would explain the involvement of the Maravi in the lucrative long-distance trade once they established themselves at Mankhamba.

Although the traditions do not reveal how long the Maravi stayed at Choma, it is clear that they liked the place. Probably they would have made it their permanent home had there been enough land for a growing population. However, the lack of land was a problem and as the population increased it became obvious that they needed to move on.[127] Chinkhole had died by then and was succeeded by his nephew, Kalonga Chidzonzi, who led the people out of Choma.[128]

Chewa Hill

One of the places they remember stopping at after they had left Choma was Chewa Hill, a site that Ntara[129] suspects was the place where the Maravi began to refer to themselves as the Chewa. Other scholars, however, have recorded different traditions about the origins of the term 'Chewa'. Citing Rangeley, Langworthy[130] said that there might already have been people called Chewa in central Malawi before any of the migrants from Luba arrived there. The original inhabitants may have intermarried with the arriving immigrants and eventually everybody adopted the term 'Chewa'. It is also possible that other people started to use it to mean 'neighbour' or 'them' and not necessarily as a way of describing a people.[131] The term 'Chewa', however, did not appear in written records until the early 1830s[132] which is more than two centuries after the appearance of the term 'Maravi'.[133] What all this really means is that even though there may have been a hill called Chewa, the origins of the use of the term 'Chewa' to describe a people have not been established with certainty.

The Maravi at Kaphirintiwa-Msinja

Their next important stop was Kaphirintiwa-Msinja where they found an established community of the pre-Maravi under Makewana.[134] Kalonga's decision to settle at a site already occupied by the pre-Maravi suggests a desire to take over the site by force. It is possible that he had heard of the area's rich physical environment. As stated by

---

126 Newitt MDD. 1972. The Early History of the Sultanate of Angoche. *The Journal of African History*. 13(3): 398.
127 Ntara 1973.
128 Ntara 1973: 8.
129 Ntara 1973.
130 Langworthy 1973: 9.
131 Ibid.
132 Marwick 1963: 378.
133 Newitt 1982: 157.
134 Schoffeleers 1973, 1992; Phiri 1975: 46.

Schoffeleers,[135] there were a number of options that Kalonga, with an invading party, could take to accomplish his goal. He could for instance destroy Makewana's ritual organisation, adapt it in some other way, accept it as it was or simply put in place a rival system. Kalonga settled on destroying the existing system. If successful, he would be king of both the pre-Maravi and the Maravi and he mounted a series of unsuccessful attacks on Makewana's symbol of authority, the shrine on Kaphirintiwa Hill.[136] Schoffeleers[137] believes Kalonga's attacks failed because of the inaccessibility of the location of the shrine, and this could well be accurate. It took me nearly four hours of vigorous uphill walking to reach the site of the shrine. It seems the pre-Maravi habitually built their shrines in inaccessible areas such as on hilltops, perhaps to protect them from invaders. In southern Malawi, for instance, two of the shrines were on Malawi Hill and on Thyolo Mountain respectively.[138] Anglican Church missionaries found the shrine on Thyolo Mountain to be well defended against slave raiders in the 1860s.[139] This example shows that the shrines also acted as a place of refuge from armed attacks. They shifted the shrines from the hills to the plains below when the threat of attacks no longer existed. For example, the Kaphirintiwa shrine was moved from the top of Kaphirintiwa Hill to the plains below, and Mbona's shrine was relocated from Malawi Hill to Khulubvi in the Lower Shire Valley.[140] Kalonga's fighters at Kaphirintiwa must have been physically tired when and if they ever got close to the shrine, as once there the fighters met well-rested soldiers of Makewana ready to defend it.

In defeat, Kalonga realised that his future success and prosperity as a king depended on Makewana's support. He therefore adapted to the status quo by accepting the Chisumphi cult and Makewana's ritual authority.[141] Kalonga and the Maravi recognised her as the perpetual principal rain-caller of all the Chewa.[142] The Banda clan was also made responsible for appointing counsellors for Kalonga and providing him with Mwali as his principal wife.[143] Upon Kalonga's death, his successor inherited Mwali, and if she died, elders of the Banda clan selected another woman to become Mwali.[144] Secular authority on the other hand became the perpetual domain of Kalonga and the Phiri clan. Being a matrilocal people, Nyangu — as the mother or sister of Kalonga — continued to occupy the highest rank,[145] an arrangement that was an

---

135 Schoffeleers 1979: 155.
136 Ntara 1973; Schoffeleers 1973: 51, 1992: 33.
137 Schoffeleers 1973: 51; 1992: 33.
138 Schoffeleers 1992.
139 Ibid: 33.
140 Ibid.
141 Ntara 1973; Langworthy 1973.
142 Rangeley 1952: 34.
143 Ntara 1973: 11; Langworthy 1973: 13.
144 Langworthy 1973: 13.
145 Ntara 1973: 12.

effective system of checks and balances of power and that worked well for a long time.[146] This was, however, more beneficial to Kalonga than to Makewana as she had been eroded of her inherent secular authority.

From Kaphirintiwa-Msinja to Mankhamba

It is not possible to figure out from oral traditions how long the Maravi were on the road before they arrived at Mankhamba, and neither can it really be confirmed how many Kalongas led them. It is possible that their journey from Kaphirintiwa-Msinja to Mankhamba lasted many years and that several generations came and went while they were migrating.[147] Their next important stop was at Mawere a Nyangu (Nyangu's Breasts).[148] The main feature of the area is two twin hills they likened to Nyangu's breasts. They settled there for a long time and it was here that Changamire, one of Kalonga's brothers, was born and raised.[149] When the population grew to a level that outstripped available arable land, they abandoned the site. Kalonga and notable leaders such as Undi, Khuthe, Kafwafwa and others proceeded in a northerly direction to the Phirilongwe area, close to Mangochi town. After the soil became exhausted, they moved on to what turned out to be their final destination, a place called Msangu wa Machete near Nadzipulu River in the Mtakataka-Mua area.[150] Like Kaphirintiwa-Msinja, the area is fertile with plenty of water. Lake Malawi is nearby and there are many perennial rivers which rise on the Dedza escarpment and drain into the lake. Kalonga liked the area so much that he finally settled down there.

Ntara[151] stated that at Msangu wa Machete the Phiri built their village, calling it Malawi, and the Banda constructed theirs and named it Mankhamba. Ntara's statement implies that the Phiri and the Banda clans arrived in the Mtakataka-Mua area at the same time. However, analyses of existing traditions[152] suggest that this could not have been the case. Further, archaeology has demonstrated, as we shall see below, that people who made Mawudzu pottery, the pre-Maravi, had settled at the site before the Maravi arrived there. There is some disagreement among scholars as to whether the site of Mankhamba was Kalonga's capital.[153] Ntara is clear that Kalonga named his village Malawi and that it was 'near the stream Nadzipulu in Mtakataka-Mua area'.[154] Other historians have different views on the matter. Phiri[155] for instance said that Kalonga

---

146 Langworthy 1973: 133.
147 Ibid: 15.
148 Ntara 1973.
149 Ibid: 10.
150 Ibid: 15.
151 Ibid: 15.
152 Hamilton 1955; Marwick 1963; Schoffeleers 1973, 1992; Phiri 1975: 47.
153 Ntara 1973; Phiri 1975, 1977.
154 Ntara 1973: 15.
155 Phiri 1975; 1977.

established his headquarters at a place called Manthimba and that Mankhamba was gradually reduced to a mere shrine centre of the Maravi kingdom. The problem with the Manthimba site, however, is that no one, including Phiri himself, is sure of its precise location. In 1975, Phiri was of the view that it was near a place called Sharpeville, some 50 kilometres to the south of Mankhamba. In 1977, he placed Manthimba about 5 kilometres northeast of Mankhamba.[156] When we attempted to locate Manthimba during our fieldwork some years ago, the local people directed us to a place beyond Chipoka, some 24 kilometres north of Mankhamba. It seems obvious that Manthimba would have been as well known as Mankhamba or Kaphirintiwa-Msinja had it been Kalonga's capital. Modern sources of oral traditions would have remembered its precise location the way they remember the locations of the other sites. As discussed later, the archaeological evidence recovered at Mankhamba is such that there can be only one explanation for it: Mankhamba was Kalonga's centre of political and economic activity. It was his capital.

Summary

Ntara's book, *Mbiri ya Achewa*, is the most prominent source of Chewa oral traditions. The Chewa consist of several clans, with the major ones being the Banda and Phiri clans. Scholars who recorded Chewa oral traditions concluded that the Banda clan left Luba before the Phiri clan, which is why they refer to the Banda clan variously as the 'proto-Chewa', 'proto-Malawi', 'pre-Malawi' or 'pre-Maravi' and the Phiri clan as the 'Maravi'. Mangadzi, a female priestess and rain-caller, whose titular name was Makewana, was the leader of the pre-Maravi. Secular authority was inherent in her ritual position and that made her both a priestess and a chiefly figure. Kamundi, the senior male member of the pre-Maravi priesthood, exercised the authority on her behalf.

Other than their reported encounter with short-statured people akin to the hunter-gatherers of the Congo forest, scholars do not know much about the pre-Maravi before they arrived at Kaphirintiwa-Msinja, where they established their primary shrine. The Chewa refer to the short-statured people variously as Akafula, Abatwa or Amwandionerakuti. The pre-Maravi, however, drove them out of their settlement areas. *Mbiriwiri*, the small drum that the Chewa still venerate, originally belonged to the Akafula.

The Phiri clan, who were led by secular leaders, settled at a number of sites after they left Luba, but found them inadequate. The sites included Choma, where they claim to have created clan names and to have appointed Chinkhole, their first king, on whom they accorded the title Kalonga. Other notable titles were 'Nyangu' for Kalonga's mother

---

156 Phiri 1975: 53; 1977: 4.

or sister, and 'Mwali' for his principal wife. They also stopped at Chewa Hill where they decided to call themselves the Chewa, but other traditions dispute this.

Their next important stop was Kaphirintiwa-Msinja, where Kalonga attempted several times to wrestle power from Makewana but failed. He abandoned Kaphirintiwa-Msinja, but not before the Maravi and the pre-Maravi struck arrangements that ensured recognition of each other's authority. The Phiri clan would maintain secular authority in perpetuity and the Banda clan would do the same with ritual authority. They also established rules of succession. Eventually, Kalonga and his followers arrived at Mankhamba in the Mtakataka-Mua area and established what turned out to be their permanent home. They called this area 'Malawi'.

CHAPTER 4

Expansion of the Chewa according to their oral traditions

According to oral traditions recorded by Ntara,[1] Kalonga began to expand his area of influence before he arrived at Mankhamba. He did this perhaps to prevent other senior members of the ruling family from unilaterally breaking away from him. Two of them, Kaphwiti and Lundu,[2] had done so already.

Kalonga's strategy for expansion was to send out some of his sons and other relatives to various places far away from him to establish new settlements. The oral traditions suggest that he started doing this when he was at Mawere a Nyangu. Among those he sent out were Changamire and Chulu, of the Phiri clan, and possibly Mkanda of the Mbewe clan.[3] Kalonga also let go certain able individuals who requested his permission to venture out on their own, as was the case regarding Mkadzula of the Mwale clan.[4] These leaders became territorial chiefs with the title of Mwini Dziko, (owner of the land) whom Kalonga dispatched with pomp and ceremony. He gave each one emblems of office, which included a flywhisk, a sword or knife, and an iron stool.[5] Once he had established himself firmly at Mankhamba, Kalonga called for a meeting of his elders to allocate land to various individuals.[6] He appointed one of his elders called Chembe to be in charge of land allocation, and Chembe in turn delegated the work to Mgawi, his younger brother. Mgawi instructed those to whom he had given land to divide the land and allocate it to others. This created many lesser chiefs who, together with territorial chiefs, regularly sent ivory and part of the initiation ceremony fees to Kalonga as a tribute.[7]

Kaphwiti and Lundu

Kaphwiti and Lundu were relatives. Kaphwiti was either Lundu's elder brother or uncle.[8] The two broke away from Kalonga and went elsewhere to establish their own settlement. Oral traditions have given various reasons for their departure. Some traditions say that

---

1   Ntara 1973.
2   Ntara 1973; Phiri 1977.
3   Ntara 1973.
4   Langworthy 1973: 91; Phiri 1975.
5   Phiri 1975: 61.
6   Ntara 1973.
7   Ntara 1973: 23.
8   Rangeley 1954: 15; Phiri 1977: 6.

they left because there was either some dispute between them and Kalonga over the practice of evil magic[9] and the administration of *mwavi*,[10] or there was some dissatisfaction with the choice of leadership after Kalonga's death.[11] *Mwavi* is a poisonous drink extracted from the bark of the Mwavi tree (*Erythrophleum suaveolens*), also known as the ordeal tree,[12] which was administered in order to find culprits in disputes involving witchcraft, theft or adultery.[13] People believed that the culprit would die within an hour or two after taking it and the innocent would vomit it up and survive. However, considering that there was no prescribed dosage, many innocent people died.[14]

According to Ntara,[15] *mwavi* was given to people when they were at Mawere a Nyangu. Many people died, which resulted in a row between Kalonga's brother, Changamire, and Kaphwiti, causing Kaphwiti and his followers to leave. Phiri,[16] however, believes that if the dispute was due to the practice of evil magic, then Kaphwiti and Lundu must have left when the Maravi were still at Kaphirintiwa-Msinja. Apparently, at that site the Maravi experienced several misfortunes including frequent lion attacks. Some had reason to believe that Kaphwiti and Lundu were responsible for those attacks and other misfortunes, which created tension in the ruling family. It is possible, therefore, that Kalonga himself may have ordered the administration of *mwavi* in order to find the real culprit and thus reduce the tension. Langworthy,[17] however, believes that Kaphwiti and Lundu left soon after the succession of a new Kalonga at Phirilongwe. The reasons for their departure from Phirilongwe are not clear but a succession dispute cannot be discounted.

It is also possible, though, that all along Kaphwiti and Lundu had their own territorial ambitions. They took advantage of the existing instability and left before a new Kalonga fully established himself in his new position. They journeyed in a south-westerly direction, and according to some traditions they stopped near Utale.[18] However, Hamilton[19] and Rangeley[20] said that they settled along the Wankurumadzi River, a tributary of the Shire River in the Mwanza-Neno area (see Map 4.1). Kaphwiti's power grew over a wide area. Besides the Lower Shire Valley, his influence extended to the

---

9   Phiri 1977: 6.
10 Ntara 1973: 16.
11 Langworthy 1969.
12 Williamson J. 1975. *Useful Plants of Malawi*. Limbe, Malawi: University of Malawi.
13 Ibid.
14 Johnston HH. 1969. *British Central Africa*. New York: Negro Universities Press; Werner A. 1969. *Natives of British Central Africa*. New York: Negro Universities Press; Williamson 1975: 108–110.
15 Ntara 1973: 16
16 Phiri 1979: 6.
17 Langworthy 1969: 157.
18 Phiri 1977: 6.
19 Hamilton, RA. 1954. The route of Gasper Bocarro from Tete to Kilwa in 1616. *The Nyasaland Journal*. 7(2): 9.
20 Rangeley 1954: 18.

Shire Highlands, Mulanje and adjacent areas of Mozambique.[21] After some time, Lundu, perhaps with Kaphwiti's blessings, moved on to establish his own settlement farther south in the Lower Shire Valley, settling at Mbewe near Chiromo.[22] Before long, Lundu's fortunes at Mbewe began to rise, and with time his area of influence extended

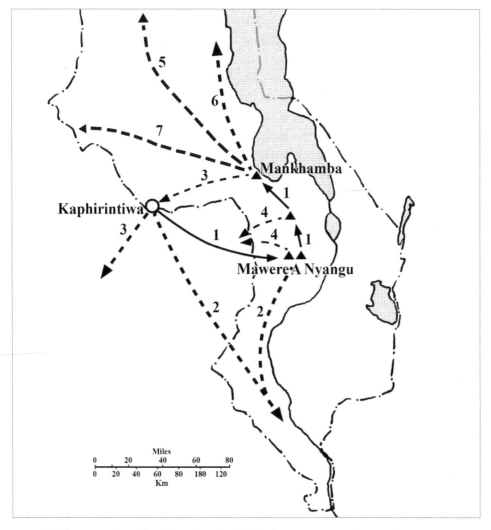

Map 4.1: The expansion of the Chewa in Malawi. (1) Kalonga's migration from Kaphirintiwa-Msinja to Mankhamba; (2) Kaphwiti and Lundu; (3) Undi; (4) Changamire; (5) Chulu; (6) Kanyenda; (7) Mkanda.
Source: The author

21 Rangeley 1954: 15; Phiri 1977: 7.
22 Phiri 1977: 7.

from the Lower Shire Valley to the Lower Zambezi Valley.[23] Part of the reason for his rapid success was that the Zambezi River Valley trade route to the gold-rich areas of southern Zambezia passed through an area under his control. Lundu took advantage of that to trade with the Portuguese and other foreign traders who used that route frequently.[24] Wealth from trade gave him power and visibility so that the foreign traders began to view him rather than Kaphwiti as the leader of the people north of the Zambezi.[25] In the end, Lundu overshadowed Kaphwiti and became the prominent Maravi personality in the area.[26]

Undi

Undi was the next prominent leader to leave but the circumstances surrounding his departure were different from those of Kaphwiti and Lundu. Langworthy says that Undi may have split off with Kalonga while they were at Phirilongwe, but he quickly adds that 'most sources which mention where it was that Undi left Kalonga indicate Mankhamba'.[27] One such source is Ntara[28] who is clear that Kalonga and Undi were together at Mankhamba. After some time, Undi began to dislike Mankhamba because of too much heat and too many mosquitoes. He tried to persuade Kalonga on at least two different occasions to abandon Mankhamba and search for a better site but Kalonga refused and so Undi left.[29] Langworthy[30] recorded two other reasons for Undi's departure. The first was that Undi left after a disagreement between him and Kalonga about who should clear away the bowls or plates from which they had been eating. Should the younger person who happened to be a Kalonga clear the plates as required by Chewa customs and traditions, or the older person who was also the *nkhoswe* or 'guardian' of the *mbumba*, that is the matrilocal kin group? Oral traditions recorded by Langworthy apparently suggest Kalonga asked Undi to clear the plates.[31] The etiquette regarding the clearing away of bowls or plates after men have eaten is similar to that of washing hands before and after eating, which is practised by many if not all of Malawi's ethnic groups. The food is brought to the men's eating area by the woman who prepared it or by children sent by her. When two or more men are eating together, the younger or youngest of them carries a container with water in it for the purpose of the older person or people to wash their hands before they start eating. Always, the oldest person washes his hands

23 Ibid; Alpers EA. 1975. *Ivory & Slaves in East-central Africa*. London: Heinemann.
24 Alpers 1975; Schoffeleers M. 1987. The Zimba and the Lundu State in the Late Sixteenth and Early Seventeenth Centuries. *The Journal of African History*. 28:3 37.
25 Schoffeleers 1987.
26 Rangeley 1954; Phiri 1977.
27 Langworthy 1969: 157.
28 Ntara 1973.
29 Ibid: 32.
30 Langworthy 1969.
31 Langworthy 1969: 161.

first. After everybody has washed his hands, the container is placed on the floor for the person who was holding it to wash his hands. Once eating has been completed, the process is repeated, after which the youngest person washes his hands and proceeds to clear the plates or bowls.

The situation involving Kalonga and Undi was a clash between seniority at the individual and socio-cultural level, and seniority at the political level.[32] According to Chewa customs, Kalonga's matrilocal kin group consisted of Undi who was an uncle to Kalonga and *Nkhoswe* or overseer of the kin group, which included his sisters and their children. In this case, Kalonga himself was one of the children and, together with the rest, looked up to Undi for support and advice. Thus, while Kalonga was ruler of the state or head of the political sphere, Undi was the *nkhoswe* or 'ruler' of the family[33] and therefore a real force with which to contend.

The second reason for his departure had to do with a succession dispute. Some sources claim that the term 'Undi' was a titular name as it is today, and therefore Undi and others believed that as bearer of this title, he would succeed his brother, the deceased Kalonga.[34] Some counsellors, however, opposed his ascension to the throne in favour of a nephew because Undi already had a title.[35] This angered him and in the end he left.

As postulated for Kaphwiti and Lundu, it is possible that these were ostensible reasons and that the real reason was an economic one. Archaeological remains at Mankhamba show that a great deal of trade was conducted there. Kalonga controlled it but it is not clear how many of the benefits trickled down to his senior relations and elders. Undi probably left to seek his own fortunes elsewhere. Kalusa[36] has suggested this would explain his decision to settle at Mano in the Tete province of Mozambique, a site close to the Zambezi River Valley which was a well-established trade route into the interior of southern Africa.

Apparently, the decision to bypass Undi did not go down well with many people at Kalonga's court. Undi seems to have been a well-liked individual[37] and when he left many people followed him. Most notably, he took Nyangu with him as well as other female members of Kalonga's royal lineage.[38] Nyangu's departure was significant. As Kalonga's sister or mother, her departure meant that the only woman who was culturally expected to provide Kalonga's successors was no longer resident at Mankhamba.[39] From then onwards, Kalonga's counsellors at Mankhamba sent messages to Undi to nominate a

---

32 Langworthy 1969: 161.
33 Langworthy 1969.
34 Ibid: 161; 1973: 31.
35 Ibid: 161; see also Schoffeleers 1979: 156.
36 Kalusa WT. 2010. *Kalonga Gawa Undi X: a biography of an African chief and nationalist.* Lusaka, Zambia: The Lembani Trust: 7.
37 Langworthy 1973: 31.
38 Ntara 1973: 31.
39 Ntara 1973; Langworthy 1973: 31.

successor whenever the position of Kalonga became vacant.[40] However, since Undi and Nyangu's departure did not disrupt the Chewa system according to which Kalonga had to marry Mwali, not all was completely lost for the people at Mankhamba. As mentioned in Chapter 3, the culture required that Kalonga must marry Mwali, whereupon she became his principal wife. Mwali came from the Banda clan. In fact, this made Kalonga's counsellors, all of whom were of the Banda clan, powerful. A new Kalonga never ascended the throne without their approval. Once approved, he had to marry Mwali who was their clan member.[41] Thus, with Nyangu's departure, Mwali's position became more important than it had been in the past. Undi, unlike Kaphwiti and Lundu and despite his unceremonious departure from Mankhamba, remained in contact with the leaders at Mankhamba for a long time.[42]

It is not possible to determine Undi's date of departure from Mankhamba but what is clear from the traditions is that from there he retraced his steps back to Kaphirintiwa-Msinja, a place that was still a thriving ritual centre under Makewana's control. Undi stayed there until his departure for Mano[43] where his power grew, and with time his influence extended to parts of Lilongwe district, including the area around Kaphirintiwa-Msinja. Some traditions say that he became so powerful he was able to appoint Makewana at Kaphirintiwa-Msinja,[44] therefore making her more aligned with him than with Kalonga.[45] By the beginning of the seventeenth century, Undi was firmly established at Mano. Bocarro[46] reported in 1614 that the Portuguese at Tete were regularly trading with a chief called 'Bundy' (his rendering of 'Undi'). The Undi chieftaincy seems to have existed without any significant interruptions to the present time when the governments of Malawi and Zambia have recognised Undi as the King of the Chewa.

Changamire

Changamire was the first person that Kalonga sent away when he began to send people to distant places to become chiefs.[47] Traditions say that Changamire's departure occurred when the Maravi were at Mawere a Nyangu. Kalonga instructed him to go in a southerly direction as he himself would go in a northerly direction following the shores of Lake Malawi. Changamire accepted the proposal and went away, taking with him his brother,

---

40 Langworthy 1973: 31.
41 Langworthy 1969: 153.
42 Langworthy 1973.
43 Langworthy 1969: 185.
44 Ibid.
45 Phiri 1975: 63.
46 Bocarro 1964: 402.
47 Ntara 1973.

Mpinganjira, and sister, Sazamanja.[48] He ended up in the area now covered by Ntcheu district and became powerful enough that at one time his influence reached back into the lowlands of Mangochi, including Mawere a Nyangu itself.[49] Later, he ceded control of the western Mangochi area to his brother, Mpinganjira, when Mpinganjira broke away from him.[50] Today, like Kaphwiti, we no longer hear of Changamire. Some historians suggested that the extinction of Changamire's chieftaincy had to do with the arrival and settling of the Maseko Ngoni in his area in the 1860s.[51]

Chulu

Chulu was next, even though oral traditions do not seem to have consensus regarding his origins. Some suggest that he was Kalonga's son and that Kalonga himself sent him to settle in northern Kasungu.[52] Others suggest that he was part of Undi's migration to the west, but he took a different route that led him to Kasungu.[53] The long distance between Mankhamba and northern Kasungu has contributed to the confusion. The Chulu chieftaincy, however, is still in possession of the iron stool that the first Chulu received from Kalonga,[54] which establishes that there was a close relationship between them.

It is not clear when Chulu arrived in Kasungu, but by the end of the seventeenth century his influence seems to have declined. Langworthy[55] mentioned a 1695 publication based on various seventeenth-century documents and reports which indicated that the Kasungu area was under the control of a king called 'Massi', or Mwase, and not Chulu. The first Mwase, who was also called Mkwangwawala (sometimes spelled Mkangowala or Mkangawala), moved to Kasungu from Bunda near Kaphirintiwa-Msinja.[56] He was a hunter who was probably looking for elephants in Kasungu and the nearby Luangwa Valley.[57] Oral traditions recorded by McFarren[58] suggest that Mwase helped local headmen in the area to get rid of dangerous animals and to win local conflicts. In their appreciation, they gave him land. As a hunter, however, Mwase must have participated in the ivory trade[59] and this was probably what made him more prominent than Chulu and the other local chiefs such as Lukwa and Kaomba.

---

48 Ibid: 17.
49 Langworthy 1973.
50 Ntara 1973.
51 Langworthy 1973: 18.
52 Langworthy 1973.
53 Langworthy 1969: 190; 1973: 69; McFarren 1986: 132.
54 Langworthy 1973: 69.
55 Langworthy 1969: 171.
56 Ntara 1973: 65.
57 Phiri 1975: 70; McFarren 1986: 133.
58 McFarren 1986.
59 McFarren 1986: 135.

Kanyenda

Mkadzula of the Mwale clan established the Kanyenda chieftaincy. He was a son of Kalonga and the most important chief of the Mwale clan, though not the head of the clan. This title belonged to his uncle, Khombe, who was Kalonga's cross-cousin.[60] According to some traditions,[61] after he left Mankhamba, Mkadzula established the Kanyenda chieftaincy headquarters along Linthipe River near Salima. Years later, he moved the headquarters to near Bua River in Nkhotakota district.

It is not clear why he did that, but Kanyenda's headquarters are still there today. The existence of an original iron stool given to the first Kanyenda by Kalonga[62] is an indication of the importance of the chieftaincy as well as its antiquity. Those who saw Kanyenda's stool early in the twentieth century described it as being 'in good condition and strong enough to hold the fattest man without being broken. It is 10 inches in diameter and 7 inches high'.[63] However, despite Kanyenda's closeness to Kalonga, we know very little about the early period of his chieftaincy.

Mkanda

Regarding Mkanda Mbewe, traditions about his position as Kalonga's son and his appointment by Kalonga to be a territorial chief in the Mchinji-Chipata area are inconsistent.[64] Langworthy[65] suggests that Mkanda's interpretation of history was distorted by two things. The first of these concerned his experiences with foreigners who intruded into his area during the second half of the nineteenth century. The second was his chieftaincy's connection with the origin of Undi's kingdom. The foreign intruders were the Ngoni and the British, both of whom were militarily stronger than he was.

The Ngoni, with Mpezeni as their leader, were the first group of foreigners to come to the area. Mpezeni raided the area from about 1860 to 1880.[66] The Ngoni raids instilled so much fear among the Chewa that when David Livingstone arrived in 1866, he could not easily find carriers to lead him to Ngoni villages.[67] One of the raids killed Mkanda Kapunza (also spelled Kapunta) and unknown people later killed Mkanda Mchochoma who had succeeded him.[68] Many people fled the area after these disturbances and became refugees under chief Mwase in Kasungu. There was no chief for a while until the rightful heir, who was still technically a refugee under chief Mwase, returned and became some kind of tributary chief under Mpezeni. He maintained this status until

60   Langworthy 1973; Phiri 1975.
61   Langworthy 1973: 91.
62   Langworthy 1973: 91.
63   Young 1970: 97.
64   Ntara 1973: 74; Langworthy 1969: 244; 1973: 76; McFarren 1986: 126.
65   Langworthy 1969: 244.
66   Langworthy 1973: 77–78; Pachai 1974: 34.
67   Pachai 1974: 34.
68   Langworthy 1973: 78.

1898 when the British defeated Mpezeni.[69] Free of Mpezeni's grip but now under the British, Mkanda's chieftaincy never regained its past glory. In fact, when the British established a boundary between Malawi and Zambia, they arbitrarily split the land into east (Malawi) and west (Zambia). Two thirds of the land remained on the western side[70] to which Mkanda initially returned from Kasungu. The Ngoni, however, were still there and occupied about half of the former area in each territory. In 1918, Mkanda decided to return to his traditional capital a few kilometres away in Malawi.[71]

These events stuck in the memory of the sources of oral traditions of the Chewa and they affected what they thought was the origin of the Mkanda chieftaincy, especially in relation to Undi whose territory was not far from theirs. Langworthy[72] listed three versions of oral traditions regarding Mkanda's origins. The first version, following the traditions of the eastern area in Malawi, depicts Mkanda and Undi as having had nothing to do with each other as they settled in different areas. Further, they claim that Mkanda was the more important of the two. To prove it, they cite the example of Mkanda whom followers carried in a hammock made from a zebra skin while Undi walked.[73] Other traditions, however, say that the reason they carried Mkanda in a hammock was that he had a bad leg due to an injury.[74] Second, traditions of the western side say that Mkanda was Kalonga's son and that his acquisition of land in Mchinji and Chipata areas had nothing to do with Undi.[75] They state that Kalonga made Mkanda stay at Bunda. Eventually, he and Mwase went to Kasungu where they settled, only to separate later following a quarrel between their followers. Mkanda then came to settle in Mchinji where he found local headmen in a struggle to contain Akafula fighters.[76] Mkanda defeated the Akafula and to thank him, the headmen gave him land or Mkanda simply took it himself.[77] It was only later that Mkanda made contact with Undi.

The third set of traditions from Undi's area, however, depict Mkanda as a subordinate of Undi.[78] They say that the first Undi and Mkanda were together as Mkanda was married to Undi's sister, Chirunje.[79] At the time, Undi was looking for a suitable settlement site and when he arrived at Mchemani in Mchinji, he instructed Mkanda to settle there. It did not mean that Undi was giving him land, but simply that his sister and Mkanda were to stay in an area that would be under his authority.[80]

---

69 Ibid.
70 Langworthy 1969: 242.
71 Langworthy 1973: 78.
72 Langworthy 1973: 76.
73 Langworthy 1969: 243.
74 Ntara 1973: 74.
75 Langworthy 1969.
76 Langworthy 1973; Phiri 1975: 66.
77 Langworthy 1973: 246; Phiri 1975.
78 Langworthy 1969.
79 Langworthy 1973: 77; see also Ntara 1973: 74.
80 Langworthy 1969: 244.

Irrespective of the uncertainty regarding his status as Kalonga's son, Mkanda became an important territorial chief of the south-western area of central Malawi and parts of eastern Zambia. Historians believe that for a while, however, he may have been a tributary chief of Undi.[81] If that is correct, then he probably did not last long in that subordinate position. Late eighteenth- and early-nineteenth century Portuguese travellers to the area 'gave the impression that Mkanda was a relatively independent ruler'.[82]

Notwithstanding the establishment of separate autonomous states by Undi, Kaphwiti and Lundu, Kalonga's strategy of sending his relatives to be territorial chiefs in different areas helped extend his area of influence. It also made him wealthy and powerful since, according to oral traditions, the chiefs remitted initiation fees and some of the ivory acquired in their domains. Traditionally, chiefs received one piece of ivory from every elephant killed,[83] some of which they sent to Kalonga. As demonstrated in Chapter 10, archaeological evidence at Mankhamba shows that the site was a major ivory processing centre.

Summary

Oral traditions say that after two of Kalonga's relatives, Kaphwiti and Lundu, unilaterally broke away from the rest of the Maravi to establish their own settlements, he decided to expand the land that he envisioned would be under his control once he settled down. He did this by sending some of his relatives to start new settlements in distant places. Changamire, Kalonga's brother, was the first one he sent away. Next were Chulu of the Phiri clan and possibly Mkanda of the Mbewe clan. Mkadzula of the Mwale clan, who founded the Kanyenda dynasty, also left after he sought Kalonga's permission to do so. These leaders became territorial or tributary chiefs. After Kalonga settled down at Mankhamba, he appointed one of his elders called Chembe to distribute land to people who became lesser chiefs. The territorial and the lesser chiefs regularly sent tributes to Kalonga.

Sometime after they arrived at Mankhamba, Undi, Kalonga's uncle, left once he had failed to persuade Kalonga to abandon Mankhamba. He settled at Mano in the Tete province of Mozambique. Among the reasons for his departure was his discontent with Mankhamba as a good site. It is also possible, however, that he wanted to be near the Zambezi River Valley trade route. He went away with Nyangu which affected succession procedures at Mankhamba. In the culture of the matrilocal Chewa, the woman bearing the title Nyangu was either the sister or mother of Kalonga. When she left, Kalonga lost

---

81 Langworthy 1973.
82 Ibid: 77.
83 Gamitto ACP. 1960. *King Kazembe: being the diary of the Portuguese expedition to that potentate in the years 1831–1832*. Translated by I. Cunningson. Lisbon: 127; Chafulumira, W. 1948. *Mbiri ya Amang'anja*. Zomba, Malawi: Nyasaland Education Department: 20.

the only woman traditionally expected to bear the next Kalonga. From then onwards, Undi became responsible for nominating one of Nyangu's sons to succeed Kalonga at Mankhamba and because of that, Undi and the Mankhamba leadership remained in contact for a long time.

CHAPTER 5

The practice of archaeology

Although many people are familiar with the term 'archaeology', very few know what the practice of archaeology entails. It is common for visitors to an archaeological excavation to ask archaeologists 'how did you know where to dig?' That question comes after they have seen some of the excavated material. How, they wonder, did archaeologists possibly know that they would find such materials at that precise location? This chapter looks at what archaeology is all about.

What is archaeology?

Archaeology is the study of humans from both the distant and recent past, using material remains—that is, the objects they made, modified, used and then discarded or abandoned. Wherever people have lived even for a short period, they leave behind evidence of their presence in the form of artefacts, ecofacts and features. Artefacts are any portable objects that human beings intentionally made or modified in order to accomplish various tasks and discarded after use.[1] Such objects include tools made from stones, metal, bone or wood; jewellery; and ceramics, including pots, smoking pipes, figurines, beads and other objects. Ecofacts, which are objects found at archaeological sites that humans did not intentionally modify,[2] include bones of both wild and domestic animals with or without butchery marks, firewood on a fireplace, charred or uncharred seeds of both wild and domestic plants, and other objects. Features are any remains of human activity that are not easily movable.[3] Archaeologists observe and study them on site and leave these features there, which include building foundations, floors, irrigation canals, postholes and other features.[4] Qualified archaeologists recover or observe these material remains when they excavate archaeological sites. After recovery, archaeologists take the portable objects to a laboratory where they analyse them in order to answer specific questions regarding the way of life of the people who made them.

Although archaeology is often seen as studying prehistory, that is, the study of cultures that existed before the invention of writing, there is also historical archaeology and the archaeology of modern society.[5] Historical archaeology is the study of complex cultures or civilisations which were literate and have some written records. Considering that biases always creep in whenever people write or produce documents, archaeologists

---

1   Thomas DH & Kelly RL. 2006. *Archaeology*. Belmont, CA. Thomson Wadsworth.
2   Sutton MQ & Yohe RM II. 2003. *Archaeology: The Science of the Human Past*. Boston: Allyn & Bacon.
3   Renfrew C & Bahn P. 2004. *Archaeology: Theories, Methods, and Practice*. London: Thames & Hudson.
4   Sutton & Yohe II 2003: 16; Feder 2008: 115.
5   Thomas & Kelly 2006; Sutton & Yohe II 2003; Feder 2008.

are able to compare if the archaeological record agrees with some of the written relics. Thus, the written records and the archaeological material often complement each other in that, together, they help bring out a more comprehensive picture of the way of life of the people who produced the relics. In some parts of the world, historical archaeology has been given distinct names: biblical archaeology or Egyptology or medieval archaeology, referring respectively to the archaeology of the time of the Bible in the Middle East, of the pharaohs in Egypt and of the post-Roman period in Europe.[6] Historic archaeology also applies to the study of any culture irrespective of its level of complexity that is undertaken after some details of its lifestyle have been recorded in some written form. Thus, the culture itself may not have been literate but literate people from elsewhere wrote about it. This was the case with people along the Indian Ocean coastal areas of East Africa. Literate people, such as the Arab traveller, ibn Battuta, provided some details of their way of life. He visited the East African coast in the first half of the fourteenth century and provided an eyewitness account of his impressions[7] and his writings have been helpful to archaeologists who conduct research along this coast.

Unfortunately for archaeologists who work in the interior of eastern and southern Africa, the earliest of these travellers rarely ventured into the region. As a result, mention of that region in early written records is rare. The entire region was therefore in the prehistoric period until the early sixteenth century. That was when some European explorers, missionaries and traders began to visit the area, some of whom recorded their observations and experiences.[8]

The archaeology of modern society, also referred to as garbology, is a new area of archaeological research. William Rathje, who was at the University of Arizona, Tucson, at the time, initiated this type of research about four decades ago. It involves the collection and examination of garbage that people throw away in their trashcans or bins, and the archaeological excavation of modern landfills and trash dumps.[9] The research has shown that there is an advantage in dealing with people's trash as opposed to interviewing them. For instance, garbage bins from homes whose owners claimed to be non-beer drinkers, or at least abstainers from drinking beer at home, consistently contained beer bottles and cans.[10] The garbage told the truth that the people themselves did not tell. Excavations at landfills and trash dumps showed that materials people believed would quickly decompose did not do so. Rathje found that decades-old paper and even some food products preserved well. The archaeology of modern society has

---

6   Sutton & Yohe II 2003: 10.

7   Gibb HAR. 1962. *The Travels of Ibn Battuta*. Vol II. Cambridge: 379–380.

8   Theal 1964.

9   Rathje WL, Hughes WW, Wilson DC, Tani MK, Archer GH, Hunt RG & Jones TW. 1992. The archaeology of contemporary landfills. *American Antiquity*. 57(3); Rathje WL & Murphy C. 1992. *Rubbish! The Archaeology of Garbage*. Tucson, AZ: University of Arizona Press.

10 Rathje & Murphy 1992: 68.

thus contributed to our understanding of the nature of information that archaeologists might garner from garbage, irrespective of its age.

The prehistoric period

The earliest archaeological evidence of culture is in the form of stone tools. In 2012, Sonia Harmand of Stony Brook University, New York, and her colleagues excavated a site called Lomekwi 3, located west of Lake Turkana in Kenya. They recovered the oldest stone tools ever, which were dated to 3.3 million years ago.[11] Archaeologists refer to the entire period, in which stone tools were the dominant cultural objects used to accomplish most tasks, as the Stone Age period. Archaeologists working in Africa recognise three stages of that period, each of which had its characteristic stone tools: the Early Stone Age, Middle Stone Age and Late Stone Age.[12] During the entire Stone Age period, humans subsisted by hunting and gathering. They were nomadic, with no permanent settlements such as villages, and their presence in any given area was dependent on the seasonal availability of wild food sources. The Later Stone Age eased into an age called the Neolithic period, a time characterised by the gathering and processing of wild cereals and, eventually, the production of food while still dependent on stone tools.[13] The last phase of the prehistoric period in sub-Saharan Africa is the Iron Age, which in some parts of the continent started during the last millennium BC,[14] a period when iron smelting and the fabrication and use of iron implements were widespread. Archaeologists recognise Early and Late Iron Age periods, with the Late Iron Age coinciding with the second millennium AD. The prehistoric period in many parts of sub-Saharan Africa ended gradually, at different times, when people from western Asia and Europe arrived and introduced writing and, consequently, the historical period.

Locating archaeological sites

For archaeological excavations to take place, archaeological sites must be found.[15] Locating sites is a two-stage process which begins with desktop assessment followed by fieldwork.[16] Discovery of a site does not necessarily mean that archaeologists will excavate it. The decision to excavate often depends on several factors, including the research questions that the archaeologist has in mind, financial and personnel resources,

11   Harmand S, Lewis JE, Feibel CS, Lepre CJ, Prat S, Lenoble A, Boës X, Quinn RL et al. 2015. 3.3-million-year-old stone tools from Lomekwi 3, West Turkana, Kenya. *Nature*. 521:310.

12   Barham & Mitchell 2008: 9.

13   Fagan BM. 2001. *People of the Earth: An Introduction to World Prehistory*. Prentice Hall: Upper Saddle River, New Jersey.

14   Phillipson 2000.

15   Smith AL. 2017a. Introduction: Finding and describing archaeological sites. In *Field Manual for African Archaeology*. A Livingstone-Smith, E Cornelissen, OP Gosselain & S MacEachern (eds). Tervuren: Royal Museum for Central Africa: 54.

16   Ibid.

permission of the owners of the land on which the site is located, and other reasons. Even if the site is not excavated, the mere fact that its existence is known is in itself a contribution to the archaeological knowledge of any given area.

Desktop assessment

Developing a research design is the first major step of the desktop assessment stage.[17] Research design is the preparatory work that enables archaeologists to come up with clear research questions or problems their research is expected to address. It also enables them to identify the kind of data required to answer those questions and to choose the field methods necessary to recover the desired data. The research design process will invariably compel them to familiarise themselves with the geographical area of their research. For instance, some of the archaeologists who work in Malawi come from western countries. Before they travel to Malawi, they get hold of literature on Malawi, which enlightens them not only on previous archaeological research in Malawi, but also on the country itself. They learn about its topography, history, culture, infrastructure, economy, politics, government and other necessary details. They also contact relevant professional institutions in the country, such as the Malawi Department of Antiquities or the National Museums of Malawi, for any recently published or unpublished archaeological and other documents on culture, and for information on how to go about obtaining a research permit. With the relevant information ready, the research design can be finalised.

Admittedly, archaeologists may be required to do site surveys and excavations without a proper research design. This happens in order to comply with laws existing in all African countries,[18] which demand that archaeological, historic and other cultural sites must be preserved and protected from destruction and any form of vandalism. While looters of cultural sites are responsible for acts of vandalism, some other types of site destruction occur unintentionally, often due to the construction of large infrastructure. Archaeologists are called upon to do site surveys and possibly excavate any discovered sites before workers begin to construct structures such as dams, roads, rail lines, airports, stadia and other forms of construction.[19] Knowledgeable people also call upon archaeologists when ongoing construction projects inadvertently damage a site that no one knew existed, or when they notice some natural processes such as water

---

17 Sutton & Yohe II 2003: 23, 112; Wotzka H. 2017. Village sites. In *Field Manual for African Archaeology*. A Livingstone-Smith, E Cornelissen, OP Gosselain & S MacEachern (eds). Tervuren: Royal Museum for Central Africa: 109.

18 Arazi N. 2017. Case study: heritage management in central Africa. In *Field Manual for African Archaeology*. A. Smith, E Cornelissen, OP Gosselain & S MacEachern (eds). Tervuren: Royal Museum for Central Africa: 32.

19 Oslisly R. 2017. Rescue and preventive archaeology: roads, thermal power stations and quarries. In *Field Manual for African Archaeology*. AL Smith, E Cornelissen, OP Gosselain & S. MacEachern (eds). Tervuren: Royal Museum for Central Africa: 42.

action from rising lake levels threatening or damaging a site. In such a situation, archaeologists do immediate salvage excavations to recover whatever is left of the site. Such was the case with the Nkhudzi Bay site in the southern Lake Malawi area.[20] In countries such as the USA, these types of rather impromptu archaeological activities are part of Cultural Resource Management (CRM). According to Feder,[21] most archaeological research projects in the USA may be viewed as compliance archaeology. People view archaeological and historic sites as resources that should be protected from all possible agents of destruction. Legislation protecting archaeological sites has been in place in the USA since 1906.[22]

In Malawi, the Department of Antiquities manages cultural resources. Organisations and individuals undertaking construction and mining projects are required to request the department to carry out a cultural heritage impact assessment of the area to be affected by the project. Such a study always includes an archaeological site survey. Once the study has been completed, the department submits a report with appropriate recommendations to the project owners and to the Malawi government. Any required archaeological excavations must be completed before the project starts or continues. In 2013, for instance, a rescue archaeology project was undertaken in southern Malawi when a railway line running from the western side of Mozambique and passing through southern Malawi to the eastern side of Mozambique was under construction.[23] The Malawi Department of Antiquities carried out an archaeological site survey throughout the entire strip of land within Malawi that was affected by the project. There was no archaeological research design. Instead, the project was driven by the desire to find archaeological sites along the affected land before construction activities destroyed them. Once found, the sites would be described, mapped and, if necessary, the material remains would be recovered through surface collections or archaeological excavations, after which the project would continue.

Projects of this nature, however, have their own unique problems,[24] particularly in countries like Malawi which have few resident archaeologists. Owners of the projects, in this case the railway company, often expect to start work without delay. The slow pace of archaeological site survey and excavation is alien to them. Therefore, they push archaeologists to work more hurriedly than they would normally do in a well-planned archaeological project. The hurried pace tends to affect the quality of their work. Further,

---

20   Inskeep 1965.
21   Feder 2008: 87.
22   Ibid.
23   Malawi Department of Antiquities Report. 2013. Report on cultural heritage impact assessment along the new railway line from Moatize, Mozambique to Nkaya, Malawi. Malawi Department of Antiquities, Lilongwe. (Unpublished).
24   Mitchell P. 2017. Cultural heritage management in Africa. In *Field Manual for African Archaeology*. A L Smith, E Cornelissen, OP Gosselain & S MacEachern (eds). Tervuren: Royal Museum for Central Africa: 35.

the dearth of resident archaeologists means that the excavated material may not be analysed timeously. As a result, the tendency is to exile this material to the storeroom where it ends up occupying storage space for many years before some interested archaeologist decides to examine it. As negative as this sounds, archaeological materials in storage are in a better position to contribute to knowledge than materials that are destroyed because there was no archaeologist to rescue them.

Site survey

How does an archaeologist begin the physical task of finding sites? Before beginning a site survey, there are several things that the archaeologist must do. These include obtaining the necessary research equipment, such as computers, compasses, binoculars, cameras and 'small handheld tape recorder or Dictaphones which can be used to record observations and impressions'.[25] Other materials include exercise books, survey forms, containers such as pails or buckets, paper bags, plastic bags, pens, pencils, markers and possibly, camp equipment. These days, use of the global positioning system (GPS) is essential. The GPS allows anyone wanting to locate anything or themselves on the earth's surface to do so accurately, and it facilitates accurate mapping of a site.[26] Vehicular transportation may be required when the survey area is large. In Malawi, archaeologists are likely to work in rural areas where they will drive on unpaved roads and cross streams without bridges. Four-wheel vehicles are always recommended. Further, the country's Department of Antiquities often insists that its experienced technicians accompany foreign researchers to the field. While some may find this requirement unnecessary, experience has demonstrated that it often works to the benefit of the researchers. It saves them money as it reduces the number of field assistants they might want to bring along from abroad or hire locally. It also creates a favourable impression as it demonstrates their willingness to work in partnership with local institutions and that is something research-funding agencies in western countries might find commendable.

Other than northern Malawi, which is sparsely populated, site surveys in the remainder of Malawi often entail trespassing on somebody's active farmland. That means the archaeologist must get special permission from the local village headman to walk over the farmlands of different people. The archaeologist must brief the village headman as clearly as possible about the project and it helps to inform the headman that the project has government approval. Once the headman grants permission, the owners of the various parcels of farmland do not take the archaeologists to task, provided they do no harm to their crops. It is in fact to the archaeologist's advantage to behave like an

---

25 Lane PJ. 2017. Archaeological field survey and the recording and cataloguing of archaeological materials. In *Field Manual for African Archaeology*. AL Smith, E Cornelissen, OP Gosselain & S MacEachern (eds). Tervuren: Royal Museum for Central Africa: 80.

26 Sutton & Yohe II 2003: 74, 398; Feder 2008: 170.

ethnographer when site surveying is taking place in a populated area. Establishing rapport by visiting and chatting with the local people, and explaining to them the educational benefits of the project, is always smart. One may be surprised at how friendly and helpful ordinary village people can be.

The method one adopts to locate sites depends on one's research topic, the topography of the area, as well as the resources at one's disposal. For instance, in hilly areas, the archaeologist might want to locate rock shelter sites, since Stone Age people routinely occupied them.[27] The reconnaissance or scanning survey method would be ideal in that situation, a method that targets both large and small boulders on individual hills. With the aid of aerial photography and a pair of binoculars, it is possible to scan and determine the distribution or layout of boulders from a distance. It is important, however, to inspect all boulders physically for the reason that, while most might not be rock shelters, prehistoric people painted some and this made ordinary boulders archaeological sites. This method of locating sites also targets gullies, road embankments, riverbanks and lake and seashore areas.

While the reconnaissance method works well in hilly regions, the pedestrian or foot survey method is the method of choice in plains and valleys.[28] It maximises site location because it involves walking over the selected landscape in an organised manner (see Plate 5.1). Using aerial photographs and topographic maps, the area to be surveyed is easily determined. Thereafter 'surveyors walk along lines (often called transects)',[29] looking for evidence of ancient human activities. The survey starts with determining the starting point. The archaeologist and the team line up, positioning themselves at regular intervals, the spacing of which is determined by the thickness of the foliage. The thicker the foliage, the closer the intervals. Then they begin to walk in the same direction[30] with their eyes fixed on the ground, looking for any evidence of ancient human activity. The evidence includes flaked and grinding stones, ceramic fragments, building foundations, iron implements, sudden changes in soil texture or colour, vegetation anomalies, mounds that might have been caused by human activity, and other forms of evidence.[31] Sometimes, an archaeologist might arrange for the surveyors to cross one another's paths to allow 'inspection of areas examined by one's nearest neighbor'.[32]

---

27 Vogelsang R. 2017. The excavation of Stone Age sites. In *Field Manual for African Archaeology*. A Livingstone-Smith, E Cornelissen, OP Gosselain & S MacEachern(eds). Tervuren: Royal Museum for Central Africa: 104.

28 MacDonald K. 2017. Field Survey in the Sahel: an informal guide. In *Field Manual for African Archaeology*. AL Smith, E. Cornelissen, OP Gosselain & S MacEachern (eds). Tervuren: Royal Museum for Central Africa: 66.

29 Smith 2017a: 54.

30 Ndanga AJ. 2017. Archaeological exploration in an urban African context: the case of Bangui in the Central African Republic. In *Field Manual for African Archaeology*. AL Smith, E Cornelissen, OP Gosselain & S MacEachern (eds). Tervuren: Royal Museum for Central Africa: 56.

31 Smith 2017a: 54.

32 Ndanga 2017: 56.

Plate 5.1: Site survey by foot in northern Malawi.
Source: The author

Once team members find traces of such evidence, they ask their colleagues to meet them at that point. If the archaeologist determines that it is indeed a site, it is photographed, and with the use of specially designed site-record forms the area is mapped and measured. The record includes the site's precise location (countries tend to develop their own system of recording archaeological sites), its size, and its possible content as determined by the nature of artefacts or features observed on the surface. Sometimes the archaeologist may also give the site a name. Thereafter, the information on the form is entered into a computer. Most of the archaeological and paleontological sites in Malawi, including the hominin and dinosaur sites in Karonga district, were discovered using the pedestrian survey method.[33] This method is ideal in areas where the ground is not thickly covered with grass, leaves or other types of vegetation.[34] In

---

33 Schrenk F, Bromage TG, Betzler CG, Ring U & Juwayeyi YM. 1993. Oldest Homo and Pliocene biogeography of the Malawi Rift. *Nature.* 365; Jacobs L. 1993. *Quest for the African Dinosaurs; Ancient Roots of the Modern World.* New York: Villard Books; Juwayeyi YM & Betzler C. 1995. Archaeology of the Malawi Rift: the search continues for Early Stone Age occurrences in the Chiwondo Beds, northern Malawi. *Journal of Human Evolution.* 28; Gomani 1999; Sandrock O, Dauphin Y, Kullmer O, Abel R, Schrenk F & Denys C. 1999. Malema: Preliminary taphonomic analysis of an African hominid locality. *Comptes Rendus de l'Académie des Sciences Paris.* 328(2).

34 Ogundiran A & Agbaje-Williams B. 2017. Ancient polities: Archaeological survey in a metropolis and its colony. In *Field Manual for African Archaeology.* AL Smith, E Cornelissen, OP Gosselain & S. MacEachern (eds). Tervuren: Royal Museum for Central Africa: 69.

Malawi and other parts of sub-Saharan Africa, where people burn the grass seasonally, the ground is often dry and bare during part of the year. This is when archaeologists do their fieldwork, and in Malawi it is from June to early November.

When sites are located, archaeologists can, depending on their financial and time constraints, restrict themselves to studying individual sites only or they can widen their study to examine how ancient humans used the entire landscape.[35] Archaeologists call this landscape archaeology[36] and it is based on the fact that individual sites are locations where artefacts, ecofacts and features are found. In other words, they are places where ancient humans carried out activities such as stone knapping, meat processing, pottery firing, metalwork, burying the dead, rituals such as rain-calling, trade and many other activities. Whereas each site can be studied and interpreted in its individual context, striving to interpret all of them as they appear across the entire landscape provides more information about the activities of ancient humans over a wide area. For instance, once archaeologists recognise whatever it was that attracted people to the area at a particular period of time, they can explain the distribution of the sites they have located and even 'accurately predict the most reasonable locations to look for sites'.[37]

Besides these methods of site survey, archaeologists use a technologically advanced method called remote sensing which allows them to investigate below the surface of a site without digging. 'Remote sensing methods range from aerial photography, to the use of side-scan sonar, to space-based laser imaging and satellite mapping.'[38]

Both piloted aircraft and remote-controlled aircraft flying below 152 metres have been used in archaeological aerial photography.[39] An observer from the air is able to see the position of some surface cultural features such as ancient roads, paths, fortifications and fields, as well as natural features including ancient shorelines, river channels and undisturbed landforms.[40] Modern multispectral infrared photography can distinguish even minute differences in soil type, vegetation, elevation and 'other characteristics that delineate ancient features'.[41] Some photography has even been done from space. In fact, such space-based aerial photography led to the discovery of the ancient city of Uber in southern Oman.[42]

Ships have towed magnetometers and side-scan sonar in order to survey the ocean floor. When they locate objects, divers or robots with cameras go in to confirm the

---

35 Dunnell RC. 1992. The notion site. In *Space, time and archaeological landscapes*. J. Rossignol & L. Wandsnider (eds). New York: Plenum Press.; Ebert JI. 1992. *Distributional Archaeology*. Albuquerque: University of New Mexico Press.

36 Feder 2008.

37 Ibid: 134.

38 Sutton & Yohe II 2003: 116.

39 Ibid: 118.

40 Ibid.

41 Ibid.

42 Ibid: 119.

finds.[43] Currently, most developing countries cannot afford the expensive equipment, apart from the GPS, that makes these site survey methods in rich countries possible.

Even though these archaeological survey methods have led to the discovery of many archaeological sites, it must also be stated that a significant number of sites are discovered by accident,[44] and by people who are not archaeologists, such as farmers, construction workers, amateur archaeologists and other non-archaeologists. In countries where knowledge of archaeology is disseminated in schools and regularly reported in the mass media, non-archaeologists are likely to report the discovery of archaeological artefacts to someone or to an organisation they think would know what to do about it.

Three of the world-famous sites that have been found by chance by non-archaeologists include the site of terracotta warriors, chariots and horses in Xian, Lintong district, in the Shaanxi province of China; Great Zimbabwe in southern Africa; and the rock art site of Lascaux in southern France. Regarding the site in China, workers digging a well discovered it in 1974[45] and brought it to the attention of archaeologists, who came in large numbers to carry out proper archaeological excavations. In the end, they uncovered thousands of life-size terracotta figures, which included warriors, chariots and horses arranged in battle formation. They represent the armies of the first Emperor of China, Qin Shi Huang Di, who became emperor in 246 BC when he was 13 years old.[46]

The largest single structure constructed in stone in Africa south of the Sahara stands at the Great Zimbabwe site. Carl Mauch, a German geologist and traveller who visited the site in September 1871,[47] was responsible for making it known to nineteenth-century Europeans. However, indigenous people and sixteenth-century Portuguese traders already knew about the existence of this ruined ancient city. Both the early Portuguese and Mauch associated it with the biblical queen of Sheba and King Solomon.[48] However, the site was the work of the ancestors of the people of Zimbabwe and it dates back to the second half of the thirteenth century AD.[49]

Turning to the site of Lascaux,[50] this was discovered by four teenage boys who were on a boyish exploration of nature in the woods above Lascaux manor.[51] When they saw

---

43   Sutton & Yohe II: 120.
44   Thomas & Kelly 2006: 372.
45   Roach J. nd. Emperor Qin's tomb. http://www.nationalgeographic.com/archaeology-and-history/archaeology/emperor-qin/ *National Geographic* (accessed 13 October 2017).
46   Ibid.
47   Pikirayi I. 2001. *The Zimbabwe Culture: Origins and Decline of Southern Zambezian States.* Walnut Creek, CA Altamira Press.
48   Dos Santos J. 1964. Eastern Ethiopia. In *Records of South-Eastern Africa.* Vol. 7. GM Theal (ed). Cape Town: Struik. 275; Summers R. 1963. *Zimbabwe: A Rhodesian Mystery.* Johannesburg: Nelson: 19.
49   Pikirayi 2001: 3.
50   Ruspoli M. 1987. *The cave of Lascaux: the final photographs.* New York: Harry N. Abrams.
51   Sutton and Yohe II 2003: 117.

the paintings, they realised they had made an important discovery and they reported the find to their schoolmaster who, having inspected the rock art, informed the well-known French archaeologist, Abbé Breuil. The paintings were made about 17 000 years ago.[52]

The opposite is true with respect to countries with high illiteracy rates. In such countries, archaeological sites are unlikely to be recognised and therefore not only are they not reported but they can also be destroyed because of ignorance. One good example of this is the way in which people in rural Malawi have damaged rock-shelter sites and the prehistoric paintings on some of them.[53] Despite the commendable outreach efforts by the Malawi Department of Antiquities to enlighten people on the importance of the rock shelters and of the paintings, people continue to vandalise them.[54] In the Chongoni-Dedza area, Mgomezulu[55] observed that some people, probably animal herders or those fetching firewood, had made fires in the shelters to cook food. At site DZ40, he found four fresh hearths and food remains like maize cobs, groundnut shells and sugarcane peels. At some sites, schoolchildren and other visitors have written their names or other messages with words such as 'I have been here' on the rock face, obliterating some paintings. Makers of bamboo baskets used a rock shelter located on Mikolongwe Hill in southern Malawi for their activities.[56] These damaged both the rock paintings and the rock-shelter floor, which is not good for archaeological research.

Sampling sites

When archaeologists find sites, they often decide on an excavation. Their decision regarding the number of sites they will sample or select for excavation will be based on the research question, the number of sites discovered in the area, where they are specifically located over the landscape, the number of personnel involved in the project, time, and financial resources.[57] Prior knowledge of the sites' subsurface material can be helpful in sampling sites and this information can be provided by test pitting or remote sensing. Test pitting is the digging of a hole or a pit in one area of the site in order to have an idea of the nature of artefacts likely to be recovered. This helps archaeologists to decide whether or not to undertake a full-scale excavation. If archaeologists have access to remote-sensing equipment, they can choose to use this in addition or as an alternative to digging a test pit. The most common and simplest of the geophysical survey instruments is the metal detector which helps locate underground iron and bronze metal objects. The more complicated equipment includes the magnetometer and ground

---

52   Ibid.
53   Juwayeyi 2010b.
54   Ibid: 137.
55   Mgomezulu 1978: 61.
56   Juwayeyi 1981: 127.
57   Feder 2008.

penetrating radar (GPR). The magnetometer 'measures the strength of the Earth's magnetic field and records variations in that strength'.[58] When the magnetometer is pulled along over a site, the strength of the earth's magnetic field in its path should remain the same. Any variation is an indication of past disturbances and may suggest the presence of walls, graves, filled in ditches and other features.[59] The GPR emits radar pulses into the ground which reflect back whenever they encounter features, and the depth at which these features are located is measured from 'the travel time of the pulses'.[60] The information obtained from the use of these tools helps archaeologists to sample sites in a systematic manner and to determine where specifically to place their excavations.[61] Archaeologists in Malawi have never used these rather sophisticated instruments for archaeological research.

Excavating archaeological sites

The first step in undertaking an actual archaeological excavation is to level the current surface[62] and to come up with a precise map of the site. A number of instruments are available to accomplish this process, including 'a standard transit, as used in road surveying, or a theodolite, plane table, or laser transit'.[63] The archaeologist is free to use either the imperial or metric system of measurement, provided the same is used in the excavations as well, and must then decide the size of excavation units to be used at the site. These units are a grid of squares laid over the area to be excavated (see Plate 5.2). Although they can be of any size, one-metre squares are commonly used. Smaller than that 'would squeeze out the archaeologist, and larger units might not allow sufficient accuracy'.[64] The squares allow excavations to be done in regularly spaced units and also enable the archaeologist to easily plot or map the precise location of finds. At the very beginning, however, the archaeologist establishes a datum point. This is a fixed spot or the '0' point at the site from which measurements, both horizontal and vertical, are taken.[65] Once excavations begin, all artefacts found in their primary context or in situ (that is where the people who last handled the artefacts dropped or left them) and features within a grid square, will be located with reference to the datum point. Thus the location of every archaeological artefact recovered in situ and every feature will be identified on the map.[66]

---

58   Sutton and Yohe II 2003: 399.
59   Feder 2008: 163.
60   Renfrew & Bahn 2004: 102.
61   Sutton &Yohe II 2003: 121.
62   Vogelsang 2017: 106.
63   Sutton & Yohe II 2003: 125.
64   Thomas and Kelly 2006: 136.
65   Vogelsang 2017: 106.
66   Sutton and Yohe II 2003: 125; Feder 2008: 183.

Plate 5.2: An excavation in progress.
Source: The author

The map gives the archaeologist a clear picture of the size of the site. Some sites can be relatively small, covering no more than a dozen or so square metres, while others can be large, covering hundreds of square metres. Irrespective of size, the archaeologist must decide where specifically to dig. Unless one has had the benefit of results from a geophysical exploration that clearly revealed subsurface materials, many archaeologists will make their decision based on what they see on the surface. In many cases, there will be artefacts scattered on the surface and sometimes there will also be evidence of a feature or two. After mapping and collecting the surface artefacts the archaeologist will often dig a test pit[67] rather than make a random decision regarding where to excavate. The test pit entails digging one excavation unit, and if the site is large, one might dig test pits in several areas of the site.[68] The results will guide the archaeologist as to where to do an extensive excavation. They will also provide some information on what to expect from the excavations, including how deep it would be before levels are reached with no archaeological material. Sometimes, however, the test pit might not produce the information that the archaeologist expected. Such a disappointing result is still useful archaeological information as it helps the archaeologist to come up with an accurate

---

67   Wotzka 2017: 113.
68   Sutton and Yohe II 2003.

map of the spatial distribution of both productive and unproductive archaeological sites.

After successful test pitting, the archaeologist is ready to excavate the site. The nature of the site, including soil type, hardness and prior knowledge of the levels where the archaeologist expects to find cultural material, will determine what excavation tools to use. When the surface soil is compact, very hard and sterile, archaeologists use picks with short handles to remove the earth and quickly reach the artefact-bearing levels. Where such sterile levels are very thick, mechanical excavation equipment can be used.[69] If, on the other hand, the very top layer contains artefacts — as is often the case — then irrespective of its hardness, the archaeologist will most likely start to probe it using the common builder's trowel, and might only turn to the pick if the trowel completely fails to work the hard soil.

The trowel is the most important and commonly used tool in archaeological excavations.[70] It is so widely used that had there been as many archaeologists as there are bricklayers, this tool would probably be called the archaeologist's trowel. Blades of trowels come in different function-related shapes. The builder's trowel is pointed and roughly diamond shaped with a handle welded to it.[71] Left- or right-handed people can use the trowel effectively. The pointed end is used to do the actual digging whereas the sides are used for scrapping soil to level the surface and to straighten the vertical walls of excavation units.[72] Other common tools used in excavations include dental picks and tweezers, root cutters, brooms, brushes (including tooth brushes), dust pans, sieves, a carpenter's bubble level, magnifying lenses, a compass and other objects.

Since archaeological excavations involve digging into a site to recover or observe material remains, they are by nature destructive.[73] The digging and recovery of artefacts destroy the site either partially or completely and permanently.[74] As a result, archaeologists excavate sites in a deliberate, slow and careful manner to ensure that they recover all the artefacts in every excavation unit at every level and uncover all features. The slow pace enables them to avoid digging through delicate and fragile features such as floors, postholes and hearths. It also enables them to notice and record certain characteristics of the soil like colour and compactness. To minimise unintended damage to features, archaeologists might set aside the trowel and turn to other more precise tools like dental pins and brushes. These two tools can also be used to remove soil

69   Sutton and Yohe II 2003.
70   Feder 2008: 179.
71   Ibid.
72   Ibid: 180.
73   Bosquet D. 2017. From the field to the lab. In *Field Manual for African Archaeology*. AL Smith, E Cornelissen, OP Gosselain & S MacEachern (eds). Tervuren: Royal Museum for Central Africa: 152.
74   Smith AL. 2017b. Introduction: How to protect archaeological sites. In *Field Manual for African Archaeology*. A Livingstone-Smith, E Cornelissen, OP Gosselain & S MacEachern (eds). Tervuren: Royal Museum for Central Africa: 102.

surrounding bones, small pieces of pottery, beads and other items, provided great care is taken not to scratch or break them.[75] Elsewhere, instead of the trowel, archaeologists fabricate scraping tools from bamboo stalks to avoid or minimise the accidental scratching of artefacts such as bones.[76] Bamboo tools are said to be hard enough for scraping soil and soft enough to prevent scratching or breaking fragile objects.

The excavation itself is done at predetermined levels. Individual circumstances will dictate how deep the levels should be, but many archaeologists prefer to excavate in 5-centimetre levels.[77] The top-most level is 0–5 centimetres, the next one 5–10 centimetres and so on, until sterile layers are reached. Those measurements are also shown on all the bags or containers in which artefacts and ecofacts from individual levels are placed. Since it is usually impossible for the excavation in the various grid squares to proceed at the same pace, it is advisable for it to be done in a chequerboard pattern.[78] Archaeologists must be careful not to increase the depth of excavation levels in a 'slow moving grid' in an effort to catch up with a 'fast moving grid'. They must maintain the 5-centimetre excavation levels at all times. This manner of consistency enables the archaeologist to maintain stratigraphic control of the excavation and also to compare material recovered from each excavation level in every excavation grid square, both vertically and horizontally. At the conclusion of the excavations, the archaeologist will take pictures of the excavation walls and draw the different stratigraphic levels.

Any excavation of features, if required, is done separately because features tend to go beyond one excavation level. Excavating them separately prevents mixing of artefacts from different levels.[79] When features are fully exposed, the archaeologist may decide to photograph them before and after cleaning them. The cleaning process should be done carefully using brushes and any other applicable tools. Features that cannot be removed from the site may be backfilled at the conclusion of excavations.

Archaeologists treat objects they find in situ more or less like features, taking great care to expose them as fully as possible so they can map and photograph them.[80] Thereafter, they collect the objects, and if no further cleaning is required they immediately label and place them in bags. The bulk of archaeological recoveries, however, are artefacts and ecofacts which are found loosely during excavations or when sieving the earth from the trenches.

Excavators in the trenches often miss small objects such as small potsherds, beads, bones of small creatures like rodents and fish, seeds and other items. They too must be found, otherwise information relating to diet and other aspects of the economy of the

---

75 Sutton & Yohe II 2003: 127; Feder 2008: 181.
76 Feder 2008: 181.
77 Thomas and Kelly 2006: 138.
78 Wotzka 2017: 113.
79 Sutton & Yohe II: 2003:128.
80 Ibid: 129.

ancient inhabitants will be severely compromised. To recover them, archaeologists use buckets to remove excavated soil from every grid square, one level at a time, which is sieved by hand or by mechanical sifters.[81] Sometimes, they use water to wash away the soil, exposing artefacts, small pebbles and other natural materials embedded in lumps of earth,[82] sifting through them to recover artefacts and ecofacts. If they expect small beads, seeds and fish bones from the site, then the sieve mesh must be of such a size that the smallest of them will still not slip through and get lost.[83] Materials recovered from the sieves are bagged and labelled separately.[84] Should they find a hearth, archaeologists may collect charcoal samples, which they will send to a specialised laboratory to be dated using the carbon-14 (C-14) dating method. Archaeologists may also collect soil for pollen analysis. Results from these activities will help give a picture of the way of life of the people who occupied the site as well as the nature of their environment.

Analysis of material remains

The excavated materials are taken to a temporary field laboratory, often part of the field camp site, where the preliminary analysis of the material is done. The analysis of material that might not require specialist attention can be done there if the volume is small. However, sometimes the volume of material tends to be large, numbering in the tens of thousands and requiring more room for the analysis exercise. Archaeologists are forced to take the material to their permanent archaeological laboratories. Analysis of archaeological material is an extremely time-consuming activity, requiring the archaeologist to examine literally every object that was recovered in the excavations. When one has well-trained students or technicians, however, the exercise is not as arduous as it sounds. Still, it is very time-consuming and may take years to accomplish.

Over the years, archaeology has become so interdisciplinary that it can no longer function without specialists from other disciplines.[85] Depending on the nature of the site and the information being sought, an archaeologist might require the assistance of specialists in geology, botany, osteology and other disciplines, including those who help with chronology. The specialists should be alerted in advance regarding the nature of the material remains coming their way.[86] Further, advances in computer technology occur so rapidly that many archaeologists fail to catch up with many of the new applications that have the potential to assist them in their work. Therefore, computer experts have become important specialists in archaeological research. They assist the archaeologist with statistical analysis, mapping and accurate illustration of certain

---

81 Sutton & Yohe II 2003: 129.
82 Ibid.
83 Ibid.
84 Bosquet 2017: 152.
85 Bosquet 2017: 152.
86 Ibid.

objects, all of which help in the presentation of research results.[87] Illustrations are important as they help to amplify what the archaeologist has to say about the site and certain objects. Photographs, scaled drawings of stone tools, pottery and objects made of bones, ivory and metal form part of the full record of the excavation.[88]

Chronology

Chronological issues require special mention. In fact, the first puzzle that archaeologists attempt to solve when they locate a new site or recover artefacts is that of age. How old is this site and how old are these material remains? The two types of dating methods in archaeology are relative dating and absolute or chronometric dating.[89] In the seventeenth century, Nicolaus Steno formulated geology's law of superposition on which relative dating is based.[90] The law states that where two or more strata or layers of earth or rocks are observed in an undisturbed context, the layer at the bottom is older than the one on top of it. In other words, the layer at the bottom was formed before the one above it, and so forth up to the top level, which is the most recent one. It is not possible to tell how many years each layer took to form and therefore no specific date is assigned to the layers. All one can point out is which one is older relative to the other.

In the nineteenth century, British geologist William Smith[91] came up with an idea called the index fossil concept, which makes it possible to correlate strata in different areas. Apparently, Smith noticed that organisms changed over time and that their remains represented by fossils distinguish geological layers or strata. It was clear that each stratum was formed in a different time. Therefore, strata in widely separated locations that contained the same fossils 'could be correlated and assigned the same time period'.[92] Strata below and above the strata containing the index fossils can accordingly be referred to as relatively older or younger.

Archaeologists adopted the index fossil concept even though they work largely with artefacts rather than fossils and this led to relative dating in archaeology. The various layers at an archaeological excavation will usually contain artefacts and archaeologists study them carefully in order to identify distinctive artefact forms in each layer. They refer to such artefacts as time markers.[93] As in geology, layers or strata that contain the same distinctive artefact forms are assumed to be of the same age.[94] Such artefacts enable archaeologists to make meaningful comparisons within and among

87   Sutton & Yohe II 2003: 131.
88   Renfrew & Bahn 2004: 115.
89   Renfrew & Bahn 2004.
90   Thomas & Kelly 2006: 153.
91   Thomas & Kelly 2006: 177.
92   Ibid.
93   Thomas and Kelly 2006.
94   Ibid.

sites. In the end, conclusions are made regarding cultural change through time, both at a single location and over a wide geographical area.

Relative dating works well in areas which have at least one site with a deep stratigraphic profile containing distinctive artefact forms in several layers. Such a site is said to contain a master sequence to which layers of all other sites in a given area may be compared.[95] One distinctive relative dating technique is called seriation. It is based on the assumption that styles of products and ways of doing things change slowly over time, and that humans tend to adopt new ones but only after an initial period of hesitation or resistance.[96] With time, however, the new style is accepted and it may become a dominant style for years until another new idea again comes on the scene.[97]

Imagine, for instance, that in 800 AD a new style of decorating pottery emerges in the southern Lake Malawi area. The style will start slowly because people will initially naturally resist or hesitate to accept it. Over time, however, they will overcome their dislike and the new style will become popular and may eventually totally replace earlier styles. Through trade or other forms of communication, the new style could spread quite far away from its area of initial introduction. Now imagine two other styles are again introduced, one in 1100 and the other in 1650. The cycle of resistance, hesitation and acceptance will be repeated. An archaeologist coming to the area in 2018 may be able to locate and excavate sites dating to those times. Some of the sites may be well stratified and show these potteries in different layers, thus enabling the archaeologist to see which pottery was replaced by the pottery introduced in 800 and which followed it through time. Should archaeologists excavate sites located over a wide area, they will be in a position to make intra-site comparisons, enabling them to draw conclusions on cultural change through time and space. Thus, seriation uses the frequencies of artefacts and or styles to date sites and artefacts relative to one another, but still without giving a specific age.[98]

In Malawi, however, deep, stratified Iron Age sites are not easily located. Relative dating has still worked, though, by carefully comparing and linking time markers at several shallow sites. Robinson[99] did this when he noticed that a type of pottery called Mawudzu consistently lay over another type called Nkope at sites along the western shore area of the eastern arm of Lake Malawi. When he moved from there to Bwanje Valley, the situation was the same, except that he was able to extend the sequence in that he discovered a third pottery type called Kapeni.[100] He noticed that where the three pottery types existed in the same excavation, Kapeni pottery was consistently between

95   Ibid: 177.
96   Feder 2008: 209.
97   Ibid.
98   Ibid.
99   Robinson 1970.
100 Ibid.

Nkope at the bottom and Mawudzu at the top. Before long, C-14 dates confirmed the pottery sequence.[101]

Absolute dating on the other hand provides the archaeologist with an actual age in years for the material remains recovered in an excavation. There are several methods of absolute dating, of which the best known and universally used is C-14, invented by University of Chicago physical chemist, Professor Willard F Libby, in 1949.[102] The C-14 dating method is such an important and powerful archaeological tool that others have referred to it as archaeology's workhorse.[103] Although called 'absolute', the dates from C-14 are never that precise as they often refer to a range of years.[104] As a result, the term 'chronometric dating', which means the 'measurement of time', is often used by some archaeologists who believe that it is more easily understood than the term 'absolute'.[105]

The chemistry involved in C-14 dating is too complex for the purpose of this book. However, to put it in simple terms, carbon exists as two stable isotopes (C-12 and C-13) and a third one (C-14), which is radioactive.[106] Radiocarbon is a byproduct of cosmic-ray bombardment in the upper atmosphere where it is 'incorporated into carbon dioxide'[107] with winds spreading it throughout the atmosphere. However, 98 per cent of C-14 enters the ocean while plants take the remainder through photosynthesis. From plants, it enters herbivores; carnivores acquire it by eating the herbivores, humans by eating both plants and herbivores.[108]

The amount of C-14 in an organism remains at an equilibrium with the atmosphere so long as the organism is alive. Once it dies, it no longer takes in C-14. Instead, the C-14 in it begins to decay and therefore decreases. It has been calculated that after about 5 730 years only half of the original amount will be left in the body.[109] It will take the same number of years for half of the remaining half to decay.[110] This number of years is referred to by scholars as the half-life of C-14.[111] Originally, it had been estimated that after 45 000 years not much C-14 would be left in the organism,[112] meaning that the method could not provide dates for objects that were older than that age. Subsequently,

---

101 Robinson 1970, 1973; Mgomezulu 1978; Juwayeyi 1981.
102 Taylor RE. 1985. The beginnings of radiocarbon dating in American antiquity. *American Antiquity*. 50(2): 309–325.
103 Thomas & Kelly 2006: 184.
104 De Maret P. 2017. Radiocarbon dating. In *Field Manual for African Archaeology*. In AL Smith, E Cornelissen, OP Gosselain & S MacEachern (eds). Tervuren: Royal Museum for Central Africa: 232.
105 Feder 2008: 214.
106 Sutton & Yohe II 2003: 176; Feder 2008: 429.
107 Sutton & Yohe II 2003: 176.
108 Thomas & Kelly 2006: 185.
109 Renfrew & Bahn 2004: 142.
110 Thomas & Kelly 2006.
111 Stuiver M & Suess H. 1966. On the relationship between radiocarbon dates and true sample ages. *Radiocarbon*. 8(1): 536; see also Taylor, RE. 1997. Radiocarbon dating. In *Chronometric Dating in Archaeology*. In RE Taylor & MJ. Aitken (eds). New York: Plenum Press: 68.
112 Thomas & Kelly 2006.

however, C-14 enrichment techniques were developed and they helped extend by up to four half-lives the maximum age limit for which the C-14 dating method could be used.[113] Only organic remains of both plants and animals can be processed to obtain dates using the C-14 dating method.[114] During excavations, archaeologists recover different types of organic remains, including teeth, shell, skin, antler, horn, bone, leather, hair, nuts, seeds, fruit and wood.[115] Although all of these remains can potentially be used in C-14 dating, the process of dating results in their destruction and so archaeologists look for charcoal first. They would use any of the other materials if charcoal was absolutely unavailable.

Samples for dating must be collected from clear stratigraphic secured contexts[116] or in close association with the material one wants to date or from features such as hearths. Great care is taken during the sample-collection process to minimise contamination with other organic objects, including the archaeologist's fingers. Therefore, inorganic objects such as clean trowels or any other applicable metal tools are used to collect the samples, after which they are put in containers and sealed.[117] The archaeologist then sends the samples to a laboratory to be processed.

The dates that the samples produce do not immediately translate into calendar years because, due to some natural factors, the amount of atmospheric C-14 has not been constant but has varied through time. It has been demonstrated through radiocarbon studies of tree rings, for instance, that there have been fairly 'consistent variations in both short-term and long-term radiocarbon production over the past 8,000 years'.[118] Therefore, radiocarbon dates do not correspond with calendar dates.[119] This has been proved by checking the radiocarbon remaining in an archaeological object of a known age, such as beams from ancient buildings, and counting their tree rings.[120] To solve this problem, dates produced by samples submitted to a laboratory must be converted to calendar years and this is where tree-ring studies have proved useful.

Tree-ring dating or dendrochronology is one of the absolute dating methods in archaeology. It is because certain trees produce rings at the rate of one ring per year: a tree with six hundred rings is 600 years old. Tree rings of bristlecone pines (*Pinus longaeva*) of California, for instance, demonstrate continuity through 8 700 years.[121] Since tree-ring dates are accurate, it has been possible for scientists to calibrate and

113 Grootes PM, Stuiver M, Farwell GW, Schaad TP & Schmidt FH. 1980. Enrichment of 14C and Sample Preparation for Beta and Ion Counting. *Radiocarbon*. 22(02): 493; Taylor 1997: 69.
114 De Maret 2017: 232.
115 Ibid.
116 Ibid: 234.
117 Ibid.
118 Sutton & Yohe II 2003: 179.
119 Thomas and Kelly 2006: 187.
120 Ibid.
121 Sutton & Yohe II 2003: 180.

convert radiocarbon years to calendar years. For instance, one of the charcoal samples from Mankhamba, which I submitted to a radiocarbon dating laboratory at the University of Arizona, Tucson, produced the following date: 365±45 BP. It was not calibrated. The last two letters 'BP' stand for 'before present,' and 'present' is defined as 1950. Why 1950? Archaeologists and chronologists simply agreed that for archaeological dating, the 'present' should be defined as 1950.[122] The date referred to earlier indicates that the age of the charcoal sample ranged from 365+45 to 365–45 BP, that is from 410–320 BP. Since 'before present' is 1950, the range of that date is 1540–1630 AD. However, when that date was calibrated to take into account atmospheric radiocarbon fluctuation, the calendar age of the sample was found to range from 1448–1636 AD, giving it a fifteenth- rather than a sixteenth-century date.

The dates that archaeologists receive from the laboratory always begin with the abbreviation of the name of the laboratory, followed by the sample number, sample type and the date, as shown in Table 7.2 in Chapter 7. Archaeologists must reproduce them in their reports so that any interested individuals can crosscheck the date in the laboratory records book.

Reporting results and curating material remains

After the archaeologist has finished analysing the material and the various specialists have submitted the results of their respective work, two important activities remain: to report the results of the research[123] and to curate the material remains. Immediate reporting of results of one's research is a professional requirement or obligation. It can be done through papers presented at professional conferences where colleagues get a chance to ask questions and seek clarifications. One may also publish reports as a monograph or as a journal article. Best of all, one can write non-technical newspaper articles for the public which is often a great fulfilment of one's professional obligation.

Curation of archaeological material is a process through which the materials are prepared for permanent storage, possibly involving special conservation techniques such as stabilising fragile bones by applying special glue that holds them together. Perishable materials, such as seeds, skins, bark cloth, wood and other materials, may have to be kept in a room where the temperature is appropriately controlled.[124] The usefulness of curating materials for permanent storage is that they become available to both contemporary and future researchers. For instance, some of the archaeological materials that were recovered in the mid-twentieth century or earlier can now be re-examined using modern computer technology or powerful microscopes to yield more

---

122 Feder 2008: 223.
123 Gérard I. 2017. Introduction to Chapter 7. In *Field Manual for African Archaeology*. In AL Smith, E Cornelissen, OP Gosselain & S MacEachern (eds). Tervuren: Royal Museum for Central Africa: 302.
124 Sutton & Yohe II 2003: 133.

information. What this means is that the home environment is not the right one to store archaeological materials: museums and large education institutions are best suited for this. Fortunately for Malawi, archaeological research is still in its infancy and so there is plenty of room to store archaeological materials. This is not true in some western countries where, over the years, they have accumulated so much material that some storage facilities no longer accept new archaeological materials.[125] Materials that are not accepted end up in less than ideal storage facilities, which may not be easily accessible to researchers.

Summary

Archaeology is the study of past and recent humans using material remains, objects that humans made or modified, and then discarded or abandoned after use. They include artefacts, ecofacts and features. Archaeology is not only about studying prehistory; it also includes historical archaeology and the archaeology of modern society or garbology. A great deal of archaeological research, however, deals with the prehistoric period, involving the Stone Age, the Neolithic and the Iron Age periods. In sub-Saharan Africa, the historical period replaced the Iron Age when writing was introduced during the second half of the second millennium AD.

Two important tasks for archaeologists before they undertake archaeological excavations involve coming up with a research design and carrying out site surveys, and this leads to the discovery of sites. The reconnaissance or scanning, and the pedestrian or foot survey methods are important in locating archaeological sites. Sometimes archaeologists undertake impromptu site surveys and excavations when they suspect that construction activities or natural processes, such as water action from rising lake levels, might destroy sites. This aspect of archaeological research is part of CRM, and in Malawi, it is carried out by the Malawi Department of Antiquities.

Once archaeologists locate sites, they may sample them and this will depend on, among other things, their research question and the location of the sites over the landscape. Archaeologists may also choose to study only one site, or they may want to study many in order to figure out how the ancient people used the landscape. Archaeologists call this landscape archaeology.

Prior knowledge of subsurface material is important and so archaeologists dig test pits. They may also use some remote sensing equipment such as metal detectors. Before undertaking a full excavation, archaeologists produce a map of the site, using equipment such as a standard transit used in road surveying or a theodolite to produce the map. After that, they determine the size of excavation units and set up a datum point that is the '0' point from which they will take all measurements. The most common excavation

---

125 Thomas & Kelly 2006: 142.

tool they use is the builder's trowel. In Malawi and in many other countries, archaeologists excavate in 5-centimetre levels.

Archaeology has become an interdisciplinary field involving specialists in geology, osteology, botany and computer technology. Chronology is important in archaeological research. Of the many dating methods available, archaeologists use the C-14 dating method the most. Finally, once analysis is completed, archaeologists curate the material remains and report research results either at conferences, in scholarly papers and even in popular magazines and newspapers.

CHAPTER 6

The Iron Age archaeology of the southern Lake Malawi area

Archaeologists refer to the period of iron-based cultural adaptation and elaboration as the Iron Age. They have divided it into the Early and Late Iron Age periods. The Early Iron Age was the time when iron tools replaced stone tools and ironworking technology became widespread. There is still some debate as to whether ironworking technology in sub-Saharan Africa was indigenously invented or not.[1] In some areas, such as the Great Lakes region, people were producing iron implements by the middle of the first millennium BC.[2] By the beginning of the second millennium AD, more cultural and economic changes began to take shape in much of sub-Saharan Africa, a period archaeologists refer to as the Late Iron Age. These changes included the development of states in areas where such institutions had been unknown, and the intensification of long-distance trade.[3] In many parts of sub-Saharan Africa, state formation and long-distance trade seem to have occurred more or less at the same time, with trade being 'seen as both a stimulus and a mechanism for state formation'.[4] These activities resulted in a great deal of population displacement and movement, as was undertaken by the Chewa.

The southern Lake Malawi area attracted more attention from archaeologists than all other areas in the country after archaeologists confirmed that the earliest Iron Age communities arrived there early in the third century.[5] During the last five decades of the twentieth century, several archaeologists carried out various research projects in the area (see Map 6.1) where they discovered and described five different Iron Age pottery types.[6] This enabled archaeologists to establish a pottery sequence which C-14 dates have confirmed. The Iron Age archaeology of the southern Lake Malawi area became the best known in the country.

The environment of the southern Lake Malawi area

Lake Malawi and the Shire River, its only outlet, dominate the environment of the southern Lake Malawi area. The lake is one of Malawi's most outstanding topographic

---

1   Phillipson 2000: 159.
2   Ibid: 188.
3   Phillipson 2000; Connah 2009.
4   Phillipson 2000: 208.
5   Robinson 1970.
6   Inskeep 1965; Robinson 1970; Davison 1991, 1992.

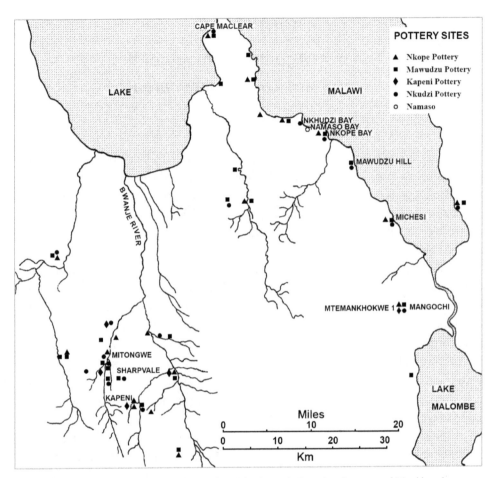

Map 6.1: Sites excavated in the southern Lake Malawi area before the discovery of Mankhamba.
Source: Adapted from Robinson 1970, used with the permission of the Malawi Department of Antiquities

features.[7] It lies within the Great Rift Valley of East Africa, which stretches from the Zambezi River in Mozambique to the Red Sea.[8] The Lake Malawi part of the Rift Valley runs almost due north for a distance of about 644 kilometres and it averages 80 kilometres in width.[9] The lake itself measures some 29 604 square kilometres.[10] It has 'the third largest surface area of all African lakes and lies between latitudes 9°30'S and

7   Pike JG & Rimmington GT. 1965. *Malawi: A geographical study.* London: Oxford University Press.
8   Shroder JF. 1972. Geological history of rocks of post-basement complex, rift-faulting, and mineral occurrences. In *Malawi in Maps.* S. Agnew & M. Stubbs (eds). London: University of London Press: 22.
9   Pike & Rimmington 1965: 12.
10   Pike JG. 1972. Hydrology. In *Malawi in Maps.* S Agnew & M Stubbs (eds). London: University of London Press: 34.

14°30'S.[11] Other topographic features include hills that form the shoulders of the Rift Valley and the many small rivers and streams that, together with the Shire River, form the drainage system of the area. All the small rivers and streams drain into the lake or into the Shire River and Lake Malombe. The annual rainfall averages 820 millimetres to 1030 millimetres[12] and although it is less than the annual rainfall on some of the highlands, it is still sufficient for dryland farming.[13] The temperature ranges from 25 °C to 27.5 °C all year round, making it neither exceedingly cold nor exceedingly hot.[14] The density of government-protected forests on nearby hills suggests that, in the past, the vegetation of the southern Lake Malawi area was thicker than it is today. There are three vegetation types in the area. The most common consists of 'woodlands, thickets, scrubs and parklands of low altitude'.[15] One of the striking features of this vegetation type is the regular occurrence of tall trees like the baobab (*Adansonia digitata*), known locally as *mlambe* and believed to be cultivation induced.[16] The second vegetation type is made up of different species of *Brachystegia* woodlands, known locally as *miombo*, which are the most common type of woodlands in Malawi.[17] The third type comprises 'woodland scrubs and thickets of the rift escarpment and its foothills'.[18] In this vegetation type, scrubs and thickets co-exist with some *Brachystegia* woodlands along with *Adansonia digitata* and bamboos (*Oxytenanthera abyssinica*).

These vegetation types supported a wide variety of wild fauna, as confirmed by the remains from various archaeological sites.[19] Wild animals ranging from very large animals such as the elephant and buffalo to small antelopes were common.[20] Today,

11 Owen RB, Crossley, R, Johnson, TC, Tweddle, D, Kornfield, I, Davison, S, Eccles, DH & Engstrom, DE. 1990. Major low levels of Lake Malawi and their implications for speciation rates in cichlid fishes. *Proceedings of the Royal Society*. B 240: 521.

12 Lineham S. 1972. Climate 4: Rainfall. In *Malawi in Maps*. S Agnew & M Stubbs (eds). London: University of London Press: 33.

13 Pike & Rimmington 1965: 71; Agnew S. 1972a. Environment and history: the Malawian setting. In *The Early History of Malawi*. B Pachai (ed). London: Longman. 33.

14 Torrance JD. 1972. Climate 2: Temperature. In *Malawi in Maps*. S Agnew & M Stubbs (eds). London: University of London Press: 29.

15 Jackson JG. 1972. Vegetation. In *Malawi in Maps*. S Agnew & M Stubbs (eds). London: University of London Press: 38.

16 Ibid.

17 Pike & Rimmington 1965; Jackson 1972: 39.

18 Jackson 1972: 38.

19 Speed E. 1970. Specialist's report on the Nkope faunal remains. In *The Iron Age of the southern lake area of Malawi*. K. Robinson. (Department of Antiquities publication no. 8). Zomba, Malawi: Government Press; Scott K, Juwayeyi, YM & Plug I. 2009. The faunal remains from Mankhamba, a Late Iron Age site of the Maravi in central Malawi. *Annals of the Transvaal Museum*. 46.

20 Speed 1970: 105; Scott, Juwayeyi & Plug 2009: 49.

however, a growing human population and uncontrolled deforestation and hunting have reduced the numbers of many species to near extinction. Elephants are an exception, though, because they are well protected by the state.

Thus, the southern Lake Malawi area has always had what Davison called 'a comparatively productive environment'.[21] People found the area very attractive for permanent settlement, as did the Chewa. The settlement pattern, however, shows that Iron Age inhabitants tended to establish more settlements on the western side of both the eastern and western arms of the lake than on the eastern side. This preference was dictated by its favourable topography as opposed to that of the eastern side which is characterised by hills and mountains. For instance, the Mangochi Hills, which form part of the Rift Valley shoulders and run parallel to the lake, constitute much of the land. In some places, the hills are only a few miles from the shoreline, therefore severely limiting the amount of land for settlement and agriculture.

Preference for the western side of either arm of the lake continued well into the nineteenth and twentieth centuries. Nineteenth-century immigrants to the area, such as the Ngoni, European missionaries and early colonial administrators,[22] established their settlements there. Further, the southern Lake Malawi area with its shallow waters[23] has 'abundant supplies of fish'.[24] In recent times, it has attracted many people from other parts of the country who have also tended to settle on the western side of the eastern arm of the lake. All major government offices, banks, hotels and other businesses are located on that same side. Just about the only important development on the eastern side of the eastern arm is a mission station of the Anglican Church which includes a hospital and a secondary school for girls.

The Shire River is viewed as an extension of Lake Malawi. Much of the land on either side of the river is relatively flat and agriculturally rich. The exception is the area between Matope and Chikhwawa where it is rocky and the river has rapids over which it falls some 384 metres.[25] The rapids blocked what otherwise would have been a navigable river from Lake Malawi to the Zambezi River. The area from Matope to the lake is referred to as the Upper Shire Valley and that below the rapids as the Lower Shire Valley.[26] Archaeological excavations along the banks, both in the Upper and Lower Shire Valley areas, have shown that, like the lake, the Shire River attracted continuous human settlement since the Early Iron Age period.[27] Some of these Early Iron Age people

---

21 Davison 1991: 25.
22 Pachai 1974; McCracken 2013.
23 Agnew S. 1972b. Fishing. In *Malawi in Maps*. S Agnew & M Stubbs (eds). London: University of London Press. 94.
24 McCracken 2013: 9.
25 Pike 1972: 34.
26 Pike 1972; Robinson 1973.
27 Robinson 1973.

migrated to the plateau areas of the Shire Highlands at the end of the first millennium AD, probably in search of a more open environment.[28]

The importance of pottery in Iron Age studies

Despite use of the term 'Iron Age', it is not iron implements but rather pottery that archaeologists study in detail. The reason is that compared to pottery, iron implements were difficult to produce and as a result they were not as numerous nor were they as regularly used and discarded as pottery was. Producing iron required many things, involving many workers, iron ore, large amounts of charcoal from specially selected trees, proper construction of iron-smelting furnaces called *ng'anjo* in Chichewa (see Plate 6.1), tuyere pipes, traditional medicine and observance of certain rituals and

Plate 6.1: *Ng'anjo*, an original iron-smelting furnace still standing in northern Kasungu, dated probably to the late nineteenth or early twentieth century AD.
Source: Cole-King 1973. Used with permission of the Malawi Department of Antiquities

---

28   Juwayeyi 1981: 467.

taboos.[29] Tuyere pipes (see Plate 6.2) are ceramic pipes that people inserted into the iron-smelting furnace to allow them to bellow in air during the iron-smelting process. The number of implements they produced was nevertheless minimal and very disproportionate to the input rendered.

An experimental project conducted among the Phoka people near Livingstonia in northern Malawi, by Nikolaas van der Merwe and Donald Avery, illustrates this point well.[30] They noted that the Phoka chose a site to build their iron-smelting furnace near the place where trees that were ideal for making charcoal grew. In this case it happened to be against a steep mountain slope and 'near the house of their chief smelter'.[31] It took fit men the whole day to walk to the iron ore mine and they brought in 6 500 kilograms of wet clay with which to build the furnace. They obtained the clay from about 600 metres away and carried it up a steep mountain slope to the site of the furnace. The smelters used 'a metric tonne of charcoal', which came from 88 cubic metres of wood. From all that work, they expected to make about 'four hoes, and some smaller tools'.[32] In other parts of the country, iron ore was scarcer than it was for the Phoka. Laws[33]

Plate 6.2: Fragment of a tuyere pipe from Mankhamba.
Source: The author

29   Van der Merwe NJ & Avery DH. 1987. Science and magic in African technology: traditional iron smelting in Malawi. *Africa.* 57(02):150; Wenner DB & Van der Merwe NJ. 1987. Mining for the lowest grade ore: traditional iron production in northern Malawi. *Geoarchaeology: An International Journal.* 2(3); Msamba F & Killick D. 1992. Kasungu and Kaluluma oral traditions. (Unpublished): 3.
30   Van der Merwe & Avery 1987.
31   Ibid: 154.
32   Ibid.
33   Laws 1979.

observed that, in some areas, people walked for as many as three days to obtain iron ore. Not surprisingly, iron implements never came close to being as common as pottery and they must have been expensive to acquire.

Another reason for archaeologists paying less attention to iron implements than to pottery is that iron implements rarely changed in design across cultures and through time. A fifth-century spear made in the Great Lakes region, for instance, might resemble a twelfth-century spear made in the same region or a ninth-century spear made on the Shire Highlands in Malawi. A further reason is that iron implements were subject to severe corrosion within a relatively short time. Archaeologists often recover unidentifiably corroded iron implements from their excavations..

All that people required to produce pottery was suitable clay, the observance of certain taboos or rituals, firewood and one's choice of temper. Temper is material such as tiny crushed fragments of old pottery, sand and charcoal that potters add to the wet clay to ensure a uniform drying process so as to prevent shrinking and cracking during firing.[34] Pottery tends to be abundant at Iron Age sites because it is heavy and cumbersome to carry around and so people simply abandoned it whenever they moved to establish new settlements elsewhere.[35] Further, pottery fractures into many fragments when dropped to the ground or when someone treads on it. While a broken pot is a loss to the owner, the many fragments and the fact that they can survive in the ground for thousands of years are huge advantages for archaeology.

Unlike iron, pottery is informative[36] because it preserves many culture-distinguishing features. Pottery shapes, including types of rims and bases, vary geographically and culturally through time. People of different cultures, regions and times designed their pottery in styles unique to themselves.

Decorations made on pots also varied geographically and changed through time. Although burnishing has decorative value and can be done on both the exterior and interior sides of the pot, the most diagnostic decorative motifs were those based on incisions, grooving, stamping and bangle impressions (see Figure 6.1). People made the motifs in different designs and usually on the exterior side of the vessel. Sometimes, they moulded bosses and ribs on the vessel. Bosses and ribs were made 'by the affixing of additional pieces of clay' on the 'surface of the vessel wall.'[37]

As shown in Figure 6.1, the terms 'incisions' and 'groovings' refer to similar decoration types made using 'a narrow-ended instrument to produce concave lines in the vessel wall, whether by depression or gouging'.[38] Incised lines are thinner or

---

34 Renfrew & Bahn 2004.
35 Smith AL & de Francquen C. 2017. Pottery analysis. In *Field Manual for African Archaeology*. AL Smith, E Cornelissen, OP Gosselain & S MacEachern (eds). Tervuren: Royal Museum for Central Africa: 173.
36 Ibid.
37 Phillipson, 1976: 23.
38 Phillipson 1976: 22.

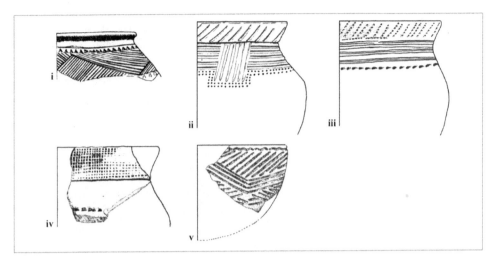

Figure 6.1: Pottery decoration types. Notes: (i) incised; (ii) grooved; (iii-iv) comb-stamped and (v) bangle-impressed decorations.
Source: Figures i-iv: adapted from Robinson 1970, 1973; Figure v: adapted from Davison, 1992

narrower than grooved lines. Observed from a section of a broken potsherd, incised lines have a V-shaped cross-section whereas grooved lines are relatively wider. Both types of lines can be made even when the clay is relatively dry. Stamping, comb-stamping and bangle impressions on the other hand were made when the clay was soft. Stamping was done with a single-toothed stamp and comb-stamping with a linear, multi-toothed stamp 'to produce depressions in the surface of the vessel wall'.[39] Bangle impressions were made by pressing wound wire or metal strip bangles into the wall of the vessel.[40] People tended to make decorations on a small area of the vessel with the preferred areas being the rim, neck or shoulders and, though not often, the lip. Sometimes, instead of making a band of decorations on the rim or shoulder, they made only a single stamped or nicked line at the point of the pot's maximum diameter, leaving the rest of the pot plain. The result is that archaeologists tend to find more undecorated fragments of pottery than decorated ones. By studying decorative designs, shapes and the changes undergone through time, archaeologists can recreate many aspects of a people's cultural history through time.

Previous archaeological investigations in the southern Lake Malawi area

Map 6.2 shows the position of Mankhamba and some of the important Iron Age sites that archaeologists excavated in the southern Lake Malawi area and along the Shire River

---

39 Ibid.
40 Ibid.

Valley. The first Iron Age archaeological site investigated in that area was Nkhudzi Bay burial site,[41] located some 48 kilometres north of Mangochi district headquarters on the western shores of the eastern arm of the lake. It is situated on what was the property of Mrs ACJ Doel in the 1950s.[42] She noticed that human skeletal remains and various artefacts such as pottery, iron spears, arrowheads, blue glass beads and other items had been eroding from the site for quite some time due to lake water action. Fortunately, she collected some of the material and sent this to the district commissioner at Mangochi district headquarters. He in turn sent the material to his supervisor, the provincial commissioner in Blantyre, who at the time happened to be WHJ Rangeley. He proceeded to get details about the site from Che Steven Mohammed, a resident of the area and caretaker of the cemetery, who remembered it being in use in the 1890s.[43] He told Rangeley that the cemetery belonged to the Mang'anja people (since Mangochi district is within a Yao and Nyanja area, Che Muhammed meant Nyanja rather than the Mang'anja). Rangeley invited the archaeologist Ray Inskeep, from Zambia, to investigate the site.

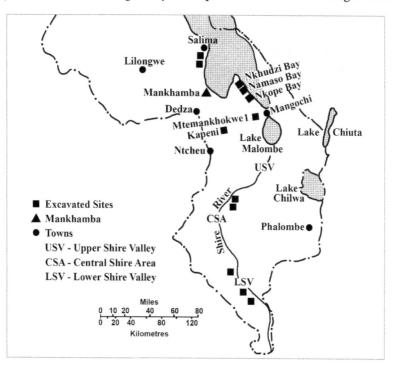

Map 6.2: The position of Mankhamba and some of the sites excavated in the southern Lake Malawi area, and along the Shire River Valley.
Source: The author

41 Inskeep 1965.
42 Ibid: 1.
43 Inskeep 1965.

Inskeep worked at the site in 1958. He quickly noticed that it had at one time been a large cemetery. However, water action caused by the rise in the level of the lake had reduced its size. In the end, Inskeep excavated a small area of a little less than 10 square metres in which he found traces of up to 12 separate burials.[44] His excavations demonstrated, among other things, that the objects Mrs Doel had collected from the shore area were indeed represented in the excavation. They were part of the burial goods that had been interred with human remains. Most importantly, however, Inskeep recovered a certain type of pottery, which he named Nkudzi. He probably meant to name the pottery 'Nkhudzi' after the name of the bay where the site was located, but he simply misspelled it as 'Nkudzi'. Archaeological publications in Malawi, including this book, have maintained the word 'Nkudzi' for the pottery and 'Nkhudzi' for the site and for the bay.

Subsequent research at another burial site called Mtemankhokwe 1, located some 10 kilometres to the west of Mangochi district headquarters and about 48 kilometres to the south-west of Nkhudzi Bay, yielded almost identical material.[45] But unlike the Nkhudzi Bay site, Mtemankhokwe 1 had not been disturbed and therefore it was not difficult to recover and record the finds. When Robinson began research in the area, he placed Nkudzi pottery in a chronological sequence with Malawi's other pottery types. Archaeologists now recognise Nkudzi pottery as the most recent of these pottery types. The dates of manufacture of the beads associated with the burials at Mtemankhokwe 1[46] suggest that the making of Nkudzi pottery began during the late eighteenth or early in the nineteenth century.

Nkudzi vessel types as described and illustrated by Inskeep[47] are bag-shaped pots, thistle-shaped pots, flattened spherical pots and two-tiered pots (see Plate 6.3). Bowls are open and flared, the vessel walls are generally thin and the rims are undifferentiated. The most common decorations include incised herringbone motifs, interlocking hatched triangles and bands of cross-hatching (see Figures 6.2a & 6.2b). Sometimes thumbnail impressions (see Figure 6.2a: iii) are present,[48] but stamping is absent on Nkudzi pottery.[49]

44 Ibid: 3.
45 Juwayeyi YM. 1991. Late Iron Age burial practices in the Southern Lake Malawi area. *The South African Archaeological Bulletin.* 46.
46 Killick D. 1987. European trade beads in southern Africa. *The Bead Forum, newsletter of the Society of Bead Researchers.*10: 6–7; Karklins K. 1990. Analysis of the beads from a Late Iron Age site on Lake Malawi, Malawi. (Unpublished); Juwayeyi 1991: 33.
47 Inskeep 1965.
48 Robinson 1970: 81.
49 Davison 1991: 16.

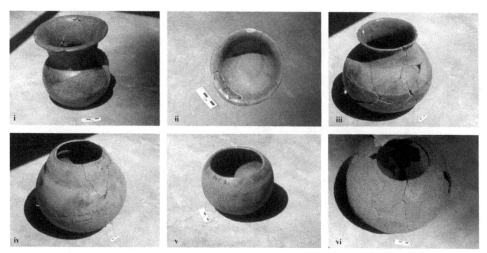

Plate 6.3: Nkudzi pottery from Mtemankhokwe 1: (i) thistle-shaped pot; (ii) flared bowl; (iii) concave necked pot; (iv) two-tiered pot; (v-vi) flattened spherical pots. The top three are lavishly burnished.
Source: The author

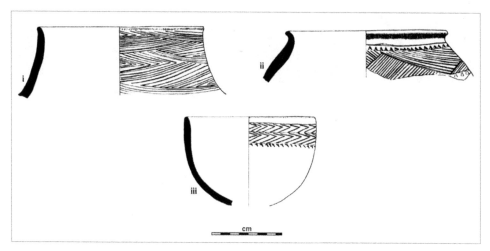

Figure 6.2a: Nkudzi pottery with incised decorations from Nkope Bay: (i) pot with a conical neck and interlocking herringbone decorations; (ii) spherical pot with interlocking hatched triangles and upward pointing triangular impressions; (iii) open bowl with herringbone decorations and thumb nail impressions.
Source: Adapted from Robinson 1970

Makers of Nkudzi pottery placed the decorations on or immediately below the rims or on the shoulders of thistle-shaped and spherical pots. Burnishing outside the vessels using red ochre and graphite was common and sometimes this was also placed inside the vessels. Some of the Nkudzi vessels were so expertly done and so beautifully decorated

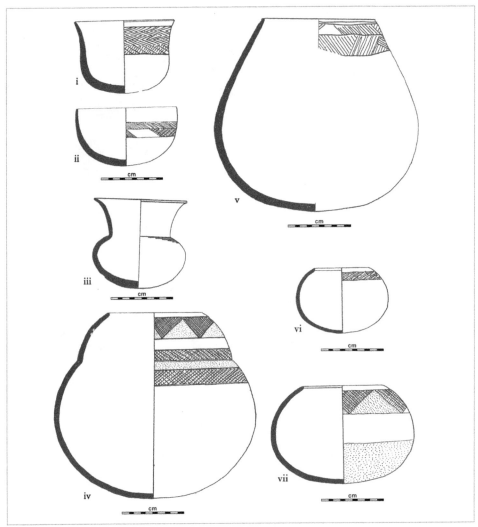

Figure 6.2b: Nkudzi pottery with incised decorations from Nkhudzi Bay: (i) flared bowl with herringbone and cross-hatched decorations; (ii) open bowl with hatched and cross-hatched bands; (iii) an undecorated thistle-shaped pot; (iv) two-tiered pot with cross-hatched triangles and bands, interspaced with those that are burnished ones; (v) bag-shaped pot with two hatched bands; (vi) flattened spherical pot with one cross-hatched band; (vii) flattened spherical pot with a band of cross-hatched triangles interspaced with those that are burnished with a wide burnished band at the bottom.

Source: Adapted from Inskeep 1965

that Inskeep was compelled to comment that 'the red surfaces almost resemble the Samian ware of the Roman period in Europe'.[50]

Robinson was the next archaeologist to work at Iron Age sites in Malawi. As stated earlier, he had been a member of Clark's research team that came to Malawi in 1966. When Clark's project concluded, Robinson decided to continue archaeological investigations in the country. He returned in 1968, which marked the beginning of his long research collaboration with the Malawi Department of Antiquities. He worked in Malawi until the early 1980s, excavating Iron Age sites throughout the country.

Inskeep's work at Nkhudzi Bay and Paul Cole-King's investigations at Michesi, about which he did not publish a report, probably influenced Robinson to start his survey of Iron Age sites in the southern Lake Malawi area first, rather than continue from where he had stopped in northern Malawi. He surveyed much of the western shores of the eastern arm of the lake, including the areas of Monkey Bay and Cape Maclear.[51] He then excavated at Mawudzu Hill, Nkope Bay and Michesi Village. At Mawudzu Hill, he excavated at the base and summit of the hill and near Nfera Lagoon, located some 300 metres south of the hill. He recovered pottery of the same tradition at all the excavations which he recognised as Late Iron Age pottery, calling it Mawudzu pottery.[52]

A charcoal sample recovered from the excavation at the base of the hill dated Mawudzu pottery to AD 1480.[53] The relatively young age of Mawudzu pottery had stratigraphic confirmation at excavations that Robinson[54] carried out later at Nkope Hill. He found out that wherever Mawudzu and Nkope pottery were together, Mawudzu pottery consistently overlay Nkope pottery.[55] Subsequent excavations by Mgomezulu[56] at site DZ40 on the Dedza-Chongoni highlands, and by Davison[57] at Namaso Bay along Lake Malawi, produced C-14 dates for Mawudzu pottery that were calibrated to the fourteenth century AD. Mawudzu pottery has some affinity with Luangwa pottery found in eastern Zambia which is dated to the second half of the eleventh century.[58] A comparison of Mawudzu, Luangwa and Namaso pottery (discussed below) suggests that Mawudzu pottery was introduced in central Malawi at some point between the twelfth and the fourteenth century.

The common shapes of Mawudzu pottery include shouldered pots, deep bowls and hemispherical bowls. The walls are generally thin and the rims are tapered, and

---

50 Inskeep 1965: 11.
51 Robinson 1970.
52 Robinson 1970.
53 Ibid: 14.
54 Robinson 1970.
55 Ibid.
56 Mgomezulu 1978.
57 Davison 1991.
58 Phillipson 1976: 213.

decorations were usually placed on both rims and areas below the rim. Incised decorations are common and the styles include scallops, chevron designs and other styles, including diagonal impressions made by impressing cords in the wet pottery (see Figure 6.3). Stamp decorations, though present, are rare. Polychrome burnishing is often present, with the burnished areas demarcated by lines of incisions.[59]

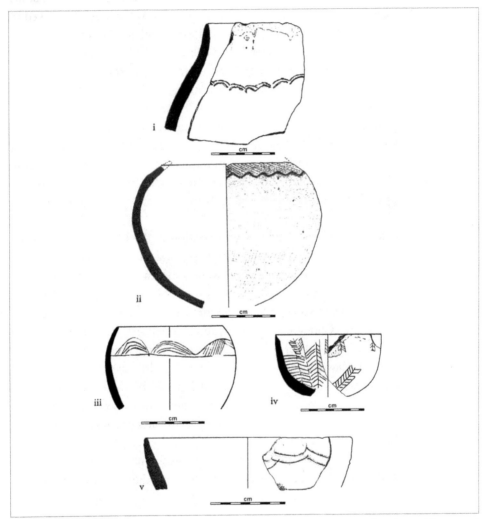

Figure 6.3: Mawudzu pottery from Mawudzu Hill and Matope Court: (i) shouldered pot with grooved scallops; (ii) globular pot with diagonal cord impressions and a grooved chevron design; (iii) bowl with in-curved rim and a band of incised loops; (iv) open bowl with incised herringbone decoration both on the outside and inside; (v) open bowl with grooved scallops.
Source: Adapted from Robinson 1970, 1973

---

59   Robinson 1970, 1973; Davison, 1992: 74.

From Mawudzu Hill, Robinson proceeded to nearby Nkope Bay where he carried out what he called test excavations at nine different locations. All of them yielded Early Iron Age pottery, which he named Nkope after the name of the hill and of the bay. Charcoal recovered from the third test excavation was dated to 775 AD and the fifth test excavation yielded a date of 360 AD.[60] In the next few years, Robinson recovered Nkope pottery from several other sites in southern and central Malawi, obtaining a range of dates, the oldest of which was 220 AD. This date came from a charcoal sample recovered in an excavation at the Mitongwe/Liwadzi confluence in the Bwanje Valley area, south of the western arm of the lake.[61] Since Nkope pottery underlay the other pottery types at all the excavated sites, Robinson recognised it as the earliest pottery ever used in Malawi.

Bowls dominate Nkope pottery. At the Nkope site, bowls 'were nearly five times as numerous as pots'.[62] Nkope bowls are hemispherical in shape and either deep or shallow with in-turned or open rims. Globular and carinated-shaped pots with everted or up-turned and thickened rims were found. The pot walls are thicker than those of Mawudzu or Nkudzi pottery and the decorative styles consist of bands of oblique or horizontal grooving and comb-stamping (see Figure 6.4). In addition, graphite was applied to the interiors of bowls.[63] In Malawi, Nkope pottery has a close affinity with Mwabulambo pottery (previously published as Mwavarambo), an Early Iron Age pottery that Robinson excavated in northern Malawi,[64] which also resembles Ziwa pottery in Zimbabwe.[65]

In 1969, Robinson began research in the nearby Bwanje River valley,[66] an area located about 32 kilometres south of the western arm of Lake Malawi. His archaeological site survey yielded 11 Early Iron Age or Nkope sites and 13 Late Iron Age sites. Mawudzu pottery was found in eight of these sites whereas Nkudzi pottery was found in five. In addition, he located four other sites whose pottery was unique, in that it had never been observed before at any of the sites along the eastern arm of the Lake. Robinson[67] called this new pottery 'Kapeni', after the name of a hill in the area. He then proceeded to excavate two of the four Kapeni sites, one located near Kapeni Hill, and the other at Nkhombwa Hill, about nine kilometres downstream at the confluence of the Nyanyangu and Bwanje rivers. Charcoal samples collected from these excavations produced dates

---

60 Robinson 1970: 18.
61 Robinson 1973: 7.
62 Robinson 1970: 41.
63 Robinson 1970, 1973; Davison 1992: 74.
64 Robinson KR. 1966a. A preliminary report on the recent archaeology of Ngonde, northern Malawi. *The Journal of African History*. 7; Robinson 1970; Robinson KR. 1982. *Iron Age of northern Malawi: an archaeological reconnaissance.* (Department of Antiquities publication no. 20). Limbe, Malawi: Montfort Press; Robinson & Sandelowsky 1968.
65 Huffman 1989.
66 Robinson 1970.
67 Ibid.

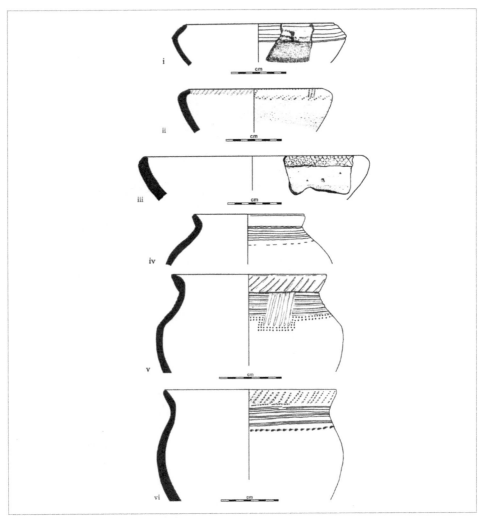

Figure 6.4: Nkope pottery from Nkope Bay, Matope Court and Phwadzi: (i) bowl with in-turned rim and a band of grooved lines; (ii) deep bowl with in-turned rim and diagonal and vertical comb-stamping; (iii) large hemispherical bowl with an in-curved rim and a band of cross-hatched grooves; (iv) globular pot with everted rim and a sinuous line, a band of grooved lines, and a line of elongated impressions below the rim; (v) carinated pot with a thickened everted rim, different patterns of grooves and parallel lines of point impressions; (vi) pot with everted rim and diagonal comb-stamping, a band of scratched lines (probably incised) and a line of point impressions below the rim.
Source: Adapted from Robinson 1970, 1973

for Kapeni pottery that range from the twelfth to the fourteenth century.[68] In subsequent years, Robinson recovered Kapeni pottery in the Upper and Lower Shire Valley areas, in Phalombe and Dedza districts and at Chilingale in Nkhotakota

---

68 Robinson 1973: 7.

district.[69] At Chilingale, Kapeni pottery was dated to the ninth century which was the oldest date Robinson ever obtained for this pottery.[70] This date convinced him that Kapeni pottery, like Mawudzu pottery, was from the Late Iron Age. Research by other archaeologists elsewhere in the country, however, produced older dates for Kapeni pottery. For instance, excavations by Mgomezulu at site DZ 13 in the Dedza-Chongoni area yielded two dates, one in the late eighth century and the other in the early ninth century.[71] At Kambiri 2 site in Salima district, Davison recovered a small collection of pot fragments displaying Kapeni-like attributes, which were dated to the seventh century.[72] Should further research in the area and elsewhere confirm this date, it will represent the earliest manifestation of this pottery ever recorded. This helps to show that Kapeni pottery co-existed with Nkope pottery in some areas for at least two centuries before Nkope pottery was phased out. It also shows that Kapeni pottery was not typical of the Late Iron Age, but rather intermediate or transitionary, spanning from the Early Iron Age to the Late Iron Age.

Kapeni pots are largely globular in shape, although pots with carinated or sub-carinated shoulders were also found.[73] The shapes of the necks vary: some are concave or flared others are short and vertical. Although incisions are present, decorations are largely in the form of grooves (see Figure 6.5) and the lips are sometimes notched or nicked.

Kapeni bowls tend to be deep, with in-turned or straight rims. Open, hemispherical and carinated bowls are also present and as with the pots, the bowls have grooved decorations on the rim. Hemispherical bowls generally have thickened and flattened rims and are more elaborately decorated, including burnishing with graphite and/or red ochre.[74]

Davison followed Robinson's footsteps in the southern Lake Malawi area. One of the sites she excavated was at Namaso Bay where she discovered a new pottery type she called 'Namaso' pottery.[75] It was dated to the ninth century and remained in use until the twelfth century.[76] Therefore, chronologically, Namaso pottery briefly co-existed with Nkope pottery and, like Kapeni pottery, was transitional. Davison also observed that its shapes and decorations were "'midway" between Early and Later Iron Age styles at

---

69 Robinson, 1973; Robinson KR. 1975. *Iron Age sites in the Dedza district of Malawi.* (Department of Antiquities publication no. 16). Zomba, Malawi: Government Press; Robinson 1977; Robinson KR. 1979. *The Nkhotakota lakeshore and marginal areas, Malawi: an archaeological reconnaissance.* (Department of Antiquities publication no. 19). Limbe, Malawi: Montfort Press.
70 Robinson 1979; Davison, 1992: 131.
71 Mgomezulu 1978: 136.
72 Davison 1992: 131.
73 Robison 1970, 1973.
74 Robinson 1970, 1973.
75 Davison 1991, 1992.
76 Davison 1992: 80.

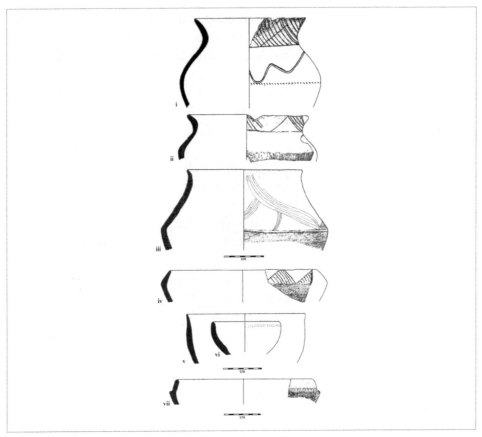

Figure 6.5: Kapeni pottery from Bwanje Valley and Matope Court: (i) concave necked globular pot with diagonal grooves on the rim, a curvilinear grooved line and a line of point impressions below the rim; (ii) carinated pot with randomly made diagonal grooves; (iii) sub-carinated pot with an irregular incised design on the shoulder; (iv) large bowl with an in-turned rim and hatched grooved triangles; (v) an undecorated bowl with a flared rim; (vi) hemispherical bowl with parallel lines of point impressions; (vii) a bowl with carination formed by an inset rim with rectangular point impressions. *Source: Adapted from Robinson 1970, 1973*

the southern end of the lake'.[77] Stratigraphic support exists for this observation. At an excavation at a spot simply called FW Ridge, Davison[78] noted that the layer containing Namaso pottery was clearly sandwiched between the layers containing Nkope pottery at the bottom and Mawudzu pottery on top.

Namaso pottery has a wide variety of shapes. Although pots were found, two types of bowls dominate the pottery: those that are sub-spherical with unlipped rims and slightly constricted mouths; and bowls that are open to hemispherical and are also not

---

77 Davison 1991: 30.
78 Davison 1992: 78.

lipped.[79] Namaso pottery was liberally decorated with decorations sometimes going over the rim to the inside.[80] The outside decorations were made in such a manner that they formed narrow or broad bands around or below the rim (see Figure 6.6). Some of the decorations were created by using wound copper-wire bangles. The preferred decoration types were either crisscross or stitched motifs made in 'either single-line impressions or impressions made by combs with elongate "teeth"-marks'.[81]

In comparing Namaso pottery with other pottery types in Malawi, Davison[82] concluded that Namaso pottery was unique in Malawi in that it appeared not to have close

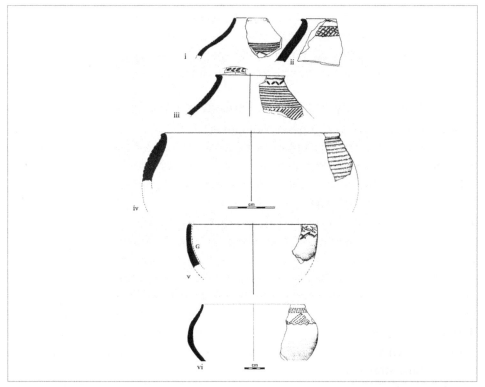

Figure 6.6: Namaso pottery with bangle impressed and comb-stamped decorations from Namaso Bay and Nkopola Swamp: (i) unlipped pot with conical neck and broad zone decoration; (ii) lipped pot with a narrow zone decoration; (iii) lipped conical necked pot with broad zone decoration covering rim and shoulder, and single bangle impressions on the top of the rim and on the lip; (iv) sub-spherical bowl with an inward leaning lipped rim and broad zone decoration; (v) unlipped open bowl with narrow zone decoration and graphite burnish on the inside; (vi) unlipped bowl with spherical body and broad zone comb-stamp decorations.
Source: Adapted from Davison 1991, 1992

---

79   Davison 1991, 1992.
80   Davison 1991: 28.
81   Davison 1991: 27.
82   Davidson 1991: 30.

relatives in the southern Lake Malawi area or elsewhere in the region. The only exception was the pottery that Mgomezulu[83] excavated at site DZ 13 on the Dedza-Chongoni highlands, which he described as being predominantly Kapeni pottery. Davison[84] felt that the two did not only resemble each other but also had almost identical dates.

Summary of the pottery sequence

Figure 6.7 is a summary of the Iron Age pottery sequence of the southern Lake Malawi area. Dating from the early third century, Nkope pottery was the earliest and the only typical Early Iron Age pottery ever used in the area. Its replacement by Kapeni pottery started in the eighth century and by Namaso pottery in the ninth century. Mawudzu pottery began to replace both Namaso and Kapeni pottery at some point between the twelfth and the fourteenth centuries AD. It was the only pottery in use in the area from that time to the late eighteenth or early nineteenth century when Nkudzi pottery predominated it. Mawudzu pottery is directly associated with the arrival of the Chewa in Malawi.

Iron Age way of life in the southern Lake Malawi area

Though extremely useful, pottery alone cannot tell us everything about the culture and other aspects of the way of life of Iron Age people. A more comprehensive picture can be obtained by also examining some non-pottery objects in their environmental and cultural contexts. The most notable thing about the southern Lake Malawi area is the large number of both Early and Late Iron Age sites that archaeologists have investigated. These sites confirm that the area had the right natural resources which Iron Age people found attractive enough that they stayed permanently. The result is that the southern Lake Malawi area has been continuously occupied since at least the third century.[85]

Among the desirable natural resources were the lake and the Shire River which made fishing the most important occupation for the area. Large-scale fishing required the use of canoes. While the archaeological evidence that these vessels were made during the Early Iron Age has yet to be recovered, it can be safely assumed that people of the area did make them just as their Bantu ancestors did, long before they dispersed from their ancestral homeland.[86]

During the Late Iron Age, people from the area traded with people deep in the interior to the west, and as far as the coastal areas of the Indian Ocean to the east.[87] Scholars refer to this as long-distance trade, which is discussed in detail in Chapter 12. Besides trade, people had enough land to grow crops and raise animals. Although the remains of domesticated plants have never been recovered in archaeological contexts in

---

83 Mgomezulu 1978: 136.
84 Davison 1991: 30.
85 Robinson 1970, 1973; Davison 1991, 1992; Juwayeyi 2010a; Inskeep, 1965.
86 Ehret 2002.
87 Robinson 1970; Juwayeyi 2010a.

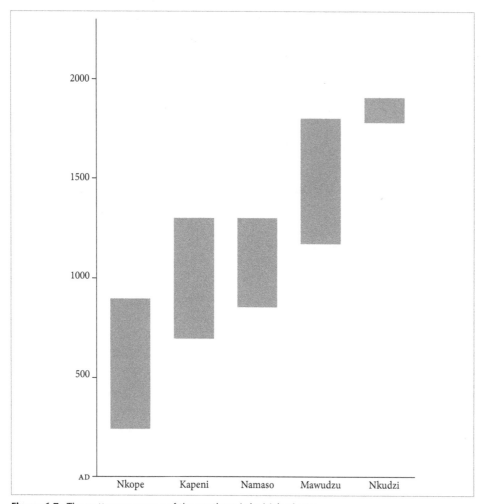

Figure 6.7: The pottery sequence of the southern Lake Malawi area.

Source: Juwayeyi YM. 2008. Wealth and affluence in southern Malawi during the proto-historic period: the evidence from archaeology, oral traditions and history. South African Archaeological Bulletin 63 (188): 105.

the southern Lake Malawi area, based on what has been found elsewhere in sub-Saharan Africa,[88] and on Chewa and Yao oral traditions,[89] it is likely that sorghum and millet were among the crops that people grew. They raised cattle too, as evidenced by the remains recovered at the sites of Nkope[90] and Mankhamba.[91] Mankhamba also yielded the remains of goats, sheep, pigs, chickens, doves and dogs. Hunting supplemented these agricultural

---

88 Phillipson 2000: 143.
89 Juwayeyi, YM. 1972–1973. The Yao chieftainship of Nkanda, its origins and growth to 1914. History seminar paper. Chancellor College, University of Malawi.
90 Robinson 1973; Speed 1970: 110.
91 Scott, Juwayeyi & Plug 2009.

activities as demonstrated by the wide range of wild faunal remains recovered at some sites in the area.[92] Finally, although the archaeological evidence for it is lacking, the rich vegetation cover provided Iron Age people with useful wild plants, as it does today, and with material for the construction of houses. The backbone of all these activities was the people's knowledge of metallurgy. Iron smelting and blacksmithing were specialised skills and archaeological records show that iron implements were widely made in the area. These implements were largely responsible for the apparent prosperous way of life. Iron implements enabled people to become efficient hunters of large animals, cultivators of large tracts of land, builders of canoes and strong houses, and makers of all kinds of utilitarian objects that made life good for them.

Summary

Archaeological evidence shows that the first Iron Age farmers arrived in the southern Lake Malawi area early in the third century and that they continued to migrate there throughout the entire Iron Age period. The abundance and distribution of Iron Age sites suggests that people liked the area's productive environment, which includes Lake Malawi and the Shire River. The area also has fertile soils and receives rain sufficient for dryland farming. Further, archaeology has demonstrated that in the past there was abundant animal wildlife, which implies that there was a rich vegetation cover. Today, the vegetation has thinned out considerably, along with the wild animals. However, fishing remains a vibrant activity and continues to draw people to the area.

Although archaeologists use the term 'Iron Age' for the period when ironworking technology became widespread, they study pottery and other material remains more than they do iron implements. This is because iron implements were difficult to produce and they corroded quickly, whereas pottery was easy to make and preserved many unique culture-distinguishing features. Pottery also preserves well in the ground, making it possible for archaeologists to recover it in large quantities. As a result, archaeologists have documented five different pottery types in the area. They are Nkope, the oldest, followed by Kapeni, Namaso, Mawudzu and Nkudzi pottery. This has made the area's Iron Age archaeology the most investigated of any area in the country.

Although archaeologists have not found the remains of seeds, evidence from other parts of sub-Saharan Africa suggests that Iron Age inhabitants practised mixed farming. Those in the southern Lake Malawi area must have grown sorghum and millet among other crops. They also raised cattle, sheep, goats, chickens, doves and dogs, evidence of which archaeologists found at Nkope and Mankhamba sites. An ability to make and use iron implements was essential in the people's accomplishment of different types of tasks.

---

92   Speed 1970; Scott, Juwayeyi & Plug 2009.

CHAPTER 7

The discovery and excavation of the Mankhamba site

Despite the existence of published oral traditions that clearly indicated where they could find the site of Mankhamba,[1] archaeologists working at Iron Age sites in Malawi made no effort to find it. There seems to be no plausible excuse for this, except perhaps they had more than enough on their plate involving research. They busied themselves with site surveys and the excavation of sites located in Mangochi district, Bwanje Valley, along the Shire River and in the Shire Highlands in southern Malawi. Their focus in central Malawi was the Dedza-Chongoni area, Salima and Nkhotakota districts; in the north, they worked in Karonga, Rumphi and Mzimba districts.

When I completed my doctoral studies, I too gravitated to Mangochi district where I discovered and excavated the Mtemankhokwe 1 site.[2] This turned out, however, to be another burial site with material remains similar to those recovered by Inskeep[3] at Nkhudzi Bay, which forced me to rethink my research strategy and to look for an area that archaeologists had never investigated before. Of the many unexplored areas in Malawi, the area between Bwanje Valley and Salima was the most attractive because, according to oral traditions of the Chewa, the site of Mankhamba was located somewhere there.[4] There was, therefore, a good chance of locating it if a well-planned site survey of the entire area were undertaken.

Current ethnic groups in the area agree that the Chewa were the earliest known ethnic group to settle there, even though they no longer wield the political power they once did. They lost political power to the Yao and the Ngoni who settled there some time during the nineteenth century.[5] Despite that, the Chewa have retained their ritual authority. For instance, they have an active rain-calling shrine, which they located at the Mankhamba site itself, and the Nyau secret society in the area continues to thrive. Retention of these structures, which are important to Chewa culture, means that the Chewa are able to play significant cultural and social roles. When I informed Group Village Headman Kafulama, the senior Chewa headman in the Mtakataka-Mua area,

---

1 Ntara 1973: 15.
2 Juwayeyi 1991.
3 Inskeep 1965.
4 Ntara 1973; Linden 1972; Phiri 1975, 1977; Langworthy 1969, 1973; Schoffeleers 1973, 1992.
5 Pachai B. 1972b. Ngoni politics and diplomacy in Malawi: 1848–1904. In *The Early History of Malawi.* B Pachai, (ed). London: Longman.

about the project, he was supportive. My interactions with Kafulama and others proved helpful in locating the Mankhamba site.

Finding Mankhamba

Despite being aware of the likely geographical area of the Mankhamba site, finding its precise location was not easy. Archaeologists in sub-Saharan Africa have always had a harder time locating Iron Age and other types of open sites as opposed to rock-shelter sites. One of the reasons has to do with land use, particularly cultivation, on previous settlement sites. Archaeological research in the southern Lake Malawi area[6] shows that Iron Age inhabitants took full advantage of iron technology to intensify land cultivation. It enabled them to clear large tracts of land for agriculture and to establish large villages. People must have practised a form of agriculture that cultural anthropologists refer to as slash-and-burn or shifting cultivation.[7] It involved repeated opening and abandonment of land, and sometimes abandonment of villages. People simply cut down trees and shrubs to open up land for cultivation. They eventually burned the vegetation and its ashes helped to fertilise the soil.

After a few years of cultivation, the fertility of the soil declined which forced people to abandon this piece of land and open up another one, repeating the slash-and-burn process. The distance of the new field from their homes or villages, and the quality of their houses, determined whether or not they would shift their homes too. Strong and well-built houses are difficult to relocate. After some years, natural vegetation returned to the previously abandoned land, making it attractive for the resumption of cultivation.[8]

Following many centuries of these activities, any material remains that previous occupants of the settlements had discarded, such as pottery and bones, were broken into tiny fragments. This made the remains prone to displacement from running water and to being covered with silt. Even if such fragments were to survive and be recovered by archaeologists, some vital information would have been lost. Archaeologists prefer to recover whole vessels, or large fragments of pottery or bones, to small ones. They obtain a lot more information from them than from tiny fragments. The relatively flat nature of the landscape in the Mtakataka-Mua area, however, minimised soil erosion. As a result, few tiny artefacts were lost to silting. The major impediment to site location was the intensive land cultivation that the area had undergone over the centuries. It was clear that if I were to find the site of Mankhamba, it would be in a cultivation-related, disturbed context.

---

6   Robinson 1970; Juwayeyi 1991; Davison 1992.
7   Kottak 2015: 138.
8   Kottak 2015.

In preparation for the project, I familiarised myself with the area by reading the few available written documents that refer to it.[9] In addition, I brought topographic maps from the Malawi Department of Antiquities to the field. When I arrived in the area, I interviewed Kafulama and some of his people and this produced information that I hoped would lead to the discovery of the Mankhamba site.

In order to increase the chances of locating as many sites as possible, I adopted the pedestrian or foot survey method and this meant working with several assistants. On any given day I had seven to ten assistants, some of whom were well-trained and experienced archaeological technicians from the Malawi Department of Antiquities. Rivers and streams were the main land demarcation markers and the research team surveyed river and stream banks first before surveying the open land.

Tiring though it might be, the pedestrian site survey method is a reliable and efficient way of locating open sites. If one has a well-experienced team, as I had, the discovery rate of sites can be significantly high, although some of them may not be suitable for excavation. The team surveyed sites six days a week for three months of the year over a two-year period. Altogether, they located 61 sites in an area of about 300 square kilometres. Accurate identification of the Mankhamba site required the input of the local people, as well as oral traditions recorded in the past. Ntara[10] had said that Kalonga and his people established the Mankhamba settlement in the Mtakataka-Mua area near a stream or river called Nadzipulu. This was not clear enough. A more precise way of putting it would have been: at the confluence of the Nadzipulu and Nakaingwa rivers ($14^{\circ}12'$ S, $34^{\circ}30'$ E).

Mankhamba and its neighbourhood

The Mtakataka-Mua area is located in the government administrative district of Dedza in central Malawi, on the lakeshore plain within the Great Rift Valley of East Africa. In this area, the lakeshore plain is at an altitude of between 472–669 metres above sea level.[11] The site is on the western margins of the Rift Valley, immediately below the hills overlooking it. It is sufficiently far away from the lake so that the intermittent flooding occurring in some areas of the lakeshore plain does not affect it. In fact, the excavation demonstrated that the site has never been flooded.

The perennial Nadzipulu and Nakaingwa rivers are just two of several perennial rivers that rise on the mountain range forming part of the Dedza escarpment. All the major rivers in the area drain into the lake, while the smaller ones disappear in the marshes before they reach the lake. The rainfall and temperature are similar to what occurs in the remaining part of the southern Lake Malawi area; that is from 820 mm to

---

9   Pachai 1972b, 1974; McCracken 2013.
10   Ntara 1973: 15.
11   Stobbs & Young 1972: 40.

1030 millimeters of rain annually, and temperatures ranging from 25 °C to 27.5 °C all year round.[12]

The vegetation is noticeably depleted, because the Mtakataka-Mua area has been continuously occupied since the arrival of the Chewa several centuries ago.[13] Further, the population of the area increased during the nineteenth century with the arrival of two other ethnic groups, the Yao and the Ngoni.[14] One Ngoni chief, Kachindamoto, settled in the area;[15] Pemba, a Yao chief, settled nearby.[16] When the British established colonial rule in the country in 1891, the colonial government took note of the area's relatively high population and included it in its development plans. For instance, when the government began to erect a telegraph line in 1894, it enabled the Mtakataka-Mua area to be connected to the line by 1897.[17] Further, the extension of the country's sole railway line from Blantyre to Salima in the 1930s meant that it passed through Bwanje Valley and Mtakataka-Mua.[18] The government built a railway station at Mtakataka itself. Other developments in the area included a post office and a police station, and a few years after Malawi became an independent country, the new government built a road running along the entire western shore of Lake Malawi. The road, which was designated M5 on Malawi road maps but is commonly called the Lake Shore Road, runs parallel to the railway line and passes through Mtakataka-Mua.

These projects attracted people to the area. Among them were the missionaries of the Order of the White Fathers of the Catholic Church, who first arrived in Malawi in 1889 and settled for a while at Mponda near Mangochi district headquarters[19] before moving on to northern Zambia.[20] They returned to Malawi in 1902 to re-establish themselves, and within three years they had built permanent mission stations at Kachebere on the border of central Malawi and eastern Zambia; at Likuni, near the modern city of Lilongwe; and at Mua.[21] As was the case with other Christian mission organisations of the time, the Mua mission station eventually expanded to include a school and a hospital. Today, Mua mission, with its enterprising head Fr Claude Boucher, a Canadian missionary, also houses the Kungoni Centre of Culture and Art[22] which

---

12 Pike & Rimmington 1965; Agnew 1972a; Jackson 1972: 38; Lineham 1972: 33; Torrance 1972: 29.
13 Juwayeyi 2010a, 2010b.
14 Gamitto 1960: 65; Cole-King PA. 1982. *Mangochi: the mountain, the people and the fort.* (Department of Antiquities publication no 12). Zomba, Malawi: Government Press: 3; Pachai 1974; McCracken, 2013.
15 Pachai 1972b; McCracken 2013.
16 Langworthy 1973.
17 Stubbs M. 1972a. Post and telecommunication services, 1969. In *Malawi in Maps.* S Agnew & M Stubbs (eds). London: University of London Press: 104.
18 Pike & Rimmington 1965: 211.
19 McCracken 2013: 53.
20 Kalinga & Crosby 2001.
21 McCracken 2013: 107; Kalinga & Crosby 2001: 249.
22 Kungoni Centre. 2012–2016. Kungoni Centre of Culture and Art, Mua Mission, Malawi. Available: http://kungoni.org/page1.html (Accessed 22 December 2018).

includes a research library and a museum displaying cultural materials of the Chewa, Yao and Ngoni. It is also a place where wood-carving activities are carried out.

Thus, the more the area became developed, the more it attracted new settlers. While this may have been beneficial, it had a negative impact on the environment. Everybody living there, including government employees and missionaries, obtained all their basic resources from within the local environment. Besides clearing land of all vegetation in order to grow crops, they also procured wood for construction and energy, and wild plants, animals and fish for food . The result was a gradual reduction of the vegetation cover and wild fauna. Today, the surviving natural vegetation is thin and found largely on the slopes of the escarpment and at burial sites where burial-related cultural norms prohibit people from harvesting trees and other plants.

Some of the development activities affected the preservation of the Mankhamba site. The railway line and the lakeshore road, for instance, cut right across the western margins of the site in a northerly direction, causing significant damage to that part of the site. Land cultivation also contributed to site damage. The entire site was cultivated to grow maize (see Plate 7.1) which left the area devoid of any natural vegetation, except for one small patch where people purposely preserved large trees and other types of vegetation in order to protect the rain-calling shrine that still exists. Fortunately, the

Plate 7.1: The Mankhamba site with maize cultivation ridges.
Source: The author

cultivation-related damage was not as destructive as that from the railway and road construction, which involved the use of heavy machinery. Local subsistence farmers cultivated the area using hand-held hoes which, unlike heavy machinery, rarely dig deeper than 25 centimetres. Subsequent cycles of cultivation simply turned over and over the same previously disturbed topsoil without causing further damage to lower levels. Below 25 centimetres, the site was undisturbed.

Excavations

Selecting a good spot to excavate on a site that had undergone some disturbances needed careful consideration of several factors. The construction of the railway line and of the road, for instance, had removed the fertile topsoil and several feet of earth in the affected area. As a result, that area was no longer attractive to agriculturists. In fact, there was no evidence that it had ever been cultivated since the railway line and road had been built. Instead, the construction activities left it exposed to running water and consequently soil erosion and exposure of material remains. It seems this research project was timely as it took place before the permanent disappearance of many of the exposed materials. In the end, I identified four spots for excavation.

There were also two mounds, one large and one small, which were close to each other and nearly half-way between the railway line and the Nadzipulu River. The rail and road construction activities had not affected them and their light-greyish surface soil contrasted with the brownish surface soil of the surrounding area. On close inspection, I noted the presence of several fragments of pottery and corroded iron objects embedded in maize cultivation ridges that farmers had made on top of the mounds. It was clear that the mounds were artificial, the result of past human activity. This was the first time that archaeologists in Malawi had located mounds at an archaeological site. Such features take a long time to form and suggest that the people responsible for their build-up had lived at the site for a long time. I dug a test pit along the margins of the large mound and the results were so encouraging that a full-scale excavation followed. The small mound was not excavated and neither was the entire large mound. Unless they have good reasons for doing so, archaeologists avoid excavating an entire site because excavations destroy sites permanently. Often, they save part of it in case there is need to return to it in the future.

The Mankhamba site was excavated intermittently from 1988 to 1991, beginning with the four locations that were identified in the rail and road construction area. Those excavations were designated A, B, C and D and they were viewed as salvage excavations. The goal was to excavate the remaining material remains before they eroded away. This book is based on the excavation of the large mound only. The fifth excavation at the site it was designated excavation E, or simply, the Mankhamba excavation (see Figure 7.1).

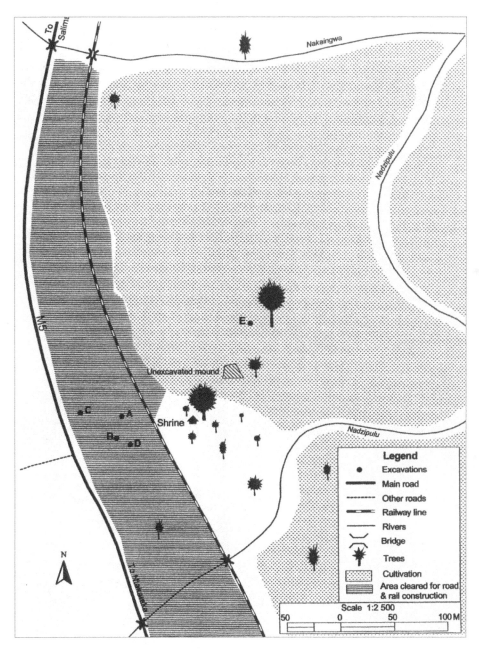

Figure 7.1: The position of excavation E.
Source: Adapted from Juwayeyi 2010a

A grid of 147 square metres was laid on top of the large mound of which 56 square metres were excavated, beginning with a careful removal of the cultivation ridges in every excavation square. The earth was sieved using a 3-millimetre square-wire mesh. The material remains from the ridges were placed in bags for storage and possible future reference. The removal of the maize ridges exposed a surface that had not been disturbed by land cultivation. Below this, excavations proceeded in 5-centimetre units. In some grid squares, the excavations went on to a depth of 220 centimetres before reaching sterile layers.

Stratigraphy

There were four stratigraphic levels in this excavation (see Figure 7.2). The top three were similar in terms of soil compactness or texture, with colour being their main distinguishing feature. What follows is a description of each of these levels.

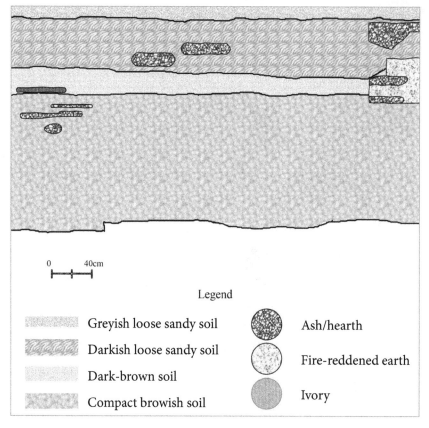

Figure 7.2: Stratigraphy.
Source: Adapted from Juwayeyi 2010a

Level 1. This level started from immediately below the ridges. There was cultivation-related disturbance at the top; the soil was sandy, loose and greyish; and material remains included pottery smoking pipes, metal, beads, bones and shells.

Level 2. The colour of the soil in this level was distinctly darker than that in Level 1. Some discrete fireplaces represented by charcoal or ashes were observed, the only features seen in this level. The charcoal and ashes may have contributed to the distinct darkening of the soil. The finds from this level were similar to those of Level 1.

Level 3. This level had a mixture of dark and brown soil. There was a layer with several objects in situ, which included a large piece of an unprocessed elephant tusk, bones of other animals, lower and upper grinding stones, pole-impressed *daga*, and fireplaces (see Plate 7.2). *Daga* comprises 'lumps of fire-hardened earth that had been used to seal the wooden framework of newly constructed houses'.[23] Some of the fireplaces were within fire-reddened earth, suggesting regular use of the same fireplaces over a long time. Although *daga* was present, there were no postholes. As a result, the boundaries of hut floors were not clear.

Plate 7.2: Artefacts and ecofacts on an excavation floor at Mankhamba.
Source: The author

---

23   Juwayeyi 2010a: 189.

Level 4. Brownish compact soil featured in this level. There were also fireplaces surrounded by fire-reddened earth. One fireplace still had a firestone, which is one of three stones that people put around a hearth to hold pots. Artefacts were recovered in diminishing quantities to a depth of 220 centimetres.

The finds

Table 7.1 shows the material remains recovered from the Mankhamba excavations. They were placed into five groups with the first group consisting of local and imported ceramic objects and *daga*. The local ceramics included smoking pipes and among the imported ceramics was Chinese porcelain. The second group consisted of lithic or stone objects, including several grinding stones. In the third group were metal objects, largely iron and copper, whereas the fourth group consisted of beads, with glass beads being overwhelmingly abundant. Faunal remains made up the fifth group, which consisted of bones, elephant ivory, shells and some cultural objects made of these elements.

Table 7.1: List of finds

LEVEL	1	2	3	4	TOTAL
GROUP 1 – Local ceramics					
Potsherds	4 108	18 554	10 408	12 780	45 850
Whole vessel	0	0	0	1	1
Smoking pipes	4	30	23	22	79
Spindle whorls	0	0	1	5	6
Other ceramic objects	1	0	1	4	6
Daga	✓	✓	✓	✓	✓
Imported ceramics					
Chinese porcelain	2	3	13	13	31
Glazed ceramics	5	31	28	25	89
Vessels with folded rims	0	3	2	0	5
GROUP II – Lithics					
Lower grinding stones	0	0	5	0	5
Upper grinding stones	0	0	2	0	2
Utilised stones	0	3	3	2	8
Soapstone	0	2	2	3	7
Other	0	0	0	2	2
GROUP III - Metal					
Iron objects	10	85	58	72	225
Tuyere pipes	✓	✓	✓	✓	✓
Iron slag	✓	✓	✓	✓	✓
Copper objects	12	136	99	130	377
Copper slag	0	0	1	0	1
Silver	0	1	0	0	1
Lead	0	0	1	0	1

⇨

LEVEL	1	2	3	4	TOTAL
GROUP IV – Beads					
Glass beads	104	1 466	2 262	1 503	5 335
Rock crystal beads	1	1	1	2	5
Shell beads	0	2	1	5	8
GROUP V – Faunal remains					
Bone specimens	4 969	17 044	9 972	6 678	38 663#
Polished ivory bangles	0	10	18	5	33
Unpolished ivory bangles	1	11	15	10	37
Other worked ivory	1	0	2	1	4
Worked bone	1	1	1	0	3
Cowrie shells	0	11	23	12	46

Notes: ✓ = Present but not counted.

= excludes fish but includes fresh water bivalve and other shell fragments.

Source: The author, originally published in Juwayeyi 2010a and modified slightly

Dating of the site

The many fireplaces observed in the excavations made the collection of charcoal for C-14 dating easy. Three samples were sent to the Radiocarbon Laboratory at the University of Arizona, Tucson, to be dated. The oldest calibrated date ranged from AD 1218–1448 and the most recent from AD 1448–1636,[24] (see Table 7.2).

Table 7.2: Radiocarbon dates

LABORATORY CODE	SAMPLE TYPE	LEVEL	UNCALIBRATED DATE BP	CALIBRATED DATE AT 2 SIGMA USING OXCAL
A - 14663	Charcoal	3	365 ± 45	1448 — 1636 cal. AD
A - 14859	Charcoal	3	625 ± 95	1218 — 1448 cal. AD
A - 14940	Charcoal	4	425 ± 110	1295 — 1797 cal. AD

Source: The author, originally published in Juwayeyi 2010a

In addition to C-14 dates, glass beads and Chinese porcelain helped date the Mankhamba site more accurately. A representative sample of glass beads was sent to Marilee Wood of the School of Geography, Archaeology and Environmental Studies, University of Witwatersrand, Johannesburg, in South Africa, for identification and analysis. Wood is an expert on glass beads from southern African archaeological sites. She developed a glass bead series for the southern African region which covers the time from the eighth

---

24 Juwayeyi 2010a; Juwayeyi YM. 2011a. Chewa migrations and the establishment of the Maravi State: a chronological perspective. *The Society of Malawi Journal.* 64(3): 51.

to the early seventeenth century.[25] She named the last of the series 'Khami' because of the abundance of the beads at Khami period sites in southern Africa. Wood determined that Khami series beads were pre-dominant at Mankhamba. These beads began to arrive in southern African during the second quarter of the fifteenth century, but it is not clear when their importation ceased.[26]

Bennet Bronson, Curator Emeritus of Asian Anthropology and Ethnology at the Field Museum, Chicago, identified the Chinese porcelain. Apparently, the materials had come from two places in China. Some were manufactured in Jingdezhen in the province of Jiangxi whereas others were produced in Zhangzhou in Fujian province, probably in the period between AD 1570–1600. The kilns that made these kinds of Chinese porcelain were only active for about 60 years from AD 1540–1600.[27]

Finally, local pottery also played a role in clarifying the site's chronology. The overwhelming presence of Mawudzu pottery and the paucity of Nkudzi pottery helped produce a picture of the time span of the site's occupation within the context of available C-14 dates.

Summary

This was the first archaeological investigation of the area between Bwanje Valley and Salima. The area was chosen for two reasons: it was archaeologically unknown and importantly, according to oral traditions, it was the heartland of the Maravi state. This was where the site of Mankhamba was likely to be found.

The vegetation along the foothill of the nearby mountain range and the small patches preserved at burial sites suggest that, in the past, the area had a thick vegetation cover. The soil is still fertile and the area, which has several perennial rivers, receives adequate rainfall and so mixed farming is practised. For a long time, the Chewa were the sole inhabitants of the area until the nineteenth century when the Yao and the Ngoni arrived and settled there permanently.

When the colonial government was established in 1891, it took note of the area's relatively large population and included it in its development plans. For instance, it connected the area to a telegraph line by 1897 and later, to a railway line and to a major road. The developments attracted new settlers, including Catholic missionaries who established a mission station at Mua that grew to include a school, a hospital and a

---

25 Wood M. 2000. Making connections: relationships between international trade and glass beads from the Shashe-Limpopo area. In *African Naissance: The Limpopo Valley 1000 years ago*. M Leslie & T Maggs (eds). Cape Town: South African Archaeological Society, Goodwin series: 82–83; Wood M. 2009a. Report on Mankhamba glass beads. Unpublished.

26 Wood 2009a: 3; Wood, M. 2009b. The glass beads from Hlamba Mlonga, Zimbabwe: classification, context and interpretation. *Journal of African Archaeology*. 7(2): 223; Juwayeyi 2010a: 180.

27 Bronson B, personal communication, 13 April 2009.

centre of culture and art. The consequent population influx brought by these developments negatively impacted wildlife.

Discussions with Kafulama, the senior Chewa village headman for the area, and some of his people led to the discovery of the Mankhamba site at the confluence of the Nadzipulu and Nakaingwa Rivers. Site disturbance came from rail and road construction, which damaged one area of the site, and from maize cultivation that affected the level comprising the top 25 centimetres of the site.

The excavation yielded both local and imported ceramics, stone artefacts, metal objects, glass and other types of beads and faunal remains. An analysis of some of the artefacts and C-14 dates have helped determine when the Chewa occupied Mankhamba.

CHAPTER 8

Ceramic and stone objects

As noted in Chapter 6, pottery designs and decorations are critically important in archaeology because they often reveal some aspects of the culture of the people who made them. This chapter presents local and imported ceramics as well as stone objects which the Chewa used for tasks that could not be accomplished using iron implements.

Local ceramics

Although the foreign ceramics are important in that they show the involvement of the Chewa in long-distance trade, emphasis will be placed on the local material because this was the handiwork of the Chewa themselves. Pots and bowls, illustrated below, dominated the local ceramics, with smoking pipes and spindle whorls following in dominance.

Pots and bowls

As shown in Table 8.1, one whole vessel and 45 850 potsherds were recovered at Mankhamba. Level 2 produced the largest number of potsherds, with over 40 per cent

Table 8.1: Ceramic and lithic objects

LEVEL	1	2	3	4	TOTAL
Local ceramics					
Potsherds	4 108	18 554	10 408	12 780	45 850
Whole vessel	0	0	0	1	1
Smoking pipes	4	30	23	22	79
Spindle whorls	0	0	1	5	6
Other ceramic objects	1	0	1	4	6
Daga	✓	✓	✓	✓	✓
Imported ceramics					
Chinese porcelain	2	3	13	13	31
Glazed ceramics	5	31	28	25	89
Vessels with folded rims	0	3	2	0	5
Lithics					
Lower grinding stones	0	0	5	0	5
Upper grinding stones	0	0	2	0	2
Utilised stones	0	3	3	2	8
Soapstone	0	2	2	3	7
Other	0	0	0	2	2

Source: The author, originally published in Juwayeyi 2010a and modified slightly

whereas Level 1 produced the smallest number, with only 9 per cent of the total potsherds. The first step in trying to obtain information from the potsherds was to sort them with an eye to finding fragments that had been parts of the same vessel.[1] The sole surviving whole vessel, recovered in Level 4, was a small shallow bowl that was missing a tiny section of its rim. Recovering a well-preserved whole vessel in an excavation characterised by heavy fragmentation was unexpected. In fact, whole vessels are rarely recovered at settlement sites, but are fairly common at burial sites where they were carefully placed in the graves as containers for burial goods. At the two Late Iron Age burial sites excavated so far in Malawi, Nkhudzi Bay and Mtemankhokwe 1, whole vessels were recovered.

Besides being small — and this was probably why it survived — the Mankhamba whole vessel was not decorated. It had a small hole with a diameter of 7 millimeters intentionally made at the bottom (see Figure 8.1 no i). Drilling holes in pots was a fairly common practice in the southern Lake Malawi area. At Nkopola Swamp, located along the western shores of the eastern arm of Lake Malawi, some potsherds were recovered which had several holes drilled in each one of them.[2] It is possible that they were drilled

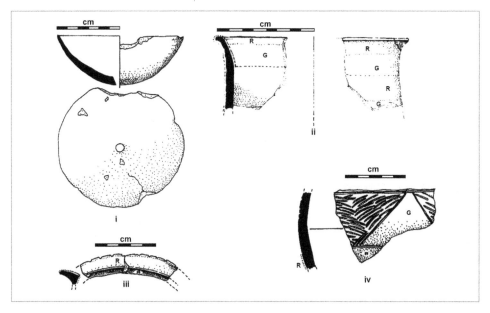

Figure 8.1: Whole vessel and other ceramic objects: (i) shallow open bowl with a hole drilled at the bottom; (ii) vessel burnished with red ochre and graphite; (iii–iv) vessels with red ochre and graphite burnish and other decorative motifs.
Source: Adapted from Juwayeyi 2010a

1   Smith & De Francquen 2017: 174.
2   Davison 1991.

for use in local salt-making.[3] The Mankhamba vessel had only one hole and so it must have been used for a different purpose.

The next step was to separate rim sherds from body sherds. This exercise is important in the analysis of pottery because body sherds, particularly when they are undecorated, are not of much use in providing information. Therefore, unless there is some good reason for keeping them, archaeologists simply count them for record purposes. They retain decorated and undecorated rim sherds though, because they provide information related to vessel design, shape and size. As shown in Table 8.2, rim sherds totalled 4 064, representing 8.9 per cent of the local pottery assemblage. Decorated pieces totalled 804, representing 19.8 per cent of all the rim sherds and a little under 2 per cent of the total pottery assemblage.

Table 8.2: Pottery decoration types.

LEVEL	1	2	3	4	TOTAL	%*	%#
Incisions	1	21	27	13	62	7.7	1.5
Stamping	3	5	9	5	22	2.7	0.6
Grooving	0	6	3	5	14	1.8	0.3
Applied decoration	126	326	173	81	706	87.8	17.4
Total decorated rim sherds	130	358	212	104	804	100	19.8
Plain rim sherds	273	1 362	817	808	3 260	–	80.2
Total rim sherds	403	1 720	1 029	912	4 064	–	100

%* total decorated sherds
%# total rim sherds
Source: The author, originally published in Juwayeyi 2010a

The majority of the vessels at Mankhamba were Mawudzu pottery. Nkudzi pottery was also found, but in very small quantities. Further, nine other potsherds were identified as belonging to Nkope, Kapeni and Namaso pottery types. They were intrusive, which means these potteries were not expected at Mankhamba, a Late Iron Age settlement site, because they are older, dating back to the first millennium. Their presence at the site is an indication that Early Iron Age people had lived in the Mankhamba area before the arrival of those who made Mawudzu pottery.

Despite the heavy fragmentation, the characteristic features of both Mawudzu and Nkudzi pottery, as described in Chapter 6, were clear. For Mawudzu pottery, deep bowls and hemispherical bowls were dominant, comprising 75 per cent of the Mawudzu

---

3   Davison 1991: 83

pottery assemblage. Shouldered pots and others were in minor quantities. The few fragments of Nkudzi pottery on the other hand consisted largely of thistle-shaped pots and open bowls.

Mankhamba pottery decoration types are also shown in Table 8.2. The most common type of decoration was one that archaeologists refer to as applied decoration, which involves burnishing the vessels with red ochre and/or graphite. As stated in Chapter 6, applied decoration also consists of the moulding of bosses or ribs 'above the surface of the vessel wall'.[4] Burnishing was present on both pots and bowls and on smoking pipes. On some vessels, it was the only type of decoration, and on others it appeared in combination with other types of decorations. In all, burnishing appeared on 706 (nearly 88 per cent) of the decorated rim sherds. On some of the vessels, both red ochre and graphite were used in an alternating fashion on and below the rim (see Figure 8.1 no ii). On others, burnishing was done together with other forms of decoration, again on or below the rim and sometimes on the lip (see Figure 8.1 nos iii–iv). Decorations showing moulded features were visible on smoking pipes only.

The rate of occurrence of other types of pottery decorations at Mankhamba, however, was very low. Incisions, for instance, appeared on only 7.7 per cent of the decorated pottery, stamping on 2.7 per cent and grooving on 1.8 per cent. Considering that plain rim sherds comprised a little over 80 per cent of the total rim sherds, it is clear that the Chewa at Mankhamba were not keen about decorating pottery.

Decorations based on incisions were observed on both Mawudzu and Nkudzi pottery. Often, the pottery showed horizontal bands of cross-hatched, diagonal incised lines (see Figure 8.2 nos i–ii), herringbone designs (see Figure 8.2 nos iii–iv), and cross-hatched upward-pointing triangles (see Figure 8.2 no v). Multiple bands of incisions on the same vessel, though present, were not common. The few that were observed included those that had cross-hatchings and those with herringbone designs, combined with external and internal red ochre and graphite burnish. One of them also had short strokes of diagonal incisions on a squared lip (see Figure 8.2 no iv). Some of the banded incisions were demarcated by single incised lines made at the top and at the bottom of the bands (see Figure 8.2 no ii). Also in evidence were other less popular motifs, such as lines of incision which were so thin they were barely perceptible, often made on the rim. There were at least two Mawudzu bowls with squared lips, on which several incised lines were made (see Figure 8.2 no vi). Placing incisions and burnishing on the same vessel, as shown in Figure 8.2 no iv, was rare at Mankhamba. Only eight vessels had both incisions and graphite burnish; six vessels had incisions and were burnished with red ochre.

---

4   Phillipson 1976: 23.

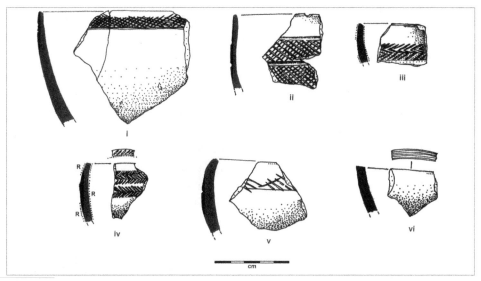

Figure 8.2: Incised Nkudzi (i–v) and Mawudzu pottery (vi): (i–ii) horizontal bands of cross-hatched designs; (iii) single band of herringbone design; (iv) two bands of herringbone design with impressions on squared lip and red ochre burnish on both sides of the body; (v) cross-hatched upward-pointing triangles; (vi) vessel with thin lines on a squared lip.
Source: Adapted from Juwayeyi 2010a

The next most popular decorative motifs were those based on stamping. Although stamp decoration was common on early pottery types such as Nkope and Namaso pottery, it was rare on Mawudzu pottery recovered at both the Mawudzu site and at other sites in the southern Lake Malawi area. Therefore, the rather relative popularity of stamp decorations on Mawudzu pottery at Mankhamba was unexpected and it is considered to be unique to that site. The significance of this fact will be discussed later. As was the case with incised decorations, stamp motifs were in the form of bands with vertical and diagonal comb-stamping as well as those with herringbone designs (see Figure 8.3 nos i–ii). The bands tend to be broad, often covering the entire rim area of the vessel and sometimes outlined by incised or grooved lines (see Figure 8.3 no iii). Besides comb-stamping, at least six vessels featured single stamps, which were made using objects with rounded, triangular or rectangular ends (see Figure 8.3 nos iv–v). The broken end of a blade-like object, probably a knife or some other object designed for the purpose, was used to stamp at least two vessels (see Figure 8.3 no vi), creating a band around the rim.

Grooving as a method of decorating pottery was also observed on Mawudzu pottery. Although the potsherds were too fragmented to be described accurately, it was noted that the most common motifs featured single or multiple horizontal lines made on the rim. The decorative motifs consisted of chevron designs, shallow arcs and zigzag

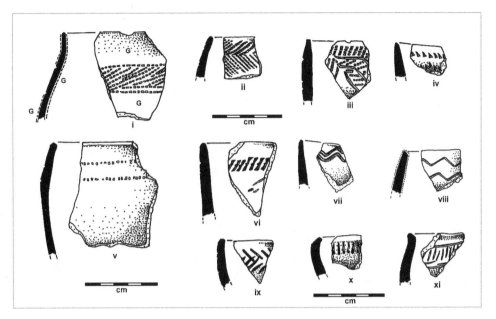

Figure 8.3: Stamped and grooved Mawudzu pottery: (i) diagonal comb-stamping; (ii) herringbone comb-stamped design; (iii) diagonal comb-stamping with irregular grooved lines; (iv–v) stamping using triangular and rectangular single toothed tools respectively; (vi) stamping using the broken end of a blade-like tool; (vii–viii) horizontal grooved zigzag lines; (ix) herringbone grooved designs; (x–xi) vertical grooved designs.
Source: Adapted from Juwayeyi 2010a

designs, and straight horizontal grooves and herringbone patterns (see Figure 8.3 nos vii–ix). Banded grooved decorations were also observed (see Figure 8.3 nos x and xi) which were in the form of short strokes of vertical, diagonal or horizontal grooves placed on and below the rim.

Smoking pipes

Besides ceramic vessels, the Chewa at Mankhamba also made ceramic smoking pipes. A total of 80 pipe fragments and 11 whole pipes were recovered throughout the sequence. Many fragments were large and so it was easy to find those that had broken from the same pipe, which helped in the calculation of the minimum number of whole pipes. It turned out that the fragments represented a minimum of 68, putting the total number at 79. Level 1 yielded four pipes only, whereas Level 2 yielded the largest number of 30; levels 3 and 4 yielded 23 and 22 pipes respectively.

The smoking pipes presented an opportunity to crosscheck the extent of mixing or displacement of artefacts between and among levels. The results showed that only two fragments representing one pipe had been displaced. One was found in Level 3 and the other in Level 4, demonstrating that intra-level mixing or vertical displacement of artefacts at this site was minimal. Smoking pipes are rare at Malawi's Iron Age settlement sites and thus their unusual abundance at Mankhamba was noteworthy.

Unlike the low rate of decoration observed on pots and bowls, as many as 53 per cent of the smoking pipes were decorated. Burnishing, though present, was noticeably rare. Incised motifs (see Figure 8.4 nos i–viii) were common, appearing on 35 per cent of the decorated pipes. Common decorative styles included bands of vertical or diagonal cross-hatchings (see Figure 8.4 nos i–iii) and plain incisions arranged in interlocking downward- and upward-pointing triangles (see Figure 8.4 nos iv–vii). One specimen

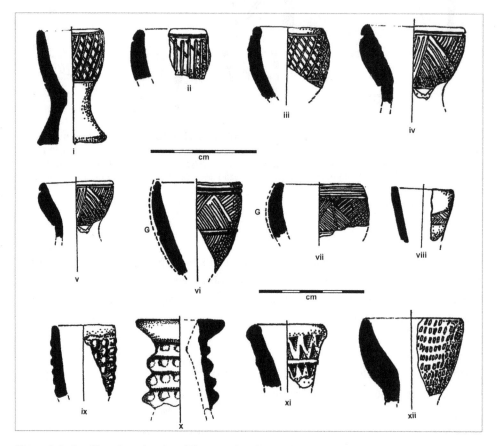

Figure 8.4: Smoking pipes showing different styles of incised and other decorations: (i–iii) vertical and diagonal cross hatching; (iv–vii) upward- and downward-pointing interlocking incised triangles with grooved lines on the rim; (viii) an incised herringbone design; (ix–x) bosses; (xi–xii) stamped decorations.
Source: Adapted from Juwayeyi 2010a

decorated in a herringbone design was also observed (see Figure 8.4 no viii). As many as 10 incised pipe fragments, two belonging to the same pipe, also had grooved decorations which were made around the lip and/or the mid-section of the pipes (see Figure 8.4 nos iv–vii). These pipes stood out because they were also the most finely finished of all the pipes. The graphite burnish on them had such a shiny finish, and the bands of incisions were so finely made, they looked almost machine-made. Other decorative motifs, such as rounded bosses (see Figure 8.4 nos ix, x) and stamping (see Figure 8.4 nos xi, xii), were observed on six fragments representing five individual pipes. However, the undecorated or plain pipes were poorly made by comparison.

Spindle whorls

These objects tend to be found at Iron Age sites in many parts of the world. They were made either of pottery or stone, and at times, of bone.[5] Spindle whorls came in different shapes, ranging from flat discs to spherical, with a hole drilled through the centre. Their diameters ranged from 25 to 100 millimetres. When inserted on a spindle, which could be any rod or stick, a spindle whorl acted as a flywheel, making it rotate with great speed. Spindle whorls found in archaeological excavations are reliable evidence that the people who lived at the site used to spin thread. The thread itself, however, does not easily survive in archaeological deposits.[6] The Mankhamba objects included a complete spindle whorl and five fragments representing five different spindle whorls. One fragment was recovered in Level 3 and the rest in Level 4, including the complete spindle whorl which was convex on both sides (see Figure 8.5 no i). This means it was not made from a potsherd but was designed specifically to be a spindle whorl. It measured 31 millimetres in diameter and its thickness around the edge was about 4 millimetres; at the centre it was 7.5 millimetres. The diameter of the hole was 6mm. Spindle whorls made from potsherds were concave in shape as they were made from body fragments of either bowls or pots (see Figure 8.5 no ii). One such spindle whorl was burnished with graphite.

Cups and other ceramic objects

This category of ceramic objects included a fragment of a cup handle found in Level 3 (see Figure 8.5 no iii.) and five rim sherds found in levels 1 and 4, each of which had a hole drilled through it. Copper wire was inserted in four of the rim sherds (see Figure 8.5 nos iv–vi), having probably dropped off the fifth (see Figure 8.5 no vii). Ceramic cups in general, and especially those with handles, are very rare at archaeological sites in Malawi. Perhaps people drank from small bowls or gourds.

---

5   Bray W & Trump D. 1982. *The Penguin Dictionary of Archaeology*. Harmondsworth, England: Penguin Books: 228.
6   Ibid: 228.

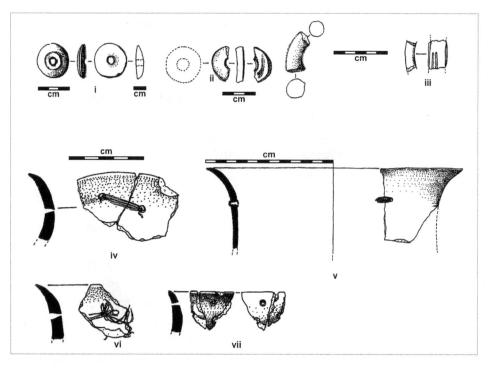

Figure 8.5: Other ceramic artefacts: (i) a complete convex-shaped spindle whorl; (ii) fragment of a concave-shaped spindle whorl; (iii) broken cup handle; (iv–vi) vessels with drilled holes and copper wire inserted in the holes; (vii) vessel with drilled hole without copper wire.
Source: Adapted from Juwayeyi 2010a

Whereas potsherds with drilled holes have been found at other Iron Age archaeological sites in the southern Lake Malawi area, the Mankhamba excavations represent the first time that drilled potsherds were recovered with strands of copper wire inserted in the holes. It is noteworthy that the holes were made only on rim sherds and the wires were inserted in such a way that the rim sherds must have been tightly pulled together. This method of repairing broken vessels may have been a common practice in the area. On display in the Lake Malawi Museum at Mangochi, there is a complete Nkudzi-type plate collected at Nkhudzi Bay which people repaired in a similar manner.

Imported ceramics

Imported ceramics, which are rare at Iron Age sites in Malawi, included Chinese porcelain, miscellaneous glazed ceramics and vessels with folded rims. This was the first time that so many were recovered at a single archaeological excavation.

Chinese porcelain

The excavation yielded 31 well-preserved fragments of Chinese porcelain which included rim, base and body fragments. They were recovered throughout the sequence as follows: two fragments from Level 1; three fragments from Level 2; and thirteen each from levels 3 and 4. Due to the large sizes of the fragments, it was possible to work out the vessel types and the minimum number of vessels represented. There were only two vessel types, plates and cups/bowls. The fragments in levels 1 and 2 represented four plates whereas those in levels 3 and 4 represented 19 large and small plates, probably saucers. There were only two specimens that were identified as either bowls or cups. These ceramics were smooth and painted with all kinds of designs, depicted largely in blue on a white or ivory background (see Plate 8.1). The designs on some vessels were made both on the inside and on the outside.

Plate 8.1: Chinese porcelain.
Source: The author, originally published in Juwayeyi 2010a

Glazed ceramics

A total of 89 fragments of glazed ceramics were recovered from the excavations. Level 1 yielded five fragments whereas levels 2, 3 and 4 yielded 31, 28 and 25 fragments respectively. Only three of the glazed ceramics were diagnostic enough for their vessel types to be identified. The remainder were body fragments with no clear diagnostic features. The three diagnostic pieces included a cup handle and two base fragments, one of a vase or a jar, and the other of a bowl.

The body fragments were glazed on the exterior side in different shades of green but their natural, unglazed brownish colour was maintained on the interior side. The exterior texture, even that of the best of these materials, did not match the smoothness of the Chinese porcelain. Some had an uneven and bumpy feel while others had a sandpaper feel to the fingertip. The interiors of most of them, including those with interior burnishing, had slight corrugations. Other than glazing, only two fragments had additional applied decorations, which were a body fragment from Level 2 and one of the base fragments from Level 4. These had plant or flower patterns embossed on the surface (Plate 8.2). The glazed ceramics probably came from south-west Asia, as some resemble the glazed ceramics described by Chittick[7] as sherds of Islamic wares.

Plate 8.2: Glazed ceramics decorated with embossed flower patterns.
Source: The author, originally published in Juwayeyi 2010a

---

7   Chittick HN. 1974. *Kilwa: an Islamic trading city on the East African coast.* Nairobi: British Institute in Eastern Africa.

Vessels with folded rims

Five undecorated potsherds with folded rims were found at Mankhamba (see Figure 8.6): three of them were recovered in Level 2 and two in Level 3. All were globular in shape. Although these vessels look very much like well-made local pottery, they had a metallic feel. Archaeologists in Malawi have not discovered this type of pottery before and its origin is not clear.

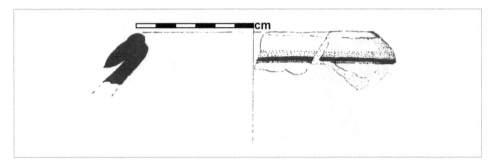

Figure 8.6: Vessel with folded rim.
Source: Adapted from Juwayeyi 2010a

Daga

As stated in Chapter 7, *daga* refers to the fire-hardened lumps of earth that archaeologists sometimes recover at Iron Age settlement sites. These were originally wet lumps of earth that people used to seal the wooden wall structures of their houses. While such houses could remain in use for many years, they were not as permanent as houses built with brick or stone. If a thatched roof leaked, for instance, the water seeped into the walls and weakened them. If the roof caught fire, the fire would at times reach parts of the wood and bamboo structures in the wall, hardening the earth surrounding these structures, forming *daga*. Some *daga* lumps recovered in levels 3 and 4 were sooty and nearly as hard as pottery. A close examination indicated that the wood encased in them had in fact been burnt, raising the possibility that fire may have caused the collapse of the dwelling. Some *daga* fragments bore imprints of material used in the construction of houses (see Plate 8.3).

Lithic objects

Whereas Stone Age people made and used stone tools as a way of life, Iron Age people utilised them as needed. Besides grinding stones, the Mankhamba excavations also yielded several pebbles and soapstone.

Plate 8.3: Fire-scorched *daga* fragments with imprints of house-construction material.
Source: The author

Grinding stones

Five lower and two upper grinding stones were recovered in close proximity of one another in Level 3. Lower grinding stones, called *mphero* in Chichewa, are large portable blocks of rocks with at least one of their sides, the grinding side, relatively flat. One of them was large (see Plate 8.4) with a utilised grinding area of about 1 188 centimetres

Plate 8.4: Lower grinding stones with upper grinding stone placed on top.
Source: The author

squared. Due to their size and weight, grinding stones were simply left behind whenever villages were abandoned. Archaeologists often find them in situ. Upper grinding stones, called *mwanamphero*, which in English translates to '*mphero's* child', are pebbles of different sizes.

Utilised stones

Eight utilised stones were recovered at Mankhamba, three in each of levels 2 and 3 and two in Level 4. Except for one stone that had soot consistent with use as a firestone, the rest were water-rolled pebbles people had collected from the nearby rivers. Four of them had been used for hammering or pounding. The others were what the Chewa call *nkhulungo*, small pebbles that have been water-rolled to such smoothness that Chewa-women use them to polish or to smooth house floors after applying a new layer of earth.[8]

Soapstone

Seven fragments of soapstone were found in the excavations. They were recovered in all the levels except Level 1. Soapstone is a magnesium-rich metamorphic rock that is composed primarily of the mineral talc.[9] It is therefore relatively soft and easily cut. Historically, people used it according to their needs and beliefs. Archaeologists working at Great Zimbabwe, for example, found that the Shona made bird effigies, flat-bottomed dishes and other objects from soapstone.[10] No such objects were found at Mankhamba and so it is not clear for what purpose the Chewa used soapstone. The nearest source of soapstone for the Mankhamba people was probably Ntonda, some 100 kilometres to the south-west in Ntcheu district.

Other stone objects

These were represented by one core and a single glassy stone found in Level 4. A core was what remained of a rock or a pebble after Stone Age people had removed flakes from the rock or pebble. They fashioned the flakes into different kinds of tools but often discarded the core. The sole core recovered at Mankhamba had been water-rolled. The Mankhamba inhabitants must have collected it along with pebbles from one of the two rivers, whereas the glassy stone may have been brought to the site, probably for ornamental purposes.

8   Topeka A, personal communication, 12 December 2017.
9   Soapstone nd. http://geology.com/rocks/soapstone.shtml (accessed 30 October 2017).
10   Pikirayi 2001: 135; Connah 2009: 252.

Summary

The Mankhamba excavations yielded both locally made and imported ceramics, and stone objects. The local ceramics included a complete vessel and thousands of pot fragments, smoking pipes and spindle whorls. Mawudzu pottery dominated the local ceramics, whereas Nkudzi pottery was minimal. Decorated rim sherds made slightly under 2 per cent of the total local pottery assemblage, with applied decoration or burnishing the most common type of decoration. Other decoration styles included incised, stamped and grooved patterns. Some 53 per cent of the smoking pipes were decorated and one of the spindle whorls was complete.

Imported ceramics included Chinese porcelain, glazed ceramics and vessels with folded rims. The Chinese porcelain was smooth and painted with various designs in blue over a white or ivory background. The glazed ceramics were greenish in colour but less smooth than the Chinese porcelain with roughly finished interiors. Vessels with folded rims looked like well-made local pottery except that they had a metallic feel.

Lithic objects consisted of five lower and two upper grinding stones, soapstone and several pebbles that people had used for hammering and other activities.

CHAPTER 9

Metal objects and beads

The Mankhamba excavations yielded the largest assemblage of iron and copper objects ever recovered at an Iron Age archaeological site in Malawi. A silver object and a lead object were also found. The discovery of the non-iron objects was significant, as these metals do not occur in Malawi in commercially exploitable quantities. Their presence at Mankhamba is more evidence that the Maravi were involved in long-distance trade. They obtained copper from the copper belt, an area that includes the Copper Belt Province of Zambia and the Katanga Province of the DRC.[1] The source of the silver and lead objects is currently not known.

The excavation also yielded beads, which included glass, shell and rock crystal beads. Foreign traders began to bring glass beads to eastern and southern Africa before the end of the first millennium,[2] whereas shell beads were made locally. Archaeological research has demonstrated that the shell beads are more common at Late Stone Age rock-shelter sites than at open Iron Age sites. Dry conditions in rock shelters favour their preservation. Rock crystal beads are rare at both types of sites, but it is possible that they too were made locally.

Iron objects

The site yielded more unidentifiable corroded iron objects than identifiable ones. The number of iron implements shown in Table 9.1 is therefore an underrepresentation of what was really available. The excavation also yielded tuyere pipes and iron slag, a by-product of iron smelting which came out of the furnace partially vitrified. The combined presence of tuyere pipes and iron slag at an Iron Age site is sufficient evidence that iron smelting happened at or close to the site.

Tangs

Commonly known as a shank, a tang is not an implement on its own but is part of a spear or a hoe hafted to or attached to a handle. Tangs are thicker than blades, and so in the archaeological record they do not rust or corrode as quickly, hence their abundance in the excavation. At Mankhamba, they comprised 70 per cent of the iron objects and since they are not implements, they should not have been listed in Table 9.1. However, because each tang represents an implement, it was necessary to list them in order to

1   Livingstone & Livingstone 1866.
2   Wood 2000; Chirikure S. 2014. Land and Sea Links: 1500 Years of Connectivity between Southern Africa and the Indian Ocean Rim Regions, AD 700 to 1700. *African Archaeological Review*. 31.

Table 9.1: Iron objects

LEVEL	1	2	3	4	TOTAL	%
Tangs	9	57	47	46	159	70
Iron points	0	12	9	11	32	14.1
Barbed iron points	0	2	0	0	2	0.9
Bangles	0	0	0	1	1	0.4
Prongs (one of silver)	0	2	0	1	3	1.3
Hoes, axes & razors	0	10	0	8	18	8.0
Misc. objects‡	1	3	3	5	12	5.3
Tuyere pipes	✓	✓	✓	✓	✓–	
Iron slag	✓	✓	✓	✓	✓	–
Nico*	✓	✓	✓	✓	✓–	–
Total	**10**	**86**	**59**	**72**	**227–**	**100**

*Non-identifiable corroded
✓ = Present but not counted
‡ = One in Level 3 was made of lead
% = percentage of total iron implements
Source: The author, originally published in Juwayeyi 2010a

demonstrate that a large number of implements would have been identified had there not been so much corrosion.

Iron points

Iron points were hunting tools (see Figure 9.1 no i) and were therefore used by men only. They comprised 14.1 per cent of the iron implements and were recovered from all the levels except Level 1. The large amount of faunal remains recovered in the excavations (discussed in Chapter 10) is a clear indication that people used these implements regularly.

Barbed iron points

Only two barbed iron points, that is less than one per cent of the iron implements, were recovered in Level 2. Their paucity had nothing to do with preservation because these implements were thick and, like tangs, they should have preserved well. People may have used them to kill large aquatic animals such as hippos.

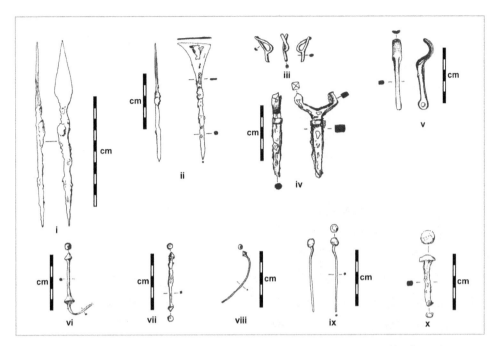

Figure 9.1: Iron objects: (i) iron point; (ii) razor; (iii–iv) pronged objects; (v) metal latch or trigger mechanism for a gun? (vi–viii) objects with conical ends; (ix) knitting pin-like object; (x) nail. *Source: Adapted from Juwayeyi 2010a*

Bangles

Only one bangle was recovered in Level 4. The poor representation of these ornaments was probably due to changing fashion trends. Iron bangles were popular during the Early Iron Age but this changed during the late Iron Age when the use of copper ornaments and glass beads increased. The archaeological evidence shows that by the middle of the second millennium, the Mankhamba community had developed a great fondness for glass beads, copper ornaments and ivory bangles.

Two-pronged objects

Also recovered at Mankhamba were three two-pronged objects. Two of them were made of iron and one was made of silver. Each of the iron objects were recovered in levels 2 and 4 respectively. They were so corroded that what remained of their prongs were more like stumps than prongs (see Figure 9.1 no iv). It was therefore impossible to estimate their original size.

Hoes, axes and razors

This group of iron objects has blades that are generally wider than iron points (see Figure 9.1 no ii). Together, they made 8 per cent of the total iron objects (see Table 9.1). Axes, however, comprised over 50 per cent of these tools. The relatively low representation of the other objects, particularly hoes, was probably due to their thin blades which made them more prone to rapid corrosion than axes.

Miscellaneous iron objects

The excavation also yielded 12 objects that were not readily identifiable. These included a heavily corroded flat object, possibly a strap; an object that looked like a metal latch (see Figure 9.1 no v); others with conical ends (see Figure 9.1 nos vi–viii); and one which looked like a knitting pin (see Figure 9.1 no ix). Others included nails or objects that were designed to be hammered into something else (see Figure 9.1 no x). Apart from the flat iron strap, the other objects were imported, but their place of origin is not currently known. A colleague who examined some of these materials speculated that the object identified as a metal latch could be part of a door latch or a trigger mechanism for a gun, whereas the knitting-needle object looks like a Victorian woman's hatpin, in both length and thickness.[3] Recovering parts of a gun at Mankhamba would not be such a surprise. According to Alpers,[4] some of the items that the Maravi imported from coastal traders early in the seventeenth century included firearms and gunpowder.

Silver and lead objects

The two-pronged silver object mentioned earlier, which was recovered in Level 2, was clearly machine made and looked like a small sounding tool except that one of its prongs was twisted (Figure 9.1 no iii). The lead object, a small ball, was recovered in Level 3. Both of these objects were imported, for a purpose that is currently not clear.

Copper objects

Objects made of copper included needles, fishhooks, rings, necklaces, bangles, a fragment of a bowl, copper rods, thick and thin wire, and other miscellaneous items, including a single copper slag (see Table 9.2). The copper objects were well preserved and thus, unlike iron objects, they were easy to identify.

---

3   Davison S, personal communication, 25 July 2008.
4   Alpers 1975: 54.

Table 9.2: Copper objects

LEVEL	1	2	3	4	TOTAL	%	THICKNESS[1]
Needles	7	66	42	57	172	45.6	1.9
Fishing hooks	2	16	11	14	43	11.4	1.6
Necklaces	0	7	0	2	9	2.4	–
Rings	0	11	10	11	32	8.5	–
Bangles	0	0	0	2	2	0.5	–
Bowl	0	1	0	0	1	0.3	–
Rods	0	12	15	3	30	7.9	5.0
Thick wire	3	23	20	41	87	23.1	1.6
Copper slag	0	0	1	0	1	0.3	–
Loose thin wire	✓	✓	✓	✓	✓	–	–
Coiled thin wire	✓	✓	✓	✓	✓	–	–
Miscellaneous objects	✓	✓	✓	✓	✓	–	–
Total	**12**	**136**	**99**	**130**	**377**	**100**	

[1] Average thickness in millimetres
√ = Present but not counted
% = Percentage of total copper objects
Source: The author, originally published in Juwayeyi 2010a

Needles

The 172 needles represented 45.6 per cent of the total number of copper objects, making them the most commonly occurring copper artefacts at the site. Their average thickness was 1.9 millimetres. One end of most needles was hammered flat with a hole drilled through it for threading (Figure 9.2 no i). Those with no holes must have been used for tasks that did not require sewing or joining objects using a needle and thread, such as making incisions on pottery or on ivory bangles.

Fishhooks

Forty-three fishhooks in various stages of preservation and completeness were recovered from all the levels, representing 11.4 per cent of the total number of copper objects. Fishhooks were a little thinner than needles, averaging 1.6 millimetres in thickness. Like needles, fishhooks also tended to have the other end flattened with a hole drilled through it for inserting a line (see Figure 9.2 no ii). In some cases, however, instead of flattening and drilling a hole, one end of the hook was simply folded into a loop for line attachment (see Figure 9.2 no iii).

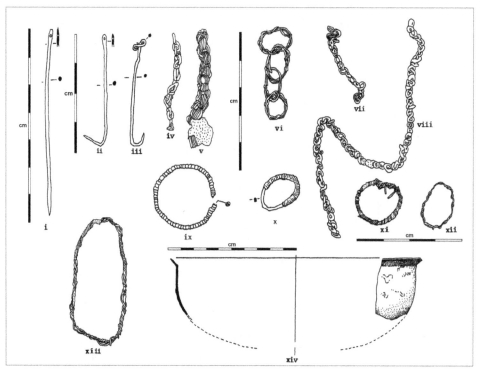

Figure 9.2: Copper objects: (i) needle; (ii) fishhook with a hole drilled on one end; (iii) fishhook with one end folded for line attachment; (iv–viii) necklaces; (ix–xii) rings; (xiii) bangle; (xiv) bowl.
Source: Adapted from Juwayeyi 2010a

Necklaces

Nine necklaces were recovered, of which seven came from Level 2 and two from Level 4. Some of them look almost modern, resembling interlocking linked gold chains (see Figure 9.2 nos iv–viii). All but one of the necklaces were imported. However, their place of origin is currently not known. One of the necklaces was unique in its thickness: although it was rather fragmented, it was clear that it had a core of three thick wires initially held together by thin wire, before they were compactly wrapped with more thin wire (see Plate 9.1). Considering that both thick and thin wire was abundant at the site, it is possible that this necklace was locally made.

Rings

The Mankhamba excavation yielded 32 rings representing 8.5 per cent of the copper assemblage. They were recovered in almost equal amounts in levels 2–4 and they were of two types: the first was made with thick wire, as the core of the ring; the second type had two or more strands of thin wire, also as the core of the ring. After shaping the core

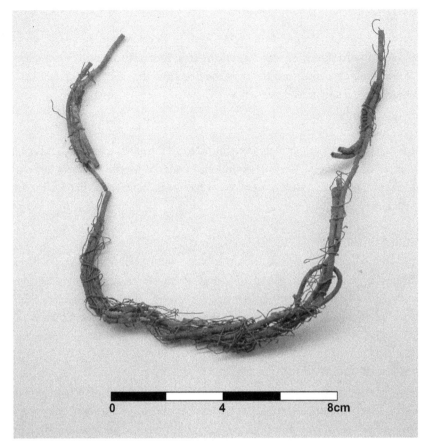

Plate 9.1: Thick copper necklace.
Source: The author, originally published in Juwayeyi 2010a.

into a ring, more thin wire was used to coil compactly around it and this had the effect of hiding the core and making the rings bulky or elaborate (see Figure 9.2 nos ix–xii). A beautifying effect was also achieved in that the rings acquired a shiny coppery appearance, making them visible from a distance. Measurements of the internal diameter of the rings indicated that most of them were too wide for fingers. Thus, while some may have been used as finger rings, the majority were used as earrings.

Bangles

Only two bangles were recovered in the excavation and these were found in Level 4. One consisted of thick wire which was the core of the bangle over which thin wire had been compactly coiled (see Figure 9.2 no xiii). The other consisted of one bare, thick wire, reminiscent of modern bangles in Malawi commonly called *chibangiri*.

Bowl

A lip/rim fragment of a copper bowl was found in Level 2 (see Figure 9.2 no xiv). Its estimated maximum diameter was 20 centimetres. Remains of metal vessels are rarely found at archaeological sites and this was the first time that such an artefact was found at an archaeological site in Malawi.

Rods

Thirty broken pieces of copper rods were found in all the levels except Level 1, averaging 5 millimetres in thickness. They were broken in such a way that it was impossible to estimate their original length. Some of them had been hammered flat for reasons that are not yet clear.

Thick and thin wire

Thick and thin copper wire was abundant at Mankhamba. With an average diameter of 1.6 millimetres, the thick wire had the same diameter as fishhooks which made it obvious that people created fishhooks from thick wire. Thin wire, on the other hand, was recovered as coiled lumps, loose broken fragments or coiled over rings. Much of it was very fragile.

Copper slag and miscellaneous copper objects

One piece of copper slag and various copper objects were also recovered from the excavations. The presence of the copper slag is an indication that some copper working took place at the site, in which imported copper ore was used and/or possibly involving the reworking of copper objects. Miscellaneous copper objects included a square rod that was pointed at both ends and some unidentifiable items.

Beads

Glass beads were by far the most popular of the three bead types recovered at Mankhamba. They were colourful, bright and more attractive than rock crystal or shell beads. As shown in Table 7.1 in Chapter 7, 5 335 glass beads were recovered from the excavations. There were also several lumps of melted glass beads, caused by fires that people made at the site. This was the largest bead assemblage ever recovered at a single, non-burial, Iron Age archaeological excavation in Malawi. Many of the beads, 42.4 per cent, were recovered in Level 3 and the fewest, only 1.9 per cent, in Level 1. As stated in Chapter 7, a representative sample of 548 glass beads and all the rock crystal and shell beads were sent to Marilee Wood. She determined that up to 98 per cent of the glass beads were Khami series beads made in Asia.[5] The remainder were made in Europe.

---

5   Wood 2009a: 3.

According to Wood: 'Several characteristics, including method of manufacture, end treatment, structure, shape, size, colour and translucency are used to classify beads.'[6] Many factors, including chemical composition, are also considered in the analysis. However, in this book, only shape, size, colour and translucency have been taken into account. Two basic shapes, cylindrical and tubular, occur in the Mankhamba Khami series beads. Cylinder beads have ends that are noticeably rounded, even though a small portion of the body may remain straight. Tubular beads on the other hand have parallel straight sides with ends that are sometimes left untreated or not smoothed.[7] The people of Mankhamba preferred cylinder to tubular beads. Cylinder beads comprised 89 per cent of the Khami series beads, with most of them medium-sized, that is ranging from 3.5 to 4.5 millimetres in diameter, irrespective of length which ranged from 1.5 millimetres to 4.5 millimetres. The colour of the beads was determined with the help of the Munsell book of colours. The most popular colours were blue (48 per cent), brownish-red (33 per cent) and blue-green (11 per cent). Less popular colours included green, yellow, white and clear, dull-orange and brown. Whereas all the brownish-red beads were opaque, 60 per cent of the blue beads were opaque and the rest were opaque-translucent. Blue-green beads on the other hand were dominated by translucent-opaque and opaque-translucent beads.

The European glass beads may date back to the sixteenth century when similar beads were first made in Venice.[8] Three different shapes of beads — tubular, cylindrical and barrel-shaped — were found. As their name implies, barrel-shaped beads have slightly rounded bodies and flat ends.[9] The size of these beads was within the range of the Khami series beads and their common colours were light brown and brownish-red.

Regarding rock crystal beads, only five were recovered and these were pentagonal to hexagonal rough spheres. Their manufacture was fairly crude and most of them had one side that was almost flat so that other facets were crowded around the remaining surface.[10] They were probably of local origin. Despite their small quantity, they were found in every level of the excavation, showing that they were in use at Mankhamba for a long time.

Eight shell beads, recovered from every level except Level 1, were made from the shells of the giant land snail (*Achatina* sp), which is very common in Malawi during the rainy season.

6   Wood 2009b: 220.
7   Wood 2009a: 1.
8   Ibid: 5.
9   Ibid: 1.
10   Ibid: 8.

Summary

Metal objects at Mankhamba included those made of iron, copper, silver and lead. Tangs, also called shanks, represented 70 per cent of the iron implements. The other iron implements included iron points, barbed iron points, bangles, two-pronged objects, hoes, axes, razors and miscellaneous objects, some of which were imported.

Copper objects included needles, fishhooks, necklaces, rings, bangles, rods, thick and thin wire, copper slag, a bowl and other items. The nearest source of the copper was the Copper Belt Province of Zambia and Katanga in the DRC. The excavation also yielded one silver and one lead object, whose origin is not clear.

Several lumps of melted glass beads and 5 335 individual beads were also recovered from the excavation. Ninety-eight per cent of them were Khami series beads which originated in Asia; the others were European beads. The majority of the beads were cylinder shaped and the most popular bead colours were blue and brownish-red. Medium-sized, that is 3.5 to 4.5 millimetres in diameter irrespective of length, was the most desired bead size. Locally made rock crystal and shell beads were also recovered from the excavations.

CHAPTER 10

Faunal remains

When archaeologists find faunal remains at archaeological sites, they often assume that humans brought them there in their quest for animal protein and other animal products.[1] There is an exception to the rule, though, when it comes to bones found at rock-shelter and cave sites, because humans were not the only users of these sites. Some carnivores and birds of prey such as owls also used them and, like humans, they sometimes brought back body parts or whole carcasses of animals that they had hunted or scavenged. Identifying remains brought in by humans is usually easy because humans butchered the animals and roasted the meat on a fire before eating it. These processes often left cut, burn or scorch marks on the bones. Archaeologists view the marks as evidence that the animal remains went through what some have referred to as a 'cultural filter'.[2] In other words, the marks on the bones are evidence that humans rather than animals of prey handled these bones.

Meat was not the only useful animal product obtained from animal carcasses. Archaeological evidence shows that humans also broke the limb bones to extract nutritious bone marrow. They used animal skins too for a variety of purposes, such as bedding, carrying children around and for clothing. During the Iron Age, animal skins and some horns were trade items too and people traded these with foreign traders, some of whom had established settlements along the coast of the Indian Ocean starting from the eighth century.[3] Further, people modified bones, ivory and shells by shaping them into useful cultural objects. Among the objects they made from bones were needles, awls, 'beads and ornaments, tubes for smoking pipes and musical instruments'.[4] From shell and ivory, they made beads, pendants, bangles and other objects.

In general, however, archaeologists tend to find more objects made from bone at Stone Age rock-shelter or cave sites than at Iron Age open sites. The reason for this is that, apart from ivory, most Iron Age people had no need for bone tools and ornaments because they had iron implements for tools, and glass beads, copper and gold jewellery for ornaments.

Success in obtaining information from faunal remains depends on how well preserved the remains are at the time they are recovered by archaeologists. Bones in a

---

1   Daly P. 1969. Approaches to faunal analysis in archaeology. *American Antiquity*. 34(2): 146; Crader D. 1984a. *Hunters in Iron Age Malawi: the zooarchaeology of Chencherere rock shelter*. (Department of Antiquities publication no. 21). Limbe, Malawi: Montfort Press: 8.
2   Daly 1969: 146; Crader 1984a: 8.
3   Phillipson 2000: 223.
4   Sutton & Yohe II 2003: 155.

good state of preservation provide a great deal of good information on human behaviour, more so than those in a poor state of preservation. Poorly preserved bones might provide environmental information regarding the cause of their poor preservation, which could turn out to be archaeologically useful. At Mankhamba, continuous land cultivation over many decades led to heavy bone fragmentation, but the general condition of the bones was good. In other words, though very fragmented, the bones were well preserved and this was helped by the relatively young age of the site. The bones simply had not been at the site long enough to be affected by agents that tend to be detrimental to bone preservation, such as extreme heat or cold, wetness or dryness.

Recovery and treatment of the faunal remains

Some of the large bones and chunks of ivory were found in situ, but most of the small fragments were recovered during the sieving of the earth from the excavation trenches. Since there was no archaeozoologist — someone trained to identify and analyse faunal remains from archaeological sites — on the research team, the material was simply kept in the field storage room until the end of the field season, when it was moved to the archaeological laboratory at Nguludi. This was where qualified technicians cleaned the material by carefully dusting off any clinging dirt and small roots. The material remained at Nguludi laboratory for some time while financial resources and expertise to identify and analyse it were sought. In the end, the bones were shipped to Karin Scott, an archaeozoologist in Pretoria, South Africa, who had kindly agreed to study them. She worked in consultation with another archaeozoologist, Professor Ina Plug, who has 'played a decisive role in the establishment of archaeozoology as a field of research in southern Africa'.[5] Besides having individual private bone collections, the two specialists also had access to an osteology collection at the Transvaal Museum (now the Ditsong National Museum of Natural History) in Pretoria, which they used for comparative purposes.

The two worked in compliance with standards acceptable all over the world, as promoted by the International Council for Archaeozoology (ICAZ), an international organisation focusing on the analysis of archaeological faunal remains. They also adopted analytical procedures that are commonly in use in southern Africa, which CK Brain, a well-known South African scientist, suggested should be used.[6] One example of these procedures had to do with the handling of the remains of bovid and carnivore animals whose species they could not identify with certainty. Bovids are the group of cloven-hoofed animals that include buffalo, oxen, sheep, goats and antelope. Often, they

5   Badenhorst S, Mitchell P & Driver JC (eds). 2008. *Animals and People: Archaeozoological Papers in Honour of Ina Plug*. Oxford: Archaeopress: v.

6   Brain CK. 1974. Some suggested procedures in the analysis of bone accumulations from southern African Quaternary sites. *Annals of the Transvaal Museum*. 29.

form the largest component of faunal remains at most archaeological sites in southern Africa. When specialists are unable to identify bones to a particular bovid species, Brain[7] proposed that they group them into classes based on live-weight ranges of adult animals. The specialists grouped the Mankhamba bovid remains into four size/weight classes as follows:

Table 10.1: Animal class/size arranged in increasing weight ranges of adult animals.

CLASS	SIZE	WEIGHT: KG
I	Small	<19
II	Medium	18–84
III	Large	77–299
IV	Very large	>367

In terms of specific live-weight examples, bovid class l applies to animals the size of oribi (*Ourebia ourebi*); bovid class II for animals the size of springbok (*Antidorcas marsupialis*) and to those of the size of puku (*Kobus vardoni*). Bovid class III are animals of the size of lechwe (*Kobus leche*) and this applies to those of the size of roan (*Hippotragus equinus*). Bovid class IV has two species only, the eland (*Tragelaphus oryx*) and buffalo (*Syncerus caffer*). Sheep and goat tend to be larger than oribi and so these were placed in bovid class II. In contrast, cattle tend to be smaller than buffalo and were therefore placed in bovid class III. It is normal for bone sizes to overlap, as was observed at Mankhamba, particularly between bovid classes I and II, and bovid classes II and III. In Table 10.2, they are shown as Bov I/II and Bov II/III.

Table 10.2 List of faunal remains expressed as NISP/QSP/MNI (NISP: number of identified specimens; QSP: quantified specimens; MNI: minimum number of individuals.

TAXA	LEVEL 1	LEVEL 2	LEVEL 3	LEVEL 4	TOTAL
Elephantulus sp. (elephant shrew)	0	2/2/1	0	0	2/2/1
Shrew	0	11/6/1	0	0	11/6/1
Homo sapiens (human)	0	3/3/1	4/2/1	0	7/5/1
cf. *Homo sapiens*	0	1/1/1	0	0	1/1/1
Papio hamadryas (baboon)	1/1/1	7/4/2	1/1/1	0	6/6/4
cf. *Papio hamadryas*	0	1/0/0	0	0	1/0/0

7   Ibid: 7.

TAXA	LEVEL 1	LEVEL 2	LEVEL 3	LEVEL 4	TOTAL
Cercopithecus pygerythrus (vervet monkey)	0	0	2/1/1	0	2/1/1
Baboon/vervet	1/1/0	3/1/1	0	0	4/2/1
Canis familiaris (domestic dog)	8/7/1	129/100/1	23/10/1	18/18/1	178/135/4
cf. *Canis familiaris*	1/1/1	1/0/1	0	0	2/1/2
cf. *Canis adustus* (side-striped jackal)	0	4/2/1	0	0	4/2/1
Canis sp.	5/5/0	8/6/0	2/1/1	0	15/12/1
Lycaon pictus (wild dog)	0	1/1/1	0	0	1/1/1
cf. *Mellivora capensis* (honey badger)	0	1/1/1	0	0	1/1/1
Atilax paludinosus (water mongoose)	0	2/2/1	0	0	2/2/1
Mongoose (not *Atilax*)	5/3/1	14/12/2	1/1/1	1/1/1	21/17/5
Felis silvestris (African wild cat)	0	0	2/0/1	0	2/0/1
Felis sp. (wild or domestic cat)	0	2/2/1	0	0	2/2/1
Panthera pardus (leopard)	0	2/2/1	0	0	2/2/1
Acinonyx/Panthera (cheetah/leopard)	0	1/1/1	0	0	1/1/1
Panthera leo (lion)	0	2/2/1	0	0	2/2/1
Caracal caracal (caracal)	0	1/1/1	0	0	1/1/1
Felid caracal size	0	1/1/1	0	0	1/1/1
Carnivore small	1/0/1	1/0/1	7/4/1	2/0/1	11/4/4
Carnivore small–medium	0	1/1/1	0	0	1/1/1
Carnivore medium	3/3/1	12/5/0	5/1/2	1/0/1	21/9/4
Carnivore medium–large	0	0	1/0/1	0	1/0/1
Carnivore large	0	1/0/1	0	0	1/0/1
Indeterminate carnivore	3/2/0	1/0/0	1/1/0	0	5/3/0
Loxodonta africana (elephant)	62/0/1	2424/5/1	887/0/1	1374/0/1	4747/5/4

⇨

TAXA	LEVEL 1	LEVEL 2	LEVEL 3	LEVEL 4	TOTAL
cf. *Loxodonta africana*	0	1/0/0	0	0	1/0/0
Equus quagga (zebra)	0	4/3/1	0	0	4/3/1
Equus sp.	0	1/0/1	0	2/0/1	3/0/2
Procavia capensis and/or *Heterohyrax brucei* (hyrax)	0	0	4/4/1	0	4/4/1
cf. *Sus domesticus* (domestic pig)	0	8/8/3	0	0	8/8/3
Phacochoerus africanus (warthog)	5/2/1	9/6/1	14/8/1	16/11/1	44/27/4
Potamochoerus larvatus (bushpig)	17/12/1	134/112/2	12/5/1	2/1/1	165/130/5
Suid	2/1/0	31/24/0	11/7/0	3/3/0	47/35/0
cf. *Suid*	1/1/0	0	0	0	1/1/0
Hippopotamus amphibius (hippopotamus)	14/13/1	68/50/2	130/25/2	13/8/2	225/96/7
cf. *Hippopotamus amphibius*	2/1/1	0	0	0	2/1/1
Non-bovid mammal small	1/0/1	0	0	0	1/0/1
Non-bovid mammal large	0	1/1/1	0	0	1/1/1
Non-bovid mammal indeterminate	14/2/0	8/4/0	10/4/0	2/0/0	34/10/0
Bos taurus (cattle)	30/29/2	94/77/3	33/30/2	8/6/1	165/142/8
Bos taurus (dwarf cattle size)	0	1/1/	0	0	1/1/1
cf. *Bos taurus*	0	4/3/0	1/1/0	3/3/0	8/7/0
Bos/Syncerus (cattle/buffalo)	1/1/1	13/10/1	1/1/1	0	15/12/4
Ovis aries (sheep)	6/6/1	47/43/3	13/9/1	4/4/1	70/62/6
cf. *Ovis aries*	0	5/5/0	0	0	5/5/0
Capra hircus (goat)	3/3/1	24/20/1	3/3/1	3/3/1	33/29/4
cf. *Capra hircus*	0	0	1/1/0	0	1/1/0
Ovis/Capra (sheep/goat)	1/1/0	80/68/4	7/1/0	15/11/1	103/81/5
cf. *Ovis/Capra*	0	3/2/0	0	0	3/2/1

⇨

TAXA	LEVEL 1	LEVEL 2	LEVEL 3	LEVEL 4	TOTAL
Connochaetes taurinus (blue wildebeest)	2/0/1	21/20/1	6/6/1	0	29/26/3
cf. *Connochaetes taurinus*	0	1/2/1	0	0	1/2/1
Alcelaphus lichtensteinii (Lichtenstein's hartebeest)	17/12/1	21/21/3	1/1/1	0	39/34/5
cf. *Alcelaphus lichtensteinii*	0	2/1/0	0	0	2/1/0
Connochaetes/Alcelaphus	0	4/3/1	0	1/1/1	5/4/2
Alcelaphine	0	3/4/2	0	0	3/4/2
Sylvicapra grimmia (common duiker)	37/29/1	130/119/3	39/26/2	6/5/1	212/197/7
cf. *Sylvicapra grimmia*	0	3/3/0	2/0/0	0	5/3/0
Oreotragus oreotragus (klipspringer)	0	2/1/1	0	0	2/2/1
cf. *Oreotragus oreotragus*	1/1/1	0	0	0	1/1/1
Raphicerus sharpei (Sharpe's grysbok)	1/1/1	21/19/1	3/2/1	0	25/22/3
Neotragus moschatus (suni)	0	1/1/1	0	0	1/1/1
Aepyceros melampus (impala)	36/30/1	214/158/4	24/17/2	30/24/3	304/256/10
cf. *Aepyceros melampus*	5/3/0	1/1/0	8/2/0	0	14/6/0
Hippotragus equinus (roan)	0	12/11/1	2/2/1	0	14/13/2
cf. *Hippotragus equinus*	0	4/4/0	0	0	4/4/0
Hippotragus niger (sable)	0	14/13/1	7/6/1	0	21/19/2
cf. *Hippotragus niger*	19/18/2	2/2/0	1/1/0	0	22/21/2
Hippotraginae	1/1/1	0	0	0	1/1/1
Syncerus caffer (buffalo)	12/8/3	116/93/3	12/8/1	0	140/109/7
cf. *Syncerus caffer*	0	2/2/0	1/1/0	0	3/3/0
Tragelaphus strepsiceros (kudu)	1/1/1	9/10/1	0	0	10/11/2
Tragelaphus scriptus (bushbuck)	0	4/4/1	0	0	4/4/1
cf. *Tragelaphus scriptus*	0	1/1/0	0	0	1/1/0
Tragelaphus oryx (eland)	35/23/1	240/195/4	36/25/2	3/2/1	314/245/8

⇨

TAXA	LEVEL 1	LEVEL 2	LEVEL 3	LEVEL 4	TOTAL
cf. *Tragelaphus oryx*	3/2/0	6/3/0	1/1/0	1/0/0	11/6/0
Redunca arundinum (common reedbuck)	3/3/1	12/11/1	0	0	15/14/2
cf. *Redunca arundinum*	0	0	1/1/1	0	1/1/1
Reduncinae	0	3/2/1	0	0	3/2/1
Kobus ellipsiprymnus (waterbuck)	6/5/1	8/2/1	0	0	14/7/2
cf. *Kobus ellipsiprymnus*	0	1/2/0	0	0	1/2/0
Bov I	77/13/0	154/51/0	56/10/2	47/2/0	334/76/2
Bov I/II	0	0	1/0/1	0	1/0/1
Bov II indeterminate	99/24/0	331/100/2	115/25/1	76/11/2	621/160/5
Bov II non-domestic	0	94/41/0	51/3/0	45/3/1	190/47/1
Bov II/III	0	1/1/1	0	0	1/1/1
Bov III indeterminate	239/52/0	371/122/2	166/60/1	154/26/0	930/260/3
Bov III non-domestic	11/7/0	77/37/2	25/3/0	25/3/0	138/51/2
Bov IV	7/3/1	134/58/3	15/3/2	19/0/1	175/64/7
Thryonomys swinderianus (greater cane rat)	6/5/1	150/124/5	25/15/1	15/9/1	196/153/8
Rattus rattus (house rat)	0	10/15/2	0	0	10/15/2
cf. *Rattus rattus*	0	16/16/3	0	0	16/16/3
cf. *Rattus* sp.	0	3/3/1	0	0	3/3/1
Paraxerus sp. (squirrel)	0	2/2/1	0	0	2/2/1
Sciuridae (squirrels)	0	1/1/1	0	0	1/1/1
Rodent small	8/7/1	45/42/3	16/11/1	2/1/1	71/61/6
Rodent small–medium	0	4/3/2	0	0	4/3/2
Rodent medium	5/1/1	75/65/5	39/31/3	48/46/7	167/143/16
Rodent medium–large	0	5/3/2	0	0	5/3/2
Rodent large	1/1	3/3/1	1/0/1	1/0/1	6/4/4
Rodent indeterminate	24/18/0	7/4/0	3/1/0	0	34/23/0
Lepus saxatilis (scrub hare)	6/4/1	0	0	0	6/4/1
Lagomorph	2/1/1	23/12/4	19/8/3	1/0/0	45/21/8

⇨

TAXA	LEVEL 1	LEVEL 2	LEVEL 3	LEVEL 4	TOTAL
Indeterminate small mammal	6/1/0	3/0/0	0	0	9/1/0
Indeterminate large mammal	2/1/0	0	0	0	2/1/0
Gallus domesticus (chicken)	2/2/1	289/84/3	81/29/4	80/34/8	452/149/16
cf. *Gallus domesticus*	0	9/5/0	0	0	9/5/0
Struthio camelus (ostrich)	1/1/1	1/0/1	0	1/0/1	3/1/3
Egretta sp. (heron)	0	0	2/1/1	3/2/1	5/3/2
Columbidae (dove/pigeon)	0	4/2/2	0	0	4/2/2
Bird small	0	8/4/1	3/2/1	0	11/6/2
Bird small–medium	1/0/1	14/4/2	0	0	14/4/3
Bird medium	38/22/2	48/20/3	17/3/2	2/0/0	105/45/7
Bird large	13/2/1	34/8/2	6/1/1	16/2/1	69/13/5
Indeterminate bird	2/0/0	1/0/0	0	0	3/0/0
Cycloderma frenatum (Zambezi soft-shelled turtle)	69/7/2	216/104/2	5/11/1	66/2/1	356/124/6
Pelomedusa/Pelusios (terrapin)	4/0/1	19/12/1	114/13/2	4/3/1	141/28/5
Crocodylus niloticus (Nile crocodile)	0	0	2/2/1	1/0/1	3/2/2
Tortoise medium	0	15/15/2	3/3/1	4/1/1	22/19/4
Tortoise large	0	2/2/1	0	0	2/2/1
Large reptile	0	1/0/1	0	0	1/0/1
Turtle medium	1/2/1	0	0	0	1/2/1
Tortoise/turtle	0	5/3/0	0	0	5/3/0
Indeterminate reptile	0	4/0/0	0	0	4/0/0
Pyxicephalus adspersus (bullfrog)	0	8/5/1	0	0	8/5/1
Frog medium	0	4/2/1	0	0	4/2/1
Frog medium–large	0	3/3/1	0	1/1/1	4/4/2
Frog large (not bullfrog)	0	2/2/1	0	0	2/2/1
Frog large	0	2/2/0	0	0	2/2/0
Indeterminate frog	0	23/18/1	0	0	23/18/1

⇨

TAXA	LEVEL 1	LEVEL 2	LEVEL 3	LEVEL 4	TOTAL
Frog/toad	3/1/1	6/4/0	17/9/1	13/7/3	39/21/5
Achatina sp. (giant land snail)	0	4/1/1	19/1/1	0	23/2/2
Cypraea sp. (cowrie)	0	11/11/11	23/23/23	12/12/12	46/46/46
Arcidae (arc shell)	0	4/2/2	1/1/1	0	4/3/3
Freshwater bivalve	0	4/1/1	3/0/1	3/1/1	10/2/3
Marine gastropod	0	0	1/1/1	0	1/1/1
Mollusc	0	2/0/1	1/0/1	2/0/1	5/0/3

Source: Scott, Juwayeyi & Plug, 2009

The archaeozoologists treated carnivore remains in a similar manner except that they put them into the three classes of small, medium and large but with different weight levels because they are generally lighter than bovids. Live-weight examples for carnivores are as follows: class I applies to carnivores that are the size of a mongoose or smaller; class II applies to carnivores of the size of canids and small felids. Canids are animals that belong to the biological family, Canidae, and they include dogs, wolves and foxes. Felids are cats, including caracals, leopards, lions and others. The caracal is a good example of a class II carnivore whereas the leopard, lion and the hyena, which is not a felid, are examples of class III carnivores.[8]

Laboratory misidentifications can sometimes affect the number of identifiable elements. These rare occurrences happen particularly with elements of closely related animals. Unless one's laboratory has a large comparative collection, elements of closely related animals are not easy to distinguish. Examples include such animals as roan and sable (*Hippotragus niger*), goat and sheep, the side-striped jackal (*Canis adustus*), the black-backed jackal (*Canis mesomelas*) and the domestic dog (*Canis familiaris*), the wild cat (*Felis silvestris*) and the domestic cat (*Felis catus*), among others. Although the Ditsong Museum has a large collection of some of these animals, the specialists took into account a margin of error as they identified the Mankhamba faunal remains. This is why there are a large number of elements in Table 10.2 shown as 'cf'.[9]

Quantification of the faunal assemblage

Quantifying faunal remains was the first important step in the analysis exercise. It meant carefully examining each bone, enabling the archaeozoologists to have a good feel of the bones and to note any human-induced modifications before they embarked on a detailed analysis. The quantification process was thorough and it included finding

8   Scott Juwayeyi & Plug 2009: 48.
9   Ibid: 53.

out the number of identified specimens (NISP) and calculating the minimum number of individuals (MNI) and the number of quantified specimens (QSP). The last category gives a better estimate than the MNI of the relative abundance of animals represented in an assemblage.[10] The Mankhamba excavation yielded 38 663 bone fragments. This figure excludes fish remains, which were also abundant but have not yet been identified and analysed. Bones that were identified according to species, genus, family or size class totalled 11 583 or nearly 30 per cent. The rest, 27 080 bone fragments, could not be identified.

Discarded bones undergo some processes that eventually transform them into fossils. Taphonomy is the study of these processes and involves examining specific natural and cultural factors that affect bones even before they are buried. As mentioned earlier in this chapter, implements used by humans to butcher animals leave marks on the bones. If meat had been roasted or smoked, some of the bones would have become partially burned or scorched. Table 10.3 shows that 1 828 or 4.7 per cent of the bones had human-induced cut and chop marks, whereas as many as 11 685 or 30.2 per cent were partially burned or scorched.[11] Burned and scorched bones were expected at this site because the excavation uncovered several hearths, some of which must have been made specifically for the purpose of smoking meat for long-term preservation, or for roasting the meat for immediate consumption.

Table 10.3: Taphonomy of the total faunal assemblage.

	BURNED	CUT/CHOP	CARNIVORE-GNAWED	RODENT-GNAWED	WEATHERED
Level 1	338	166	12	8	8
Level 2	3 894	478	224	39	343
Level 3	4 431	221	138	15	157
Level 4	3 022	963	71	6	262
Total	11 685	1 828	445	68	770

Source: Adapted from Scott, Juwayeyi & Plug, 2009

Once discarded, bones become food for other creatures. For instance, some 445 bones, a little over 1 per cent, had marks consistent with carnivore tooth marks and 68 of them had marks consistent with rodent tooth marks. Further, some bone fragments showed green discoloration resulting from their association with the many copper objects at the site. About 2 per cent of all the bones were more weathered than the bones with which

---

10   Ibid: 48.
11   Ibid: 52.

they were associated. This was interesting because it meant that these bones were on the surface long before the bulk of the bones was deposited at the site. They were probably related to the nine potsherds that were identified in Chapter 8 as belonging to an age earlier than that of Mawudzu pottery.

When people exploit animals, they make choices based on two criteria: whether to target female or male animals, and whether to target aged, adult, sub-adult or juvenile animals. The specialists attempted to identify male and female animals as well as their ages at the time of death. Unfortunately, the Mankhamba faunal assemblage was too fragmented to allow any meaningful sexing of the animals. As a result, no animal larger than bovid II was sexed. Birds, however, were easy to sex based on the presence of spurs on the tarsometatarsus or lower leg. In all, the following male and female animals were found: eight male and eleven female domestic fowls; three male birds whose species could not be identified; one male common duiker (*Sylvicapra grimmia*); a male and a female class II bovid and one male domestic dog.[12] Heavy bone fragmentation also made it impossible for the exact ageing of the animals represented in the material. Instead, they were identified simply as neonate, juvenile, sub-adult, adult and aged. Adult animals formed the bulk of the remains, followed by juveniles and sub-adults, with the aged and neonates in minor quantities.[13]

Wild animals

People hunted the majority of the wild animals at Mankhamba for food. However, a high or low number of specimens representing a particular animal is not necessarily an indication of how often the animal was hunted, or of the level of likeability of its meat. There are several factors that affect the level of wild animal representation at an archaeological site. The most common of these factors are the environment of both animals and humans, and human actions involving technology, beliefs, traditions and other activities. For instance, Table 10.2 shows that people hunted the zebra (*Equus quagga*) less often than they did other large animals. The impression given is that people targeted the elephant (*Loxodonta africana*), the eland, the impala (*Aepyceros melampus*) and some of the other large animals more than they did the zebra. Interestingly, the zebra also was absent or poorly represented at other Iron Age sites in the southern Lake Malawi area and in the Upper and Lower Shire Valley areas.[14] However, the environment of these areas as well as nineteenth-century ethnographic observations show that the zebra was, and still is, widespread in Malawi.[15] The zebra associates with the roan and

12 Ibid: 52.
13 Ibid: 51.
14 Voigt E. 1973. Faunal remains from the Iron Age sites of Matope, Namichimba and Chikumba, southern Malawi. In *The Iron Age of the Upper and Lower Shire, Malawi*. KR Robinson. (Department of Antiquities publication no. 13). Zomba, Malawi: Government Press: 138.
15 Smithers RHN. 1966. *The Mammals of Rhodesia, Zambia and Malawi*. London: Collins: 86.

the eland, and evidence from elsewhere shows that it must have done the same with the wildebeest before the wildebeest became extinct in Malawi.[16] The archaeological record, however, shows that hunters of Mankhamba preferred the other animals to the zebra and reasons for their preference can only be speculative. Perhaps as is the case with a few other African societies in southern Africa,[17] the Chewa either had taboos against the zebra or they simply disliked its meat. Research at other large Iron Age sites in southern Africa suggests that the rarity of zebra elements at Mankhamba was normal. The quantity of zebra elements at sites in areas where the zebra was common fluctuates greatly from total absence to good representation.[18] It shows there were some societies in southern Africa that either had taboos against this animal or that they did not like its meat. One current example are the !Kung foragers of Botswana. They dislike the meat of the zebra because they 'say its meat smells bad'.[19] If the people of Mankhamba disliked the meat of the zebra or had taboos against it, then the reason they hunted the zebra was to acquire its skin. As mentioned earlier, animal skins were trade items and the zebra happens to have a distinctively well-patterned skin which, very likely, fetched better prices than the skins of bovids. We can therefore conclude that people actually hunted the zebra as aggressively as they did some of the large bovids. They skinned the animal at the kill site and, more often than not, they left the entire carcass behind and took the skin home. Occasionally, some among the hunters would go against the norm and take home some of its body parts, probably for ritualistic or medicinal purposes, thereby accounting for the minimal zebra elements recovered in the archaeological excavations.

The high number of specimens of the Zambezi soft-shelled turtle (Trionychidae) is a good example of the nature of an animal affecting its level of representation in the archaeological record. This creature can grow to as much as 350–450 millimetres in length.[20] Its high representation in the faunal assemblage gives the impression that people exploited it often. However, archaeozoologists do take extra caution when they examine the remains of this creature. The physical characteristics of its shell are such that it fractures into many small fragments which are easier to identify than small bone fragments.[21] Therefore, unless sufficient bone fragments are also recovered, the shell fragments alone do not give a true picture of the level of exploitation of this animal. Fortunately for Mankhamba, limb and toe bones of this creature were also represented. Besides, research has demonstrated that the Zambezi soft-shelled turtle was relatively

---

16 Smithers: 87; Hayes GD. nd. *A Guide to Malawi's National parks and game reserves*. Limbe, Malawi: Montfort Press.
17 Lee 1980.
18 Plug I & Voigt EA. 1985. Archaeozoological studies of Iron Age communities in southern Africa. *Advances in World Archaeology*. 4; Scott, Juwayeyi & Plug 2009: 53.
19 Lee 1980: 233.
20 Branch B. 1988. *Field guide to snakes and other reptiles of southern Africa*. Cape Town: Struik.
21 Scott, Juwayeyi & Plug 2009: 53.

common in the southern Lake Malawi area and the Upper Shire Valley.[22] It is therefore clear that this turtle was indeed heavily exploited by the inhabitants of Mankhamba.

Examples of animals whose habits may have contributed to their high representation in the faunal assemblage are the hippopotamus (*Hippopotamus amphibius*) and the bush pig (*Potamochoerus larvatus*). Hippos are large animals and they were represented by 225 specimens. Even though it is possible that the people at Mankhamba may have found some use for hippo ivory, fragments of which were found in the excavations,[23] these animals were hunted mainly for their meat and to stop them ruining crops. Although they are aquatic, hippos are nocturnal feeders, feeding on land, and known to be 'a great raider of crops in which they do tremendous damage'.[24] Bush pigs, which should not be confused with warthogs (*Phacochoerus africanus*), their relatively smaller cousins, were represented by 165 specimens. These animals are also nocturnal feeders and although they are known to 'eat meat and take carrion on occasion',[25] they are notorious for their regular invasion of gardens and for destroying both maize and root crops.[26] Thus, the feeding habits of both animals inevitably brought them closer to human habitations. To kill them, people simply set game traps in strategic places along their regularly used tracks.

Some of the reasons why the eland and the rest of the bovid animals were well represented have to do with the area's favourable environment, and the fact that they are relatively less dangerous to hunt than large carnivores and large non-bovid animals. The faunal list shows that the hunters at Mankhamba,[27] like those who lived on the Shire Highlands,[28] preferred medium- and large-size antelopes to small-size antelopes. Since the Mankhamba environment was ideal for both browsing and grazing animals, and for mixed feeders, all were widely exploited. Browsers are animals that eat stems, leaves and bark; grazers are those that eat grass and other ground-level vegetation; mixed feeders both browse and graze. Thus, the eland, a very large antelope, was the most highly represented of the antelopes, followed by the impala. Both are mixed feeders. The common duiker, a browser, was represented with 212 specimens and the buffalo, a grazer, was represented with 140 specimens.

The good representation of the common duiker was interesting because, like other small bovids, it tends to be territorial and is likely to browse alone or in pairs or in family

---

22   Speed 1970: 110; Voigt 1973: 140.
23   Scott, Juwayeyi & Plug 2009: 57.
24   Smithers 1966: 93.
25   Ibid: 89.
26   Smithers 1966; Hayes nd.
27   Scott, Juwayeyi & Plug 2009: 57.
28   Juwayeyi YM. 2008. Human and animal interaction on the Shire highlands, Malawi: the evidence from Malowa rockshelter. In *Animals and People: Archaeozoological Papers in Honour of Ina Plug*. S Badenhorst, P Mitchell & JC Driver (eds). Oxford: Archaeopress: 88.

groups.[29] Therefore, the relative abundance of such animals in an area cannot be expected to be as great as that of animals moving in herds. The duiker's high representation in the faunal assemblage may have been due to preferential targeting by hunters or to an unusually high abundance in the general environment.[30] Below these highly represented bovids was a host of other antelopes with various levels of representation. Special mention must be made of the blue wildebeest (*Connochaetes taurinus*) because it became extinct in Malawi many decades ago.[31] At one time, this wildebeest was widespread, at least in central and southern Malawi. Besides Mankhamba, other sites that have yielded remains of wildebeest are Chencherere,[32] Chencherere II[33] and Malowa rock shelter.[34] Remains of wildebeest were also observed at the sites of Matope Court, Namichimba and Chikumba, all in the Upper Shire Valley where a total of four bone fragments were recovered.[35] Despite their extinction in Malawi, wildebeest are still abundant in East Africa.

The overwhelming occurrence of elephant specimens at Mankhamba was a total surprise because there was no precedent for this in Malawi. Until the Mankhamba excavation, only one site in the country, the Matope Court site, had yielded elephant remains, but this was one specimen — an ivory fragment.[36] The Mankhamba site was thus an exception. A huge number of the elements were ivory shavings or chips rather than bones. The abundance of the shavings could be attributed to the fact that people hunted the elephant more for its tusks than for its meat. Besides, it is not entirely clear if the Chewa liked elephant meat. Ethnographic observations of other ethnic groups in the region show that they ate elephant meat selectively. The Lambas of Zambia, for instance, preferred the trunk, feet and the flesh above the eyes.[37] The ivory shavings at Mankhamba were the residue from the manufacture of ivory objects, the most common of which were bangles. The abundance of these elements indicates that elephants were common in the area. They can still be seen on some of the hills on the eastern side of the lake where they are protected by the state. When hunters killed an elephant, they simply removed the tusks at the kill site, and if a hunter needed meat, then he would cut out chunks of it to take home, preferably without the bones. This explains why elephant postcranial remains in the faunal assemblage are not well represented.

---

29   Skinner JD & Chimimba CT. 2005. *The Mammals of the Southern African Sub-region*. Cambridge: Cambridge University Press; Scott, Juwayeyi & Plug 2009: 54.
30   Scott, Juwayeyi & Plug 2009: 54.
31   Hayes nd: 81.
32   Crader 1984a: 14.
33   Crader DC. 1984b. Faunal Remains from Chencherere II Rock Shelter, Malawi. *The South African Archaeological Bulletin*. 39.
34   Juwayeyi 2008.
35   Voigt 1973.
36   Ibid: 138.
37   Doke CW. 1931. *The Lambas of Northern Rhodesia: A study of their customs and beliefs*. London: George G. Harrap: 102.

Two species of primates and several carnivores were also exploited at Mankhamba. The primates were baboons (*Papio hamadryas*) and vervet monkeys (*Cercopithecus pygerythrus*), both of which are common in the country. Like hippos and bush pigs, these two primates endanger themselves by going into people's gardens to steal their crops. Since they feed during the day, it is normal in Malawi for people to go to their fields accompanied by their dogs to fend off monkeys and baboons. It is such a full-time job, particularly in some of the well-forested areas of the country, that people build temporary shelters in the middle of their gardens, to shield themselves from rain or intense sunshine because they know they will be there all day protecting their crops.

Many of the wild carnivore remains could not be identified to species. Those that were identified included the wild dog (*Lycaon pictus*); shrews, including a possible elephant shrew (*Elephantulus sp*); the African wild cat, caracal (*Caracal caracal*); and possibly a honey badger (*Mellivora capensis*). There were also several mongooses but only one was identified to species, a water mongoose (*Atilax paludinosus*). It is possible that among the unidentifiable mongooses was the slender mongoose (*Herpestes sanguineus*), called *nyenga* locally. This animal was found in archaeological contexts at Chencherere[38] and at site DZ40 in the Dedza-Chongoni area.[39] Malawians are familiar with the *nyenga* because it is 'a great raider of chickens'.[40] Medium to large carnivores included the side-striped jackal, the lion (*Panthera leo*), leopard/cheetah (*Panthera/Acinonyx*) and the Nile crocodile (*Crocodylus niloticus*). Whereas the small carnivores may have been acquired for food, people would not ordinarily hunt large carnivores unless they had become a threat to domestic animals or to humans; or in the rare cases when it was culturally imperative to obtain certain body parts for use in various traditional activities, particularly magic.

Hares (lagomorphs) locally known as *kalulu*, are common in rural Malawi. At Mankhamba, only the scrub hare (*Lepus saxatilis*) was identified to species and it was represented by six specimens. There were also 45 other lagomorph specimens that could not be identified to species. However, since the red rock hare (*Pronolagus crassicaudatus*) and the Cape hare (*Lepus capensis*) currently exist on the adjacent Dedza-Chongoni highlands[41] and their remains were found at various excavations there,[42] it is possible that both are also represented in the Mankhamba faunal assemblage.

Besides the scrub hare, other very small animals that were identified to species at Mankhamba included the greater cane rat (*Thryonomys swinderianus*), the house rat (*Rattus rattus*), and either the rock dassie (*Procavia capensis*) or the yellow-spotted dassie (*Heterohyrax brucei*). The greater cane rat was the most common of the rodents,

---

38 Crader 1984a: 38; 1984b: 41.
39 Mgomezulu 1978: 267.
40 Smithers 1966: 47.
41 Crader 1984a: 14.
42 Mgomezulu 1978: 267; Crader 1984a: 38; Crader 1984b: 41.

with 196 specimens represented, followed by the house rat. Some of the unidentifiable rodents must have included remains of field mice. Unlike the house rat, which no ethnic group in Malawi considers as food, field mice are regarded by some as a delicacy. In fact, one common sight in the dry season along Malawi's main roads, particularly in central Malawi, is that of young boys carrying kebabs of roast mice for sale to motorists. Going by such ethnographic observations, it is clear that people were responsible for the presence of the remains of rodents at the site, even though this is hard to justify with respect to house rats. Ethnographic observations suggest that house rats make their way into houses to feed on the same food as humans. Whenever house rats infest a house, people bring in cats to help eradicate them and since cats cannot possibly eat all of them, people throw the rest away. As shown in Table 10.2, however, the identification of cats at Mankhamba was doubtful. If indeed there were no cats at the site, then the people must have had some creative ways of eradicating house rats.

The ostrich (*Struthio camelus*), the heron (*Egretta* sp) and possibly the pigeon (Columbidae), whose bones were hard to distinguish from those of doves, represented wild birds. Surprisingly absent were partridges and guinea fowl which, along with pigeons, are currently some of the most exploited wild birds in Malawi. They are widely exploited because partridges, and guinea fowl in particular, are notorious for recovering and eating newly planted seeds in gardens and fields where people either trap them or kill them with bows and arrows. It is therefore possible that some of the remains of medium-size birds that specialists could not identify to species were of these two birds. Whereas people acquired most birds for food, they may have targeted herons for their feathers or for medicinal purposes. Elsewhere, people use certain body parts, including heads and hearts of such birds, in this way.[43]

Frogs were also recovered, but only the bullfrog (*Pyxicephalus adspersus*) was identified to species and was represented by eight specimens. Many other specimens were identified simply as frog/toad or by size as either medium or large. At least 23 specimens were indeterminate, even by size. Although bullfrogs and other types of frogs are eaten by various people, including the !Kung,[44] and legs of certain frogs are considered to be a delicacy by some people in the western world, frogs in general are not considered as food by the Chewa or any ethnic group in Malawi. Frogs at Mankhamba were thus self-introduced. Often, they hide in burrows and other objects to shelter from the heat or cold.[45]

Besides the Zambezi soft-shelled turtle discussed above, the Mankhamba excavation also yielded other shelled creatures, including other turtles, terrapins

---

43 Gelfand M, Mavi S, Drummond RB & Ndemera B. 1985. *The Traditional Medical Practitioner in Zimbabwe.* Gweru, Zimbabwe: Mambo Press; Scott, Juwayeyi & Plug 2009: 57.
44 Lee 1980; Quin PJ. 1959. *Foods and feeding habits of the Pedi.* Johannesburg: University of Witwatersrand Press.
45 Passmore NI & Carruthers VC. 1979. *South African Frogs.* Johannesburg: University of Witwatersrand Press.

(*Pelomedusa/Pelusios*), medium- and large-size tortoises, freshwater bivalves and the giant land snail. There were also Indo-Pacific marine molluscs, including arc shells, as many as 46 cowrie (*Cypraea* sp) shells and an unidentified gastropod. Humans had modified the shells of the giant land snail only.

The Mankhamba site also yielded a huge quantity of fish remains, but archaeozoologists have not yet identified them. Some of the most popular fish found in Lake Malawi are *utaka* (*Copadichromis otopharynx*), tilapia, locally called *chambo* (*Oreochromis* sp), *mcheni* (*Rhamphochromis* sp), *kampango* (*Bagrus meridionalis*) and *usipa* (*Engraulicypris engraulicyprisardella*). Other fish species are *mulamba* (*Clarias gariepinus*) and *matemba* (*Barbus paludinosus*) found in rivers, marshes and ponds.[46] When the fish remains are identified, it is very likely that these same types of fish will be dominant.

Conspicuous by their absence in the archaeological record are the remains of the black rhinoceros (*Diceros bicornis*). Studies show that this animal was very widely spread in southern and central Malawi.[47] Its total absence in the archaeological record at Mankhamba is therefore surprising. The Chewa probably tabooed it, or they did not like its meat, or most likely, they found it hard to hunt. The black rhinoceros is not a herd animal — it is often alone or roams in a pair or as a female and a calf.[48] Large animals with such habits were difficult to hunt using traditional hunting implements and techniques.

An understandable absence, though, is that of insects. Although archaeologists recovered a roasted edible caterpillar, known locally as *chitsenda*, at a Late Stone Age rock-shelter site in southern Malawi,[49] insects rarely survive in the archaeological record. Malawians, however, do eat insects of one type or another, the most common edible insect being the winged or flying termite of the genus *Macrotermes*, locally called *ngumbi* or *inswa*. It is consumed by probably all the ethnic groups in the country.

Domestic animals

Remains of both food and non-food domestic animals were identified in the Mankhamba faunal assemblage. They were cattle, sheep, goats, chickens, doves/pigeons and dogs. Cattle (*Bos taurus*) were prominent among the large food animals and they were represented by 166 specimens, one of which was identified as dwarf cattle. There were also 70 specimens representing sheep (*Ovis aries*) and 33 specimens representing goats (*Capra hircus*). A further 103 specimens were identified as either sheep or goats (sheep/goat). As indicated earlier in this chapter, the term 'sheep/goat' is used because it is difficult to distinguish very fragmented bones of the two animals. When unable to tell

---

46 Fishes in Lake Malawi. nd. http://www.est.ryukoku.ac.jp/est/yuhma/FLM-pamph/ (accessed 21 October 2017).
47 Smithers 1966: 83; Hayes nd: 70.
48 Smithers 1966: 83.
49 Juwayeyi 1981: 99.

if the bone is that of a sheep or a goat, archaeozoologists list the bone as that of sheep/ goat (*Ovis/Capra*). Sometimes they are termed simply as ovicaprines.

The high representation of domestic animals makes Mankhamba a unique site. Apart from Nkope and Matope Court sites, which yielded one and two cattle bones respectively, no other Iron Age sites have yielded remains of cattle, sheep, goats or pigs in the southern Lake Malawi area, or along the Shire River Valley.

The people at Mankhamba raised more cattle than sheep or goats. This confirms research elsewhere, which has shown that during the Iron Age there were more cattle than either sheep or goats in the region north of the Zambezi.[50] In fact, European travellers, who passed through the land of the Maravi during the late eighteenth century, commented that they did not see goats, pigs or sheep.[51]

The size of the cattle from Mankhamba was noted to be generally small compared to modern skeletal samples located in the Ditsong Museum. Even the dwarf specimen was small compared to specimens of dwarf cattle observed at Nyanga in Zimbabwe.[52] Inadequate grazing, hot conditions and overpopulation in relation to available food resources are usually the reasons for small stature in modern cattle populations.[53] At Mankhamba, however, those reasons were contradicted by the fact that wild grazers were of normal size. Perhaps the small size of the cattle had to do with how the Chewa herded them, which calls for more research.

The abundance of cattle at Mankhamba suggests that during the time that the Chewa occupied the site, the area was relatively free of tsetse flies (*Glossina* spp). These flies carry the nagana or trypanosomiasis (sleeping sickness) disease, which is fatal to both cattle and humans. Unlike the highlands of Malawi, which were tsetse free,[54] the lowlands were not. However, the abundance of tsetse flies in the places where they thrive fluctuates, with their numbers expanding and contracting at different times.[55] The low incidence of domesticated cattle at Nkope and Matope Court sites in comparison to Mankhamba may therefore be related to tsetse fly fluctuation. The former two sites were occupied during a period of expansion and Mankhamba during a period of contraction.

50 Plug & Voigt 1985; Scott, Juwayeyi & Plug 2009: 56.
51 Burton RF. 1969. *The Lands of Cazembe: Lacerda's journey to Cazembe in 1798.* New York: Negro University Press.
52 Plug I, Soper R & Chirawu, S. 1997. Pits, tunnels and cattle in Nyanga, Zimbabwe: new light on an old problem. *The South African Archaeological Bulletin* 52; Plug I & Badenhorst S. 2002. Appendix B: Bones from Muozi midden trench II. In *Nyanga. Ancient Fields, Settlements and Agricultural History in Zimbabwe.* R Soper (ed). London: British Institute in East Africa; Scott, Juwayeyi & Plug 2009: 56.
53 Scott, Juwayeyi & Plug 2009: 56
54 Smith AB. 1992. *Pastoralism in Africa: origins and development ecology.* Johannesburg: Witwatersrand University Press.
55 Fuller C. 1923. Tsetse in the Transvaal and surrounding territories: an historical review. *Entomology Memoirs.* 1(1): Department of Agriculture, Union of South Africa. Pretoria; Punt WHJ. 1975. *The First Europeans in the Kruger National Park.* Pretoria: Simon van der Stel Foundation.

It is worth pointing out that tsetse flies still exist in Malawi despite tremendous efforts to contain them.[56] Eight specimens represented domesticated pigs at Mankhamba which is the first and only Iron Age site in Malawi ever to yield these specimens. Pigs are a recent import to southern Africa, with European settlers having introduced them in the region after AD 1500.[57] Over time, the Chewa and other ethnic groups acquired them.

Chickens (*Gallus domesticus*) were represented with 452 specimens. They were and continue to be the most common domestic animals found in Malawian villages. Despite the abundance of chicken remains at Mankhamba, only a few Iron Age archaeological sites in southern Africa have yielded them, and this has been in small amounts.[58] The Mankhamba site was therefore unique. It is not too difficult, though, to speculate the reasons for their abundance at the site. Most Malawians have the habit of eating both the meat and most, if not all, of the bones of well-cooked chickens. They throw away those they fail to eat due to the hardness of the bone or to tooth loss, and often dogs and cats find the bones. This scenario indicates that there should not have been so many chicken bones at Mankhamba. The site was unique, however, in that a large population of people occupied it for several centuries. Given such a time span, chicken bone accumulation of this nature is possible.

Only four specimens represented doves and it was not entirely clear if they might have been the remains of pigeons. Assuming they were doves, then their low representation is probably normal. Malawians tend to raise chickens more than they do doves.

Dogs were the only clearly identified non-food animal at Mankhamba and were represented by 178 specimens. It is worth pointing out, though, that there were also two specimens identified as wild or domestic cats. Assuming they were domestic cats, the low representation would align with ethnographic observations. Unlike dogs, cats are not popular in Malawi because, other than their ability to kill house rats, they do not have any other social or economic use.

Worked objects

Despite the large faunal assemblage, modified objects made of bone, shell and ivory were limited. Only three worked objects made of bone were identified and one each was recovered in levels 1, 2 and 3. Two of them were shafts, one of which was made into

56 Gondwe N, Marcotty T, Vanwambeke SO, De Pus C, Mulumba M & Van den Bossche, P. 2009. Distribution and density of tsetse flies (Glossinidae: Diptera) at the game/people/livestock interface of the Nkhotakota game reserve human sleeping sickness focus in Malawi. *EcoHealth*. 6(2).

57 Plug I & Badenhorst S. 2001. The distribution of macromammals in southern Africa over the past 30000 years as reflected in animal remains from archaeological sites. In *Transvaal Museum Monograph no. 12*. Pretoria: Transvaal Museum.

58 Plug I. 1996. Domestic animals during the Early Iron Age in southern Africa. In *Aspects of African archaeology: Proceedings of the 10th congress of the Pan-African Association for Prehistory and Related Studies*. G Pwiti & R Soper (eds). Harare: University of Zimbabwe Publications; Plug & Voigt 1985.

some kind of a bangle, and the other was simply polished. The third object was a rounded piece and it had a hole drilled through its centre. It is possible that these worked bone objects were intended to be ornaments. However, since no comparable material has ever been observed ethnographically, this remains a conjecture.

Worked shell included one large shell of the giant land snail, which had a hole drilled through it, and eight shell beads. The drilled shell would probably have resulted in a bead had the modification process on it continued. All the eight shell beads were made from the shell of the same creature. Surprisingly absent were ostrich eggshell beads. This was surprising because ostriches were represented in the archaeological record, and at some sites such as Ndondondwane in South Africa ostrich eggshell beads have been recovered.[59] In Malawi, these beads had never been recovered at an archaeological site and, until the Mankhamba site was excavated, neither had the remains of ostriches.

Thousands of ivory fragments with chopping damage, four unidentifiable objects and many bangles represented ivory objects. Two of the four unidentifiable objects were recovered in each of levels 1 and 3. Neat and evenly spaced cut marks had been made on them probably in preparation for cutting out bangles (see Plate 10.1). The average width of the marks was not any different from that of finished bangles. The third was a half disk with diagonal striations and a hole drilled through its centre. The last one, found in Level 4, was a small piece of ivory that was cut through, exposing a section in the middle of which a small hole had been drilled to a depth of 12 millimetres. Its external side was then worked until it looked like a roughly made cone with its tip sliced off. Its height was only 65 millimetres. Whereas the first two objects were most likely part of ivory bangle manufacturing activities, it is not clear what the others were intended to be.

Plate 10.1: Fragment of elephant ivory marked for cutting out bangles.
Source: The author

---

59   Maggs T. 1984. Ndondondwane: A preliminary report on an Early Iron Age site on the lower Tugela River. *Annals of the Natal Museum.* 26(1): 89.

As many as 78 fragments of both polished and unpolished bangles were recovered at Mankhamba. They represented a minimum of 70 bangles, of which the majority (77 per cent) were recovered in levels 2 and 3. Level 4 yielded 22 per cent and Level 1 only one bangle. I am not aware of any site in southern Africa or anywhere else that has yielded so many ivory bangles.

Polishing was observed on 33 fragments, constituting 47 per cent of the total yield, of which 32 fragments were polished on both sides and one on the dorsal side only. The polished bangles had a smooth finish with a distinct, dull yellowing reminiscent of ageing white or ivory-coloured objects. These bangles had been worn for a long time and some may have been passed down one or more generations. Twenty-three polished bangles, constituting 70 per cent of these bangles, were also decorated. The most common form of decoration featured very fine incised lines that went around the bangle. On most bangles, two or three such lines were made, either evenly spaced (see Figure 10.1 nos i–ii) or with one line on one side and two on the other side of the bangle (see Figure 10.1 no iii). Five bangles had single incised lines (see Figure 10.1 v). Two bangles showed other types of decorations in addition to incised lines. On one, two incised lines were placed on one side and a row of bosses was made on the other (see Figure 10.1

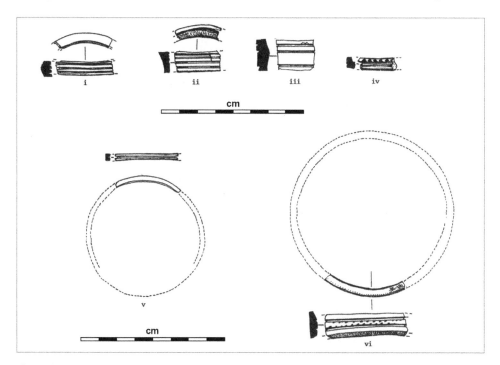

Figure 10.1: Ivory bangles: (i–ii) bangles decorated with three evenly spaced incised lines; (iii) bangle with three incised lines, two on one side and one on the other; (iv) bangle with two incised lines on one side and a row of bosses on the other; (v) bangle with one incised line; (vi) bangle with a patterned decoration in between two incised lines.
Source: Adapted from Juwayeyi 2010a

no iv), and on the other, a patterned design was placed in between two incised lines (see Figure 10.1 no vi).

Amounting to nearly 53 per cent of the total yield, the unpolished bangles had sharp edges, rough surfaces and a dull or dirty appearance; suggesting that they had probably never been used. It is very likely that they never became full bangles in the first place. They represent objects that fractured during manufacture.

Both polished and unpolished bangles were measured for width and thickness, averaging 7 millimetres in width and 5 millimetres in thickness. The average width allowed for ample room for the various decorations that were made on them.

Summary

The faunal remains from Mankhamba were largely the result of animal food processing by humans. Two archaeozoologists identified nearly 30 per cent of the 38 663 bone fragments, excluding fish, to species, genus, family or size class. Some of the well-represented animals included adult large bovids and non-bovids like elephants, the hippopotamus and Zambezi soft-shelled turtles. Other finds included ostriches and other birds, hares, rodents, frogs and snails. All of them were probably food, except frogs and snails. About 4.7 per cent of the bones had cut and chop marks and 30.2 per cent had burned or scorch marks. Some had marks consistent with carnivore and rodent tooth marks. The many copper objects at the site resulted in a green discoloration in some of the bones.

People hunted some of the large animals for both food and their skins and this includes the zebra, whose meat the Chewa seem to have tabooed. They targeted elephants largely for ivory. Some animals such as hippopotamus, bush pigs, baboons and monkeys were targeted for both food and crop protection.

People hunted and killed large carnivores whenever they had become a threat to domestic animals or to people. In some rare and exceptional cases, they hunted large carnivores to acquire certain body parts, including skins, claws, teeth and other items for use as symbols of power, and for traditional rituals.

The abundance of cattle suggests that the Chewa occupied Mankhamba when the area was relatively free of tsetse flies, which cause sleeping sickness, an illness that is fatal to both cattle and humans.

The people of Mankhamba were not fond of making objects from bones. However, they used ivory to make bangles and other objects.

CHAPTER 11

The Chewa at Mankhamba

Oral traditions and the current distribution of ethnic groups in central and southern Malawi make it rather obvious that the Mankhamba site was founded by people who spoke Chichewa, a Western Bantu language. Archaeology has provided a time span for the occupation of the settlement but has not given a depiction of what the settlement might have looked like. For this, one may extrapolate from modern village settings in Malawi and from observations made by Portuguese explorers and traders in southern Africa during the seventeenth century. This will help to establish an image of what the Mankhamba settlement might have looked like when Kalonga and his people occupied it. The material remains from the excavations have provided ample evidence regarding the way of life of the Chewa, which will be covered in this chapter. The discussion will concentrate on how they made a living. Long-distance trade will be discussed in detail in the following chapter.

Founding the Mankhamba settlement

Scholars who have analysed oral traditions of the Chewa believe that the pre-Maravi were the first Chewa group to arrive in Malawi and that they were followed by the Maravi.[1] According to Schoffeleers,[2] the pre-Maravi were in full possession of the land when the Maravi arrived. Some of them had settled at Mankhamba, where they established a rain-calling shrine.[3] However, oral traditions provided no reliable dates for the arrival of either of the two groups. In fact, for a long time, historians and other scholars have grappled with the chronology of the migration of the Chewa.[4] Their main problem was that the only sources of information they had were documents written by the early Portuguese and the oral traditions themselves.

The earliest of the Portuguese documents were written in the sixteenth century, long after the Chewa had settled at Mankhamba. They contain records of events that took place after, and not before, the fifteenth century. Oral traditions are also problematic in their own way. Unlike archaeology, which involves analysing material remains recovered at archaeological sites and scientifically dating them, oral traditions can be unreliable when they refer to events that occurred many centuries ago because people

---

1   Hamilton 1955; Marwick 1963; Schoffeleers 1973, 1992; Phiri 1975.
2   Schoffeleers 1973: 48.
3   Schoffeleers 1992: 152; 180.
4   Alpers 1975; Shoffeleers 1973; Phiri 1975; Newitt 1982.

tend to modify narratives through time. Archaeology has now stepped in to help clarify the chronology and the settling of the Chewa at Mankhamba and other sites.

Dating Mawudzu pottery and the arrival of the Chewa

Mawudzu pottery was the dominant pottery in Malawi during much of the second millennium and it is associated with the arrival of the Chewa.[5] The oldest C-14 date for Mawudzu pottery at Mankhamba was calibrated to AD 1218–1488,[6] a period of over 200 years, which is not precise enough. Other sites have produced relatively more precise dates. Mawudzu pottery was dated to the late fifteenth century at Mawudzu Hill on the shores of Lake Malawi, and to the mid-sixteenth century at Mitongwe homestead in the Bwanje Valley.[7] Calibrated dates from sites DZ40 and Chencherere on the Dedza-Chongoni highlands and from Namaso Bay along Lake Malawi have pushed back the age of Mawudzu pottery to the fourteenth century.[8] These dates provide some context for the imprecise dates obtained at Mankhamba.

When these dates are examined together with some pottery attributes observed on eleventh-century Luangwa pottery, ninth- to twelfth-century Namaso pottery, and Mawudzu pottery itself, a clear picture regarding the introduction of Mawudzu pottery and the arrival of the Chewa in Malawi begins to emerge. As demonstrated in Chapter 8, Mawudzu pottery from Mankhamba featured stamp-based decorations. This was unique to Mankhamba because this type of decoration was rare on Mawudzu pottery from late fifteenth- and sixteenth-century sites. However, it was present on older Mawudzu pottery recovered at sites on the Dedza-Chongoni highlands, Salima and Nkhotakota districts.[9] Stamp-based decorations were also observed on Luangwa pottery in eastern Zambia, which resembles Mawudzu pottery, and on Namaso pottery in the southern Lake Malawi area.[10] The resemblance between Luangwa and Mawudzu pottery is not surprising considering that eastern Zambia and central Malawi are adjacent to each other and the Chewa passed through this area to reach central Malawi.

These pottery attributes present an interesting picture. They show that stamping as a decorative technique on Mawudzu pottery was localised to the Mankhamba area, the Dedza-Chongoni escarpment and areas to the west of Lake Malawi, including eastern Zambia. This localisation and the small percentage of stamp-decorated vessels represented at Mankhamba suggest that stamping as a decorative style was in decline. It is clear from this evidence that stamp-decorated Mawudzu pottery represents what Davison called cultural mixing and transition over time, from earlier pottery traditions

---

5   Robinson 1970; Mgomezulu 1978; Juwayeyi 1981, 2010a.
6   Juwayeyi 2010a: 196; Juwayeyi 2011a.
7   Robinson 1970: 32; 1975: 44.
8   Mgomezulu 1978: 213; Davison 1991: 54.
9   Robinson 1975, 1979; Mgomezulu 1978; Davison 1992.
10 Davison 1991, 1992; Phillipson 1976: 213.

to Mawudzu pottery.[11] The transition period was between the twelfth century, when Namaso pottery phased out, and the fourteenth century, the earliest date available for Mawudzu pottery. This shows that the Chewa began to settle in central Malawi, Mankhamba and the remaining southern Lake Malawi area at some point during that transition period.

There was some significant change, though, in the way of life of the people at Mankhamba during the fifteenth century, reflected in their use of glass beads from Asia.[12] Some glass beads were also recovered by Davison[13] at Namaso Bay in levels that were dated to the fifteenth century. These beads began to arrive in southern Africa during the first half of that century.[14] The presence of the beads at Mankhamba suggests that the inhabitants of the site were already active players in long-distance trade by the fifteenth century. As demonstrated in the following chapter, it was the secular leadership of the Maravi that coordinated long-distance trade. This evidence shows that the arrival of the Maravi at Mankhamba dates to at least the first half of the fifteenth century.

However, some scholars are unlikely to accept these dates. For instance, Smith[15] argued that the pre-Maravi arrived in Malawi in the sixth or seventh century. He based his argument on the fact that the pre-Maravi were a Western Bantu-speaking matrilocal people[16] and that pottery at some sites in Zambia where they settled suggests that they were in that area by that time. While Smith's argument seems plausible, the archaeological evidence at Mankhamba and elsewhere in the southern Lake Malawi area does not support it. Nkope pottery, which was gradually replaced by Kapeni pottery between the eighth and the tenth century, was the only pottery in use in the area during the sixth and seventh century. Both Nkope and Kapeni pottery were made by Early Iron Age Eastern Bantu speakers, who first settled in the southern Lake Malawi area in the third century.[17] Western Bantu speakers replaced the Eastern Bantu speakers sometime during the first half of the second millennium AD. Other than the Chewa, who also speak a Western Bantu language, no other ethnic group is known to have settled in the area from that time until the nineteenth century. Therefore, these Western Bantu speakers must have been the pre-Maravi, the first people to settle at Mankhamba and who were joined later by the Maravi.

---

11 Davison S, personal communication 25 July 2008.
12 Arkell AJ 1936. Cambay and the bead trade. *Antiquity* 10: 299.
13 Davison 1991.
14 Wood 2009a: 3.
15 Smith BW. 1995. Rock art in south-central Africa. A study based on the pictographs of Dedza district, Malawi and Kasama district, Zambia. PhD thesis. University of Cambridge; Smith BW. 2001. Forbidden images: rock paintings and the Nyau secret society of central Malawi and eastern Zambia. *African Archaeological Review.* 18(4).
16 Vansina 1984; Huffman 1989; Phillipson 2000.
17 Robinson 1970.

What did the Mankhamba settlement look like?

The best one can do to visualise what the Mankhamba settlement might have looked like is to compare it with some of the prosperous-looking modern villages in which Malawian chiefs with the rank of traditional authority or that of a senior or paramount chief reside. In making such a comparison, however, one would initially have to assume that Kalonga was the equivalent of these modern high-ranking chiefs. In Malawi, traditional authority is hierarchically arranged. The lowest rank is that of village headman. Above that and in increasing order of authority are the ranks of group village headman, sub-chief and chiefs of a rank simply called traditional authority. Then there are the top ranks of senior chief and paramount chief.

The top-ranked chiefs tend to have large houses that are often surrounded by smaller houses belonging to members of their immediate family. They keep an open area at a respectable distance from their house where they conduct hearings and meetings. The rest of the village, featuring clusters of houses of individual families, spreads from there. Each village also has a name and often it is the name of the founder of the village. The typical, modern Chewa village also features a wooded area called *mzinda*, which they use for Nyau performances, the hiding of Nyau costumes and the burial of the dead.

One Portuguese traveller, Gaspar Bocarro, has given us an idea of what Mankhamba must have looked like in the early seventeenth century. In March 1616, Bocarro began a journey from Tete to Kilwa.[18] He passed through the Maravi kingdom where he visited Kalonga Muzura, who will be discussed in detail in the next chapter. At the time, Muzura was not at Mankhamba, but at a settlement he had established along the Wankurumadzi River in the Mwanza-Neno area.[19] Bocarro described settlements of some of Muzura's tributary chiefs, such as Bunga, as large villages. When he arrived at Muzura's settlement, however, he described it as a town.[20] As demonstrated below, this town was established not only later than Mankhamba, but it was also secondary to Mankhamba in terms of political influence. Mankhamba was the capital of the Maravi state. It was also a major trading centre and was at a crossroads for long-distance trade. Maravi leaders distributed imported goods from there and exports, particularly elephant ivory, originated from this location too. Bocarro did not reach Mankhamba, but considering that people had settled there continuously for more than two centuries before the founding of the town in Mwanza-Neno, Mankhamba was most likely the larger of the two.

What were some of the features of this town? Geographically, it was situated at the confluence of the Nadzipulu and Nakaingwa rivers, in an area that was and is still fertile. The specific position of the excavation and the nature and abundance of the material

---

18 Bocarro 1964; Hamilton 1954; Rangeley1954.
19 Rangeley 1954; Hamilton 1954.
20 Bocarro 1964: 416.

remains show that the centre of activity at Mankhamba was closer to the confluence of the two rivers than farther away from it. This suggests that Kalonga's residence may have been near there. The rest of the village extended backwards from the confluence, with thatched houses or huts spread between the two rivers. How far back it extended is impossible to say because the evidence was destroyed by land cultivation that has continued at the site since its abandonment.

Mankhamba was not an isolated settlement. There were small satellite settlements in the Mtakataka-Mua area that were located during the site survey. They must have been connected in one way or another to Mankhamba, but confirmation of this must await the excavation of some of the other settlements.

The Mankhamba settlement, like Kaphirintiwa-Msinja, had its own rain-calling shrine and sacred water pool. The shrine at Mankhamba still exists and is located in a small thicket about 80 metres to the south of the excavated mound. It is used whenever the group village headman and other leaders feel it necessary to conduct a rain-calling ceremony. Its current location, however, cannot be the original one. Historically, shrines used to be located far away from the village and sometimes in hard-to-reach places, such as on hilltops.

As stated in Chapter 3, the sacred water pool was located eight kilometres to the east of the site. Unlike the rain-calling shrine, the pool is no longer in use, nor is it venerated in any way, except for the fact that they named it after Nyangu, the perpetual mother or sister of Kalonga.

Metallurgy

The people of Mankhamba, like other people in the world, strived to make a good living by involving themselves in various productive activities for which the archaeological evidence is either direct or indirect. Where the evidence is indirect, ethnographic-based reports were taken into account to help clarify relevant aspects of the people's way of life.

Metallurgy was perhaps the most important industry at Mankhamba, involving finding and smelting iron ore, fabricating iron implements and copper working. Iron smelting was the most difficult part of the process of making iron tools. It required experts who could accurately identify good iron ore and good charcoal-producing trees, and who had the ability to calculate accurately the quantity of charcoal required to smelt a given amount of iron ore.[21] Such knowledge was important if good iron was to be produced and iron implements were to be fabricated successfully. After smelting the iron, blacksmiths began to fabricate the implements. The Maravi were in fact well-known to the Portuguese and to other ethnic groups for the high quality of their hoes and other iron implements.[22] Besides their durability and usefulness in agriculture, iron

---

21   Van der Merwe & Avery 1987.
22   Alpers 1975.

implements were also useful in the manufacture of frequently used objects such as mortars, pestles, mats, baskets, drums, canoes and other items.

Although identifiable objects made of copper at Mankhamba were abundant compared to iron, copper working was a minor industry. This was due to a lack of commercially exploitable copper deposits in the area. It is likely that many of the copper rings, necklaces and thin wire found there were brought to Mankhamba by traders who travelled between the copper belt and the southern Lake Malawi area. This trade continued well into the nineteenth century.[23] As mentioned in Chapter 9, limited copper work did take place at the site itself, perhaps through using imported copper ore or by reworking copper objects.

Other industries

Other industries included the production of cloth, wicker objects and pottery, and food processing and house construction. Nineteenth-century ethnographic observations and oral traditions suggest that before the introduction of cotton cloth, people wore bark cloth and *dewere*, that is cloth made from the fibre of the *bwazi* plant (*Securidaca longipedunculata*).[24] Bark cloth, which was made throughout Malawi,[25] was produced from the bark of the *mombo* tree.[26] As stated in Chapter 6, this tree is ubiquitous in the country. Its bark is easier to remove than that of other trees.

The evidence for spinning the fibre of *bwazi* and cotton is indirect, in the form of spindle whorls, not from the remains of *bwazi* and cotton thread or cloth. It is rare for cloth of any kind to survive in the archaeological record, particularly at an open site like Mankhamba. Although spinning and weaving of *bwazi* fibre to make *dewere* is rarely mentioned in Malawi's oral traditions, early twentieth-century ethnographic reports by European travellers[27] suggest that *bwazi* fibre was commonly used for making cloth and fishing nets. They also suggest that the wearing of *dewere* was common in the southern Lake Malawi area and probably elsewhere in the country.[28] For instance, one of the observations that Laws[29] made in Dowa district was that *bwazi* was plentiful. On at least one occasion, he saw a native loom at work weaving *bwazi* fibre into cloth. It is possible that people either cultivated the *bwazi* plant or at least nurtured it to ensure its continued productivity.

---

23 Livingstone & Livingstone 1866: 410; Kirk J & Foskett R. 1965. *The Zambesi journal and letters of Dr. John Kirk, 1858–63*. London: Oliver & Boyd.

24 Macdonald 1882. Juwayeyi 1972–1973; Williamson 1975.

25 MacDonald 1882.

26 Werner 1969: 200.

27 Laws 1879; Waller H. 1970. *The Last Journals of Livingstone in Central Africa*. Westport, Connecticut: Greenwood Press; Werner 1969.

28 Williamson 1975: 212.

29 Laws 1879.

Cotton cloth replaced both bark cloth and *dewere*, but the process was gradual because the availability of cotton was not universal. The cloth was readily available in areas where cotton was grown and rare where the soil and the environment were not ideal for cotton growing. Mankhamba was within a cotton-growing area and so cotton spinning must have been a common activity at the site. By the early colonial period, however, the use of bark cloth, *dewere* and cotton cloth was in decline due to the abundance of European cloth. Only the thread of the *bwazi* fibre remained in use for a long time and was widely used to thread beads and to make fishing nets.[30]

Indirect evidence for making wicker ware, such as mats and baskets, comes in the form of copper needles. The two most popular mats made in Malawi are the *mphasa* and the *nkeka*. The *mphasa* is made from a type of reed locally called *bango* (*Phragmites mauritianus*), whereas the *nkeka* is made from the leaves of a type of palm called *mgwalangwa* (*Hyphaene* spp). Unlike the *nkeka*, which is woven, the *mphasa* is sewn. To make *mphasa*, the reeds are split into thin slips and then sewn or joined together with string using needles similar to those recovered at Mankhamba. Besides its many uses, such as being slept on or having foodstuff spread on it that needed to dry in the sun, the *mphasa* was used in the past to wrap dead bodies for burial.[31] The *nkeka* plays more of a social than a utilitarian role. Although it is sometimes substituted for the *mphasa*, the *nkeka* is used mostly by women to sit on when socialising. In some parts of the country, particularly in areas where mosquito infestation was heavy, the *nkeka* was sewn into a sleeping bag as a form of protection against mosquito bites.[32]

The *dengu* or *mtanga,* and the *lichero* are the most popular baskets in Malawi. Both are made by weaving flat slips of bamboo and they come in different sizes. The *dengu,* which is a deep basket, is shaped specifically for carrying on the head; hence its use primarily by females. The *lichero* is a winnowing basket, again used by females. The largest of the baskets is called *mseche*. Some can be as high as 1.5 metres and up to a metre in diameter. Women use them to keep locally brewed beer in readiness for consumption during celebrations or any other event involving the entire village. To prevent beer from leaking, the external side is sealed using a mixture of sap squeezed from the roots of the *nkhunga* (*Sphenostylis marginata*) plant and ground charcoal. Rims are fastened to baskets using a needle and the stem of a climbing plant with the local name of *chilambe* (*Cissampelos mucronata*).

Making pottery was a common activity at Mankhamba. In Malawi, ceramic pots are made by women only[33] and so it can be assumed that the same was true at Mankhamba. Being a centre with a large population, Mankhamba must have had women who

---

30 Werner 1969: 195; Williamson 1975: 212.
31 Juwayeyi 1981.
32 Werner 1906: 200.
33 Macdonald 1882: 39.

specialised in making different types of vessels, such as those for cooking *nsima*, for brewing beer, carrying water from the river or the well and for other domestic activities.

Locally made ceramic plates and cups are rare both archaeologically and ethnographically. Their rarity suggests that Iron Age people had better alternatives. They probably used *nsengwa* and *chikho* as plates and cups respectively. *Nsengwa*, shaped more like a bowl than a plate, is made of woven bamboo stripes or some other suitable fibre; whereas *chikho* is a gourd (*Lagenaria siceraria*), used for drinking water.[34] However, with only less than two percent of the pottery decorated, the Mankhamba potters seem to have cared less about the aesthetic value of the pots and more about their utilitarian benefits. The opposite was true with smoking pipes in that over 50 percent were decorated. As noted in Chapter 8, incisions and grooves made on some of the pipes were so evenly spaced, it was as if modern calibration machines had been used to make them.

Another industry at Mankhamba was the processing of elephant ivory. The people did not sell all of their raw ivory to Indian Ocean coastal traders, keeping some for their own use and producing various objects, the most popular of which were bangles. The abundance of bangles in the excavation is an indication that there was a viable local market for them. Other notable activities were food processing and house construction. Food processing was an ongoing activity. The presence of grinding stones suggests that plant food was locally processed for consumption. As it is today, women must have been responsible for processing plant food whereas men processed animal food. For large wild animals, meat processing started at the kill site, where the carcass was butchered in order to make it easy for people to carry the meat home. As was the case with hunter-gatherers,[35] the meat was distributed to the people immediately or fire-cured for preservation. Fish was also fire-cured and some of the fireplaces observed in the excavations were made probably for this purpose.

House construction at Mankhamba is represented by fire-hardened *daga*, some of which had imprints of wood, bamboo poles and reeds or grass. These building materials were so readily available in the local environment that it was both cost- and time-effective to use them, rather than moulding and firing bricks or quarrying and dressing stones. Besides, building houses using these materials takes no more than a few days compared to the much longer time it takes to use bricks or stones. Unfortunately, no hut floors were observed at Mankhamba, but elsewhere, archaeologists have found evidence of huts.[36] Circular houses appear to have been the only house construction style in Malawi during the Iron Age. Elsewhere, however, remains of sub-rectangular houses have been observed.[37]

---

34 Werner 1969.
35 Lee RB. 2003. The hunters: scarce resources in the Kalahari. In *Conformity and Conflict: Readings in Cultural Anthropology*. J Spradley & DW McCurdy (eds). Boston, MA: Allyn & Bacon.
36 Mgomezulu 1978: 119.
37 Phillipson 1977b: 142.

Mixed farming

Although the archaeological excavations at Mankhamba did not yield any botanical remains, the presence of hoes, pottery, grinding stones and bones of domestic animals indicates that the people practised mixed farming, that is the cultivation of crops and the raising of livestock. This manner of making a living goes back to the arrival of Early Iron Age people in the southern Lake Malawi area.

Crops

Land cultivation and the growing of different types of crops were some of the important economic activities at Mankhamba. Nineteenth-century European explorers in Malawi[38] reported seeing sorghum, millet, beans, groundnuts, cassava, sweet potatoes, pumpkins, dagga (*Cannabis sativa*) and other crops. It is possible that the people of Mankhamba grew some or all of these crops too.

Archaeology elsewhere in Africa has proved that crops such as sorghum and millet were indigenous to the continent. The growing of pearl and finger millet, sorghum and African rice started at different periods in various parts of Africa beginning from around 1500 BC.[39] Phillipson[40] indicated that excluding maize and cassava — which were introduced in Africa from the Americas within the last five centuries and bananas that arrived earlier from Asia, most of the crops that have been grown, or are still being grown in Africa are indigenous to the African continent and were probably first cultivated there.

Although direct archaeological evidence is still lacking, one can safely assume that Early Iron Age people introduced sorghum and millet in Malawi during the first millennium AD. They were still popular at least until the late nineteenth century.[41] Use of indigenous cereals in Malawi began to decline with the introduction of foreign crops, the most popular of which are maize, cassava, pumpkins and sweet potatoes. All of these were imported from the Americas and were introduced in Malawi probably by people who had contact with early Portuguese settlers.

Non-food plants that were grown at Mankhamba were cotton and either dagga or tobacco or both. Once introduced, cotton quickly became popular, with people growing both indigenous and foreign varieties. At least three or four varieties of cotton were grown, the most popular of which were a foreign variety called *thonje manga* and an indigenous

---

38   Livingstone & Livingstone 1866: 123.
39   Amblard S. 1996. Agricultural evidence and its interpretation on the Dhars Tichitt and Oualata, south-eastern Mauritania. In *Aspects of African Archaeology: Papers from the 10th Congress of the Pan-African Association for Prehistory and Related Studies*. G Pwiti & R Soper (eds). Harare: University of Zimbabwe Publications; Marshall F & Hildebrand E. 2002. Cattle before crops: the beginnings of food production in Africa. *Journal of World Prehistory*, 16 (2).
40   Phillipson 2000: 118.
41   Livingstone & Livingstone 1866.

variety, *thonje kaja*. David Livingstone noted that the quality of *thonje manga* was comparable to the cotton that England imported from New Orleans in the USA.[42]

The many smoking pipes recovered at Mankhamba show that the Chewa were avid smokers. It is likely that they smoked dagga before the introduction of tobacco in the country. Dagga, a plant native to Asia, was introduced in the interior areas of east Africa before Europeans arrived along the east African coast.[43] Smoking dagga appears to have been a normal and expected activity. People viewed it as an alternative to alcohol in that it provided 'some relaxation from the rigours of daily toil'.[44] They did not regard it as an undesirable habit as some people do today.

It was probably the Portuguese who who introduced tobacco in southern Africa in the sixteenth century. It is not clear when the Chewa acquired tobacco, but they were growing it before Europeans settled in the country.[45] Today, the Chewa are the largest tobacco producers in Malawi. Five of the six districts in Malawi where tobacco is widely grown are in central Malawi,[46] which is where the Chewa are the dominant ethnic group. This makes the Chewa economically significant because, small as it is, Malawi ranked fourteenth in the world in tobacco production in 2017, and tobacco is the country's top export.[47]

Livestock

The people of Mankhamba raised animals for both food and non-food purposes. The food animals were cattle, sheep, goats, pigs, chickens and doves whereas non-food animals were represented by dogs only. Cattle were an important possession at Mankhamba and they are still found among all ethnic groups in Malawi and elsewhere in southern Africa. Cattle represent wealth and status and as such they play a significant role in the social and economic way of life of the people.

The role of cattle varies however, depending on whether the people are patrilocal or matrilocal. In patrilocal northern Malawi where people use cattle to make bride-wealth payments, families strive to own cattle. As a result, the cattle density per square kilometre is nearly double that of the other two matrilocal regions.[48] The Chewa,

---

42   Ibid: 123.
43   Williamson 1975: 57.
44   Ellert H. 1986. *The Material Culture of Zimbabwe*. Harare: Longman: 125.
45   Haviland WE. 1955. The rise of the African tobacco industry in Nyasaland and its production problems. *South African Journal of Economics*. 23(2):141.
46   Drope J, Makoka D, Lencucha R & Appau A. 2016. *Farm-level economics of tobacco production in Malawi*. Center for Agricultural Research and Development (CARD). Lilongwe, Malawi: 16.
47   Food and Agriculture Organization (FAOa). nd. Tobacco production quantity. Available: https://factfish.com/statistic/tobacco%2C%20production%20quantity (accessed 5 November 2019).
48   Food and Agriculture Organization (FAOb). 2005. Livestock sector brief. Available: http://www.fao.org/ag/againfo/resources/en/publications/sector_briefs/lsb_MWI.pdf (accessed 2 December 2017).

however, perceive cattle only as a symbol of wealth and status. Kalonga and the local elite must have acquired cattle to enhance their already high social rank in the society.

Although archaeology has consistently shown that in prehistoric times, people who lived north of the Zambezi River had more cattle than either goats or sheep,[49] the evidence shows that the situation has reversed, at least for Malawi. According to the Food and Agriculture Organisation,[50] there are now more goats and sheep than cattle in the country. The data shows that the combined population of goats and sheep is more than twice that of cattle.[51] The change from raising more cattle to raising more goats and sheep was gradual and most likely dictated by changes in the country's environment, including a growing human population, which in 2018 reached 17.5 million people from about 4 million people in 1966.[52] As an agricultural but mountainous country, the growing population brought about pressure on its limited arable land. Feeding cattle simply became a difficult exercise for many people. Further, the presence of tsetse flies affects the population of cattle more than that of goats and sheep. Infected goats and sheep are less likely than cattle to die from trypanosomiasis.[53] Due to their small size, the heavy presence of goats and sheep in many of Malawi's villages is easy to miss because most households raise only a few animals at a time. They do this more for ease of accommodation than lack of animal feed. Malawians tend to keep small livestock indoors overnight for fear of carnivorous predators, the most notorious of which are hyenas. Thus, they tend to raise just enough animals that can be accommodated in their houses.

Pigs on the other hand are relatively recent arrivals in southern Africa. European settlers introduced them after 1500 AD[54] and they were adopted by many ethnic groups including the Chewa. The archaeological evidence at Mankhamba, however, shows that they were less popular than goats and sheep. That trend apparently continued throughout the centuries. Today, pigs make up about 25 per cent of the combined population of sheep and goats.[55] Religious beliefs may have played some role in the unpopularity of pigs in Malawi. Over 23 per cent of Malawi's population belongs to religious organisations that prohibit the consumption of pork;[56] this is a lot of people, perhaps enough to discourage would-be pig farmers.

---

49 Plug & Voight 1985.

50 FAOb 2005: 2.

51 Ibid.

52 Stubbs M.1972b. Distribution of population, 1966. In *Malawi in Maps*. S Agnew & M Stubbs (eds). London: University of London Press. 56. See also National Statistical Office (NSO). nd. 2008 population and housing census. Available: www.nsomalawi.mw (2017, December 2).

53 Gifford-Gonzalez D. 2000. Animal disease challenges to the emergence of pastoralism in sub-Saharan Africa. *African Archaeological Review*. 17: 120.

54 Plug & Badenhorst 2001.

55 FAOb 2005: 2.

56 NSO 2018.

The people of Mankhamba also raised a great number of chickens but very few doves and no ducks. Chickens are easy to raise and are kept indoors. Until money began to circulate widely in the country, chickens were a reliable medium of exchange.

Cats were not definitively identified at Mankhamba, but dogs were. People raised dogs not for food but for both hunting and companionship. In fact, there are no traditions among the Chewa that suggest they ever considered dogs as food. Citing Frank,[57] Scott et al[58] said that other than the Nyika people of the Nyika Plateau who ate dogs in the past, there are no ethnic groups in Malawi that eat dogs. However, the Nyika were not alone in eating dogs in Africa. Frank[59] also mentioned other people, including those in the Congo basin, Lesotho, the southeastern shore of Lake Victoria and the southwestern shore of Lake Rukwa, which are both in Tanzania, who ate dogs. He said that German anthropologists who worked in Africa in the later part of the nineteenth and early twentieth century reported that the eating of dogs by Africans was usually done on special occasions or as a ritual or during famine.

Hunting

The faunal remains from the excavations show that the people of Mankhamba undertook large-scale hunting expeditions. They targeted large- and medium-size adult animals, mainly antelope, and this required planning and good preparation. Werner[60] reported that hunting expeditions had a recognised leader who made decisions regarding the animal's size, and this depended on the types of animals they were after. Besides regular hunting weapons, hunters offered sacrifices and carried charms and medicines to ensure safety, good luck and a good catch. The lead hunter carried the medicines.

African people had several methods for hunting different types of animals. These included pitfall traps, spears, bows and arrows, and nets.[61] Werner[62] described one hunting technique that an unnamed ethnic group in Malawi devised for killing elephants. It involved hanging a heavy log in a tree, vertically above the pathway of the animals. Attached to the lower end of the log was a poisoned spear. A catch was then set along the tracks, which when trod on by the animal, released the log and the spear stabbed the animal. Often, the animal did not die instantly. The poison, locally called

57 Frank B. 1964. Der hund als opfertier und kulturheros in Afrika. In *Festschrift für Ad. E. Jensen*. E Haberland, MA Schuster & H Straube (eds). Munich: Klaus Renner Verlag.
58 Scott, Juwayeyi & Plug 2009: 56.
59 Frank 1964.
60 Werner 1969.
61 Casalis E. 1861. *The Basutos*. London: James Nisbet; Douglas M. 1968. The Lele of the Kalahari. In *African Worlds*. D Forde (ed). Oxford: Oxford University Press; Roscoe J. 1966. *The Northern Bantu: An Account of some Central African Tribes of the Uganda Protectorate*. London: Frank Cass & Co; Reynolds, B. 1968. *The Material Culture of the Peoples of the Gwembe Valley*. Manchester: Manchester University Press; Hall M. 1977. Shakan pitfall traps: hunting techniques in the Zulu kingdom. *Annals of the Natal Museum*. 23(1).
62 Werner 1969: 189.

ulembe and mentioned a great deal in Malawi's oral traditions, did the rest of the work. The hunters simply followed the injured animal until the poison took effect. Marks[63] referred to a similar method, which was used by the Bisa of Zambia, as the 'harpoon downfall'.

The Banyoro and other ethnic groups in Uganda also killed elephants from trees.[64] They would first locate a herd of elephants, then climb and hide in the branches of trees along the tracks the animals were likely to take, and spear a chosen animal as the herd passed under the trees. They aimed to spear it between the shoulders. If they were unable to bring down the animal in one blow, they would follow it until due to the injury it became weak and separated from the herd. They would then kill it with their spears.

The most common hunting methods, however, involved the use of traps, spears, barbed iron points and bows and arrows. The preferred method for killing elephants was the pitfall trap,[65] a method that required hunters to study the movements of elephants in their area by observing them from a distance or by following their tracks. Then they dug pitfall traps along the tracks where the animals often tended to pass. They dug them with sloping sides and carefully camouflaged the opening with vegetation to make the spot look natural. Sometimes, but not always, they put sharpened stakes in the traps with the pointed ends up.[66] The sloping sides meant that a falling elephant was stuck, with its feet never touching the bottom and being injured by the pointed stakes. The hunters then finished off the elephant with spears. This method also worked well for other large herd animals such as buffalo but was difficult or impossible to implement for solitary or mother-and-calf animals such as rhino.

From his study of pitfall traps that the Zulu of South Africa dug in the early nineteenth century, Hall[67] found that the Zulu re-used the traps. The Zulu used to erect fences with openings leading to where the traps were located. They would then drive animals towards the openings in the fence and those in front fell into the traps. Although oral traditions in Malawi have never suggested that people re-used pitfall traps, the idea makes sense because animals tend to use the same tracks regularly.

Barbed iron points were effective tools against the hippos when they were still in the water. Werner[68] described how the Apodzo of the Lower Zambezi hunted hippos. Apparently, when hunters spotted a hippo in the water, they stood on the bank or in canoes, carrying barbed points or spears with strong, long ropes attached to the shafts of these points or spears. When the animal dived after they struck it several times, the

63 Marks SA. 1976. *Large Mammals and a Brave People: subsistence hunters in Zambia*. Seattle: University of Washington Press: 80.
64 Roscoe 1966.
65 Werner 1969.
66 Ibid: 189.
67 Hall 1977: 6.
68 Werner 1969: 190.

shafts would float on the water, revealing the position of the animal to the hunters. Using the ropes, the injured animal was then pulled out of the water. Once on land, and held by ropes, the hapless animal was killed by means of spears. The Chewa probably used both barbed iron points and pitfall traps placed in the tracks frequented by these nocturnal feeders to reach feeding fields.

Werner[69] also described traps designed to kill lions and leopards. Hunting and killing large carnivores was rare because they are dangerous animals. As stated earlier, people hunted them to protect their livestock and themselves. Whereas people may have eaten the meat, the main sought-after items were skins, canine teeth, claws and tails. They used these as symbols of power, ceremonial attire, and to add potency to some traditional medicines and charms.[70] People at Mankhamba also hunted small animals, including small bovids, rodents, hares, monkeys, birds and other animals. They gathered those that crawled on the ground, such as tortoises. An interesting exception, however, was the giant land snail, a creature that was represented in the archaeological record. However, although it is food in some parts of Africa such as Nigeria, it is not food in Malawi and there are no traditions that suggest it ever was in the past. The shells recovered in the excavations may have been brought to the site for the production of shell beads, some of which were recovered in the excavation. It is also possible that some snails simply died there in their burrows. As indicated in the previous chapter, missing from the archaeological record, are insects, including caterpillars, grasshoppers, flying termites and others, which in all likelihood were as widely exploited by the people of Mankhamba as they are by the Chewa and other ethnic groups today.

Fishing

The abundance of fish remains in the excavations shows that fishing was an important activity at Mankhamba. Fishing had the advantage of not being as dangerous as hunting unless one ventured far away from the shoreline. The people did not need to go all the way to the lake for small quantities of fish as the nearby rivers had and still have fish in them.

Hooks and barbed iron points were the only fishing tools recovered in the excavation. It is possible that people also used traps, weirs and nets. One common trap is the *mono*, a basket trap which fishermen place behind a weir. In swamps or slow-moving streams, people use poison to cause the fish to go into a stupor for easy catching. Williamson[71] identified at least seven plants that produce such poison.

---

69 Ibid: 189.
70 Scott, Juwayeyi & Plug 2009: 56; Plug & Badenhorst 2001; Gelfand et al 1985; Quin 1959.
71 Williamson 1975: 305.

Aesthetics

Finally, although people at Mankhamba seem not to have cared much about decorating their pottery, the archaeological evidence shows that they took time to beautify themselves. The recovery from the excavations of glass beads, copper rings, copper necklaces and ivory bangles suggests that they invested time and resources in this activity. Ethnographic observation among Chewa women suggests that besides adorning themselves with jewellery, the women of Mankhamba may have scarified their faces and other parts of the body to enhance their beauty.

Summary

Pottery attributes and C-14 dates of Luangwa, Namaso and Mawudzu pottery suggest that the pre-Maravi settled at Mankhamba and other areas of central Malawi at some point between the twelfth and the fourteenth centuries. Dates of importation of glass beads show that the Maravi had joined them by the first half of the fifteenth century.

Mankhamba was more than a large village — it was a town, with its own satellite villages. It was both the capital of the Maravi and a major trading centre of local and imported products.

The Chewa made iron implements, copper objects, cloth, wicker and ceramic objects, and ivory bangles. In addition, they practised mixed farming. Nineteenth-century ethnographic observations and oral traditions suggest that they grew food crops including sorghum and millet, and non-food crops such as cotton and dagga. It is also possible that they grew the *bwazi* plant to make *dewere* or they nurtured it to ensure its continued productivity.

The Chewa raised food animals but obtained a great deal of their meat from hunting and fishing. Hunters used pitfall traps to kill large animals such as elephants, buffalos and hippos. Otherwise, the regular hunting tools were nets, spears, arrows and other types of traps. Fishing implements included barbed iron points, fishhooks, traps and nets. The wearing of various ornaments was also part of the Mankhamba lifestyle.

CHAPTER 12

Long-distance trade and the rise of the Maravi empire

To appreciate the extent to which the Maravi were involved in long-distance trade, one needs to examine this in relation to what was going on in southern Zambezia, the area south of the Zambezi River controlled by the Mwene Mutapas in Zimbabwe. Long-distance trade has a long history in that area compared to other areas in the interior of southern Africa. Early seventeenth-century written records of the Portuguese show that the Kalongas in Malawi had dealings with the Mwene Mutapas. One of them, Gatsi Rusere, is said to have 'affirmed that a number of Maravi chiefs, including Kalonga Muzura, were his military allies'.[1] Such an alliance must have had economic benefits too.

Commenting on the nature and intensity of the trade in southern Zambezia, Chirikure[2] pointed out that imported items, such as glass beads, cowrie shells and bronze items began to appear before AD 900. The earliest glass beads were recovered at many archaeological sites, including Chibuene in southern Mozambique, Makuru in south-central Zimbabwe, Schroda in the Limpopo River Valley, and at sites in north-eastern Botswana.[3] They belong to a time that archaeologists refer to as the Zhizo period, dated between AD 600 and 900.[4] Bronze was recovered at the site of Berryl Rose Claims in northern Zimbabwe where it was dated to AD 800 and cowrie shells appear elsewhere in the hinterland at about the same time.[5] The distribution of the sites shows that both the elite and ordinary people in southern Zambezia participated in the trade. Some of the commodities used in the exchange of these items were ivory, cattle and perhaps gold.[6] Although the role of gold during this early period is not that clear, the evidence shows that it was being exploited at least by AD 1000.[7] The same might apply to the exploitation of copper. Remains of copper in southern Zambezia were found at several

---

1   Alpers 1975: 73.
2   Chirikure 2014.
3   Sinclair PJJ, Ekblom A & Wood M. 2012. Chibuene, understanding the dynamics between social complexity, long distance trade and state formation in southern Africa in the late first millennium AD. *Antiquity* 86: 728; Wilmsen EN, Killick D, Rosenstein DD, Thebe PC & Denbow, JR. 2009. The social geography of pottery in Botswana as reconstructed by optical petrography. *Journal of African Archaeology.* 7(1): 4; Chirikure 2014: 709.
4   Chirikure 2014.
5   Ibid.
6   Chirikure 2014: 709.
7   Ibid.

sites, including those that had been occupied by non-elites.[8] This metal was so widely used, it has been argued that Africans considered it more valuable than gold.[9]

The evidence in northern Zambezia, where the site of Mankhamba is located, shows that long-distance trade was not as well established as in southern Zambezia. Although rich copper deposits exist in the north-west of the area, the extent to which copper was exploited during this early period is not clear. It seems traders did not venture into northern Zambezia regularly during this period. One reason could be that they saw no need to go there since southern Zambezia provided all they wanted. It is also possible, however, that the topography of the region discouraged them from making regular journeys to northern Zambezia. Some areas were not easily accessible from some of the trading posts along the Indian Ocean coast. They were blocked by Lake Malawi and by a series of mountain ranges, leaving the Zambezi River Valley as the most viable trade route to northern Zambezia. But it was too circuitous to make trade profitable. As a result, southern Zambezia remained the major source of the important export commodities sought by foreign traders until well into the second millennium.

Trade at Mankhamba

Long-distance trade at Mankhamba has been examined with this background in mind. The archaeological evidence shows that not much trade was conducted in the southern Lake Malawi area before the arrival of the Chewa. In fact, the paucity of imported objects is one of the many aspects that Iron Age sites in the area have in common. Only one site, the Namichimba site in the Upper Shire Valley, yielded an imported object belonging to a pre-Chewa arrival period. It was a fragment of a cowrie shell dated to the tenth century.[10]

Thus, the extraordinary abundance of imported objects at Mankhamba makes the site unique. It shows that it was the Chewa who intensified long-distance trade in the area once they became firmly established at the site. Glass beads from Asia and Europe[11] were one of the commodities obtained from Indian Ocean coastal traders. The Chewa also imported different objects made of copper and copper ore, probably from the copper-producing areas of Zambia and the DRC. Furthermore, the excavation yielded objects made of iron which could not have been produced locally. It is also likely that the people of Mankhamba imported perishable items such as cloth to supplement their own locally made material.

The abundance of Khami series glass beads at Mankhamba suggests that the Chewa liked them immensely. Early Portuguese records show that the beads originated in India.

---

8   Ibid: 720.
9   Herbert EW. 1984. *Red Gold of Africa: Copper in Precolonial History and Culture*. Madison: University of Wisconsin Press.
10   Robinson 1973: 22.
11   Arkell 1936; Wood 2009a.

At least two Indian ports, Cambay on the west coast and Nagapattinam (previously spelled Negapatam) on the south-east coast of India, were the major export centres of the beads. The first traders to bring them to the east African coast were the Moors during the first half of the fifteenth century. The Moors were described as Mohammedan sea-faring traders who, among other products, traded in Cambay beads.[12] During the early sixteenth century, the Moors were joined by Portuguese traders and later, by other European traders. The beads from the two ports became popular on the east African coast because according to some sources, Africans did not like European beads.[13] When the Portuguese monarch heard about the African dislike of European beads, he directed his governor at Nagapattinam to load his ships with the beads liked by Africans in East and southern Africa.[14] In 1660, the port of Nagapattinam was taken over by the Dutch and after that the export of beads from Nagapattinam 'either ceased altogether or could only be carried on as contraband'.[15] European beads probably found a greater place in the African beads trade from that date, but they never became as popular as Khami series beads.

Chinese porcelain, glazed ceramics and pots with folded rims were the next most visible connection between Mankhamba and Asia. Unlike glass beads, however, the antiquity of Chinese ceramics in southern and northern Zambezia before the thirteenth century has not been confirmed. It seems the earliest were Ming Dynasty ceramics which were dated to the second half of the fourteenth century[16] and were found at many sites, including Great Zimbabwe, Khami and Danangombe. The Chinese porcelain recovered at Mankhamba was introduced there in the sixteenth century.[17] It was the Portuguese who from the late sixteenth century began to export a great deal of this porcelain from Macao to India, Africa and Europe.[18] Currently, Mankhamba is the only site in Malawi to have yielded Chinese porcelain. In Zimbabwe, however, Chinese porcelain has been found at a number of sites that were early Portuguese trading stations, suggesting that Portuguese traders rather than local middlemen brought the materials into the interior.[19] The ceramics were virtually absent outside the major ruins, which

12   Arkell 1936: 299.
13   Axelson E. 1973. *Portuguese in South-East Africa: 1488–1600.* Johannesburg: Struik; Van der Sleen WGN. 1956. Trade wind beads. *Man.* 56: 28; Van der Sleen WGN. 1958. Ancient glass beads with special reference to the beads of east and central Africa and the Indian Ocean. *The Journal of the Royal Anthropological Institute of Great Britain and Ireland.* 88(2): 212; Schofield JF. 1958. Beads: southern African beads and their relation to the beads of Inyanga. In *Inyanga: Prehistoric settlements in southern Rhodesia.* R Summers (ed). Cambridge: Cambridge University Press: 183.
14   Van der Sleen 1956: 28
15   Schofield JF. 1938. A preliminary study of the prehistoric beads of the northern Transvaal and Natal. *Transactions of the Royal Society of South Africa.* 26: 366.
16   Chirikure 1914: 713.
17   Juwayeyi 2010a.
18   Bronson B, personal communication, 2009.
19   Garlake PS. 1968. The value of imported ceramics in the dating and interpretation of the Rhodesian Iron Age. *The Journal of African History.* 9.

were also centres of power in Zimbabwe. Garlake[20] believes that the reason for their absence was because the ceramics were treated not as trade items, but as gifts to be given to leaders in order to obtain their goodwill. While this sounds reasonable, it seems highly unlikely that the material could have been brought by traders solely to be freely distributed to local leaders.

Chirikure[21] has offered an alternative explanation. Apparently, the ceramics were brought over to be traded but the local people did not like them because they were culturally unsuitable. They could not, for instance, 'be used in making beer for ancestors, in serving food, in rainmaking ceremonies …'.[22] The situation in Malawi was somewhat different in that Mankhamba was the domain of the local potentates. It is also the only site in the southern Lake Malawi area to yield late sixteenth-century Chinese ceramics, the total absence of which at other sites is therefore interesting. The majority of the Chinese ceramics at Mankhamba were plates and no remains of locally made plates were recovered in the excavations. In fact, locally made plates are rare at Iron Age sites in Malawi, which shows that ceramic plates were not part of the indigenous ceramic tradition. Therefore, the presence of Chinese ceramics at Mankhamba, and their absence at all other sites, suggests that these objects were status symbols which were more ornamental than functional. Only the ruling elite and probably the few others who could afford them had them. The same was true with glazed ceramics, which originated probably in south-west Asia and were brought to the east African coast by Arab or Asian traders. Like Chinese ceramics, they were well represented at Mankhamba but were rare at other sites in Malawi. They too were ornamental objects. Vessels with folded rims were also imported from elsewhere and have never been found at any other archaeological site in Malawi. Although they seem not to have been popular, their globular shape may have made them somewhat useful at Mankhamba. Their lack of popularity was probably due to the fact that vessels of this nature are heavy and rather cumbersome for traders to transport over long distances.

One other foreign item commonly occurring at Mankhamba, but whose usefulness to the community is entirely unclear, is the cowrie shell. Like imported ceramics, cowrie shells are very rare at other archaeological sites in the southern Lake Malawi area. Elsewhere in Africa, cowrie shells had economic and cultural value. In West Africa, for instance, they were used as currency from the thirteenth century to the nineteenth century.[23] Achebe asserts their use in bride-wealth payments in late nineteenth-century eastern Nigeria.[24] Ethnographic observations in southern Africa suggest that cowrie shells also make good jewellery. They are perforated, strung in a cord and worn as a

---

20   Ibid: 30.
21   Chirikure 2014: 719.
22   Ibid.
23   Ehret 2002: 312.
24   Achebe 1994:73.

necklace and sometimes used as decorations on clothing. Other ethnic groups elsewhere in Africa view them as symbols of fertility.[25] At Mankhamba, however, all the 46 shells were whole, with no evidence of any attempted modification. Further, cowrie shells do not feature in the oral traditions of the Chewa. It is therefore not clear what economic, social or ritual role these objects played among the Chewa at Mankhamba.

The people of Mankhamba were also great users of copper products. Considering that Luba, their original home, was located within a major copper-producing area, it is likely that they were familiar with copper workings before they arrived at Mankhamba. Some of the objects recovered at Mankhamba, such as copper rings and bangles, were used as a medium of exchange.[26] One type of object not recovered at the site, but nearby, was the copper ingot. In 1967, a man removing a tree stump on the adjacent Dedza escarpment, not far from Mankhamba, found a hoard of eight, large H-shaped ingots[27] (see Plate 12.1). This shows that despite their absence in the Mankhamba excavations, these objects circulated in the area. Their absence in the excavation was value-related as ingots were expensive objects and unlikely to be disposed of carelessly. In contrast, rings, bangles, necklaces and other objects were readily available to the general population.

The value of copper depended on the principle of supply and demand, in relation to location. Freeman-Grenville[28] indicated that objects like bracelets were used as a medium of exchange for small expenses in much of southern and eastern Africa. According to Waller,[29] however, a journal entry made by Livingstone on 1 May 1871 indicated that two rings of copper were enough to buy an elephant tusk among the Bisa of Zambia. That does not sound like a small expense. The person who hoarded the ingots and never came back for them lost a great fortune.

The recovery of a copper vessel at Mankhamba was totally unexpected. The fact that only one was recovered suggests that copper vessels were rare. It is not clear what this type of vessel was used for, but many ethnologists and museum collectors in Africa observed that copper objects were used largely for ceremonial and ornamental purposes.[30] It is possible that the Mankhamba specimen was used in some ceremonial

---

25 Ellert 1986: 119.
26 Freeman-Grenville GSP. 1962. *The East African Coast*. Oxford: Clarendon Press: 165; Waller 1970: 120; Bisson MS. 1975. Copper Currency in Central Africa: The archaeological evidence. *World Archaeology*. 6: 280.
27 Cole-King 1973: 48.
28 Freeman-Grenville 1962: 165.
29 Waller 1970.
30 Bisson, 1975: 279

activity. The abundance of copper and total absence of gold objects at Mankhamba makes the argument acceptable that Africans viewed copper as being more valuable than gold.

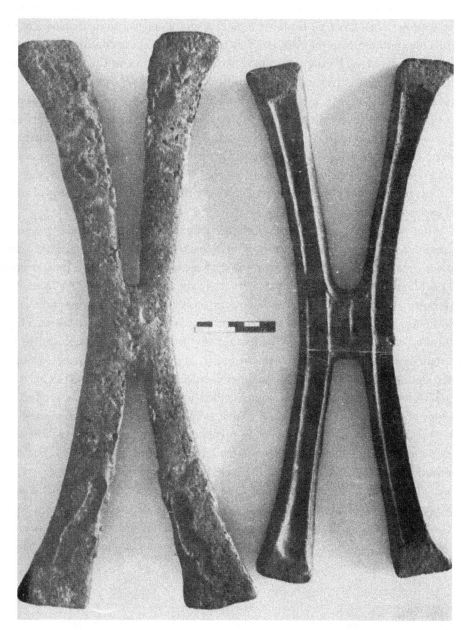

Plate 12.1: Copper ingots. Part of a hoard of eight similar ingots dug up at Chombe village, in Dedza district.
Source: Adapted from Cole-King 1973.

What were these foreign products bartered for at Mankhamba? Malawi, unlike southern Zambezia, did not have gold, copper or silver in commercially exploitable quantities. With respect to silver, however, an exception might be made even though the extent of its exploitation by the people of Mankhamba is far from clear. Apparently, silver deposits existed not far from Mankhamba, and it appears some members of the Portuguese community in the Zambezi Valley had heard of these deposits. In 1678, the captain or leader of the Portuguese called João de Sousa Freire sent Theodósio Garcia to the land of Kalonga to investigate exploitability of these silver deposits.[31] Garcia and the Kalonga of the time were said to have been friends. However, when he arrived at Mankhamba, Kalonga would not allow him to see the mines. Instead, he sent his men and two of Garcia's slaves, who brought back some silver that they had mined and smelted. Garcia took back a sample, but no further action was taken, probably because Sousa Freire died two days after Garcia's return.[32] It is also possible, however, that the silver was of low quality and that is probably why there are no other records of silver exploration in the area.

Iron implements and cotton cloth are often mentioned in the Portuguese documents as major trade commodities of the Maravi. It seems that once the Portuguese began to establish plantations in the interior, the need for iron implements became great and the Maravi became important suppliers. They are said to have exported 'from their lands every quality of agricultural and domestic tools'.[33] Hoes were the most popular of the iron implements. In fact, hoes made by the Maravi were reputed to be of such high quality and were so much liked by the Portuguese that other ethnic groups such as the Yao sometimes attempted to pass their hoes off as Maravi hoes.[34] The same was true of cotton cloth. This might initially sound dubious since one of the commodities Africans bought from the foreign traders was cloth. But the Maravi were known for the production of a type of cloth called *machila*. It was coarse, tough and less expensive than the cloth that came from India. In fact, many people preferred it to imported cloth.[35] *Machila* is a Portuguese word for 'litter' and this is what gave the cloth its name. It refers to a hammock-like structure fitted with shafts held by bearers to carry passengers to their chosen destination. Unlike a hammock, a litter could be fitted with curtains on the sides and a cover on top to provide privacy and a shade. The Portuguese became a ready market for the *machila* cloth. They liked its durability and it became their choice cloth for litters.[36] Cloth made by the Maravi was also highly sought after by other African

31 Axelson E. 1960. *Portuguese in South-East Africa: 1600–1700*. Johannesburg: Witwatersrand University Press.
32 Ibid: 153–154.
33 Alpers 1975: 26.
34 Ibid.
35 Livingstone & Livingstone 1866: 123.
36 Alpers 1975: 25.

people of the interior. It was one of the commodities with which traders from Katanga exchanged their copper.[37] The Chewa adopted the name and today call a hammock *machila*.

Three other commodities not as well documented as iron implements and cloth were animal skins, beeswax and salt. Trade in animal skins should not surprise anyone in view of the intense hunting that went on at Mankhamba. People carried them along with ivory to Tete or to the coast. Wax may also have been sold at this early period. Oral traditions recorded by the Malawi Department of Antiquities are clear about wax as a trade commodity.[38] Johnston[39] also listed wax as a commodity that newly established trading companies bought from the indigenous people.

Salt from the southern Lake Malawi area was traded more in the interior than at the coast. It was at one time such an important commodity that it was described as 'a staple of regional trade and…a source of capitalization for international trade'.[40] According to Abdallah,[41] salt had been a trade item for a longer time than ivory or slaves. The salt made by the Maravi was described as being so good that it competed very well with the salt available at the coast. Nineteenth-century Europeans who used it felt that it was comparable to good table salt used in England.[42] Other ethnic groups in the region, such as the Bisa and the Yao from western Zambia and northern Mozambique respectively, often came to the southern Lake Malawi area to buy it.[43] None of these commodities, however, compare with ivory in importance and value. The Maravi were fortunate in that elephants were readily available in the area. The Luangwa Valley, Kasungu, the Lower Shire Valley and the southern Lake Malawi area itself teemed with elephants. Further, if nineteenth-century lakeshore trading practices are anything to go by, the people of Mankhamba must have obtained additional ivory by acting as middlemen between traders of the interior and those from the coast. The people from Katanga whom Livingstone met in the southern Lake Malawi area in 1859 also carried ivory which was to be sold in the area.[44] In view of the large quantity of manufacture residue and the many ivory bangles recovered at Mankhamba, it is very likely that the Maravi exported both raw ivory and manufactured ivory products.

---

37 Livingstone & Livingstone 1866: 410.
38 Malawi Department of Antiquities oral traditions collection. 1973–1974. Malawi Department of Antiquities, Lilongwe. (Unpublished).
39 Johnston 1969: 182.
40 Alpers 1975: 20.
41 Abdallah 1973: 28.
42 Rowley H. 1969. *The story of the universities' mission to Central Africa; from its commencement under Bishop Mackenzie, to its withdrawal from the Zambesi.* New York: Negro Universities Press: 179.
43 Abdallah, 1973: 27–28; Alpers, 1975: 26.
44 Livingstone & Livingstone 1866: 410.

The Maravi state

Early seventeenth-century Portuguese settlers and traders made it clear that there was a large and powerful political entity in one part of northern Zambezia. They referred to it as the 'empire of Maravi', which was 'governed by its emperor named "Caronga"'.[45] They distinguished that political entity from other smaller political entities in the area such as the one ruled by Rundo (Lundu), whom they referred to as 'the second person in the empire of Maravi'.[46] What this demonstrated was that successive Kalongas had, in a period of about two centuries, succeeded in gaining political and economic control of a large area of the eastern part of southern Africa.

Whereas the Portuguese records are clear about the existence of the Maravi state, late twentieth-century scholars disagreed on whether or not the original Maravi state had existed as a single entity under one Kalonga or if there had been more than one state each with its own Kalonga. It was an interesting debate and the three disputants were Alpers,[47] Newitt[48] and Schoffeleers.[49] The fact that the Portuguese never used the term 'Maravi' until the early seventeenth century added some confusion to the debate, with Newitt[50] declaring that a Maravi state or states did not pre-date the seventeenth century.

According to Alpers,[51] there were two rival Maravi states—a northern and a southern state—by the sixteenth century. The northern state ran from the southern Lake Malawi area to the central Shire and Mwanza/Neno area. It was ruled by a Kalonga, and by the early seventeenth century an individual called Muzura was the Kalonga. The southern state stretched from the Lower Shire Valley to the Zambezi Valley and was ruled by Lundu. Schoffeleers,[52] on the other hand, believed that there were during that time not two, but three Maravi states and three Kalongas. He agreed with Alpers regarding the geographical location of Lundu's state, but he split Kalonga's state into two. One state started from the central Shire River area and extended westwards to include the Mwanza-Neno area. This, according to Schoffeleers, was the state ruled by Muzura. The third state, ruled by an unnamed Kalonga, was the one based at Mankhamba. It included the southern Lake Malawi and Upper Shire Valley areas (see Map 12.1).

Newitt[53] was the only one of the three who believed that there had never been a Maravi state or states before the seventeenth century and that, therefore, there never had been a king with the title Kalonga in the area north of the Zambezi before that date. He

---

45   Barretto 1964: 480.
46   Ibid.
47   Alpers 1975.
48   Newitt 1982.
49   Schoffeleers 1987.
50   Newitt 1982: 159.
51   Alpers 1975: 48.
52   Schoffeleers 1987: 338.
53   Newitt 1982: 156–158.

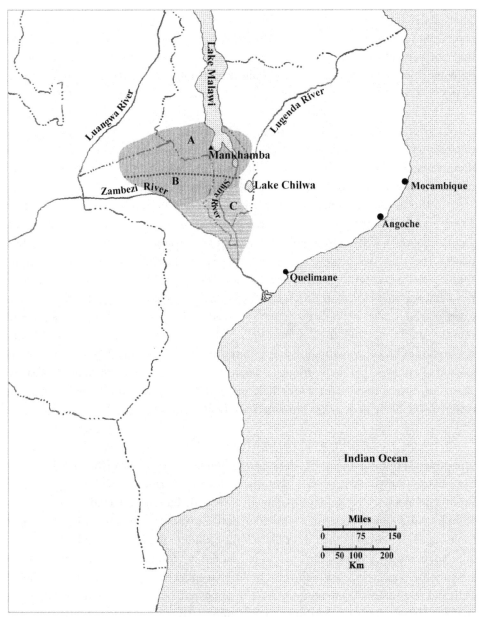

Map 12.1: Maravi states before the seventeenth century. According to Alpers,[54] there were only two Maravi states. A & B was one state ruled by Kalonga at Mankhamba. C was the other state ruled by Lundu. According to Schoffeleers,[55] there were three states—A, B and C—for Kalonga at Mankhamba, Muzura and Lundu respectively.

Source: Adapted from Alpers, 1975; Schoffeleers 1987

---

54 Alpers 1975.
55 Schoffeleers 1987.

believed that the Maravi state was established only in the first two or three decades of the seventeenth century. He cited sixteenth-century Portuguese sources which had stated that northern Zambezia experienced the arrival of several migratory groups under different chiefs. This caused social and political disruptions as well as trade interference in the area. By the early seventeenth century, the chiefs had joined together to form a kind of loose political entity of Maravi chieftaincies. He cited the example of the chieftaincies of Lundu and Undi, which were first mentioned by the Portuguese early in that century.[56] The title Kalonga, however, was never mentioned until 1661.[57] With such disagreements among the three scholars, it was clear that agreeing on an acceptable date for the establishment of the Maravi state was not going to happen.

Until relevant settlement sites are discovered and excavated in the Lower Shire Valley and the Mwanza-Neno area, to complement what we know about Mankhamba and the Chewa, it will not be possible for archaeology to contribute meaningfully to this debate. The issue does, however, raise a very important question: Why did the sixteenth-century Portuguese write about Lundu and not Kalonga and Mankhamba? Archaeology has demonstrated that by the sixteenth century, Mankhamba was a rich and vibrant town located near one of only three unobstructed trade routes to the Indian Ocean and into the interior north of the Zambezi Valley. The routes were located at the south and north ends of Mulanje Mountain[58] and at the Shire River crossing in Mangochi town. As such, it is unlikely that the Portuguese would not have known about Mankhamba. So again, why were they silent about Kalonga and Mankhamba until the seventeenth century? The likely reasons are presented below.

Emperor Muzura and the Maravi empire

The presence of more than one Maravi state should not surprise anyone familiar with the oral traditions of the Chewa. I have already noted in Chapter 4 that, in the past, three prominent relatives of Kalonga — namely Kaphwiti, Lundu and Undi — broke away from him and established their own settlements. Lundu, who became more prominent than Kaphwiti, settled in the Lower Shire Valley, Undi in western Mozambique and the adjacent areas of Zambia. Kaphwiti and Lundu did not last long as a ruling duo. By the time the Portuguese arrived in the area in the sixteenth century, it was Lundu they dealt with and not Kaphwiti who seems to have disappeared. Lundu became the sole ruler of the area. His proximity to the all-important Zambezi River Valley trade route to southern Zambezia put him in a very enviable position. He ruled until 1622 when Muzura defeated him with the help of the Portuguese.[59] Muzura turned out to be the most

---

56   Ibid: 157.
57   Alpers 1975: 68; Newitt 1982: 157. See also Barretto 1964: 480.
58   Johnston 1969: 119.
59   Schoffeleers 1987: 345.

interesting Chewa personality of the first half of the seventeenth century. Newitt[60] cited an uncorroborated story by a Jesuit missionary, Father Antonio Gomes, who said that Muzura had been an escapee slave of some Portuguese settler, and that he eventually built up a following on the north bank of the Zambezi due to his good hunting skills and generosity to his followers. Schoffeleers,[61] citing the same Jesuit, said that Muzura was an employee of one Portuguese settler on the south bank of the Zambezi. He worked as a *capataz* (supervisor) and was a very energetic person and a good hunter, qualities that helped him build up a loyal following. In the end, he was able to unite several smaller chiefdoms or states into a large kingdom.[62] This background would have been difficult to believe had the Portuguese not dealt directly with Muzura after he escaped or left his employer. They dealt with him as someone with power and great authority. For instance, they recorded in 1608 that they sought his help in their fight against the rivals of Mwene Mutapa Gatsi Rusere in Zimbabwe. Muzura had the capacity to offer them 4000 warriors.[63] In 1616, the Portuguese traveller, Gaspar Bocarro, visited Muzura for two weeks at his headquarters called 'Marauy' (Bocarro's rendering of the word 'Malawi'). After examining some written sources, Rangeley,[64] who believed that Muzura was either Kaphwiti or Lundu, and Hamilton[65] concluded that 'Marauy' was probably located on the Wankurumadzi River in Mwanza district. Calling the place 'Malawi' was apparently in keeping with the traditions of the Chewa. According to Ntara,[66] Chewa leaders tended to call some of their newly established settlements 'Malawi', perhaps in order to not forget their Mankhamba origins.

The record shows that Muzura entertained Bocarro quite well.[67] Bocarro and Muzura exchanged gifts and among the gifts Bocarro gave Muzura were calico, beads and silk cloth. He also gave him his bed and sheets because 'it was a great encumbrance to carry such a large bed on the shoulders for such a long journey'.[68] Muzura in turn gave him two ivory tusks, food for the number of days he stayed at Marauy and a slave girl.[69]

In 1629, Muzura went into an alliance with Mwene Mutapa Kapararidze[70] who had succeeded Gatsi Rusere in Zimbabwe.[71] Their aim was to end Portuguese presence in Zambezia, but Muzura's attack on the port of Quelimane failed. Schoffeleers[72] says that

---

60 Newitt 1982: 159.
61 Schoffeleers 1987: 345.
62 Ibid.
63 Alpers 1975: 33.
64 Rangeley 1954.
65 Hamilton 1954.
66 Ntara 1973: 15.
67 Bocarro 1964: 416.
68 Ibid.
69 Ibid.
70 Schoffeleers 1987: 345.
71 Ibid.
72 Ibid: 346.

after failing to take the port, Muzura's power for the next quarter century was overshadowed by that of Kalonga at Mankhamba, which was apparently not the case. As demonstrated below, Muzura himself was the power at Mankhamba. He was so well-known to the Portuguese that had there been another personality in the area more powerful than he was, they would have recorded it. Instead, there is evidence that the Portuguese continued to revere Muzura. For instance, although they were now at peace with him, in 1635 the Portuguese described him as a king who was cunning and so powerful that he wanted to be called 'Emperor' like the Mwene Mutapa in Zimbabwe.[73] Muzura's desire was not surprising because, according to Alpers,[74] at the time he was more powerful than the Mwene Mutapa. Schoffeleers' views were based probably on the fact that from the mid-1630s until the end of that century, the area north of the Zambezi experienced no major wars,[75] a situation that allowed Muzura and the Maravi to prosper.

Under Muzura's leadership, trade continued to flourish,[76] generating a great deal of wealth for him and for the Maravi in general. In fact, the Maravi became so dominant and prosperous that they were the envy of other ethnic groups. One Portuguese individual commented in 1667 that as any local person 'is offended at being called a Bororo or Macua, so it is a great honour to be a Maravi'.[77] Muzura's kingdom extended from Nkhotakota to the Zambezi River in the south (see Map 12.2); and his influence eastwards to 'the Indian Ocean opposite Mozambique Island and south to Quelimane'.[78] Since much of that land had originally belonged to other rulers, the term 'empire' and the title 'Emperor' were appropriate.

Muzura conducted the affairs of state from Mankhamba, and there is some documentation to support that fact. This was in the form of a letter written in 1624 by one Jesuit missionary resident at Tete, called Luis Mariano. He referred to Lake Malawi as Lake Hemosura or Muzura's lake. He said Muzura's capital was called Maravi, and it was located about two miles from the lake.[79] Clearly, that capital was Mankhamba. After 1635, Portuguese traders who came to Mankhamba praised Muzura's hospitality. Some commented that the king wanted carpenters sent to him because he wanted better boats built for him for sailing on the lake.[80]

Perhaps the question is, how could the 1624 report by Mariano be reliable when in 1616 Muzura was at his town in the Mwanza-Neno area? Langworthy[81] believes that

73 Alpers 1975: 54.
74 Ibid: 68.
75 Newitt 1982: 161.
76 Ibid.
77 Barretto 1964: 480.
78 Langworthy 1969: 169.
79 Langworthy 1969: 169; Schoffeleers: 1972: 93.
80 Alpers EA. 1969. The Mutapa and Malawi political systems to the time of the Ngoni invasions. In *Aspects of Central African History*. TO Ranger (ed). London: Heinemann: 23.
81 Langworthy 1969: 169.

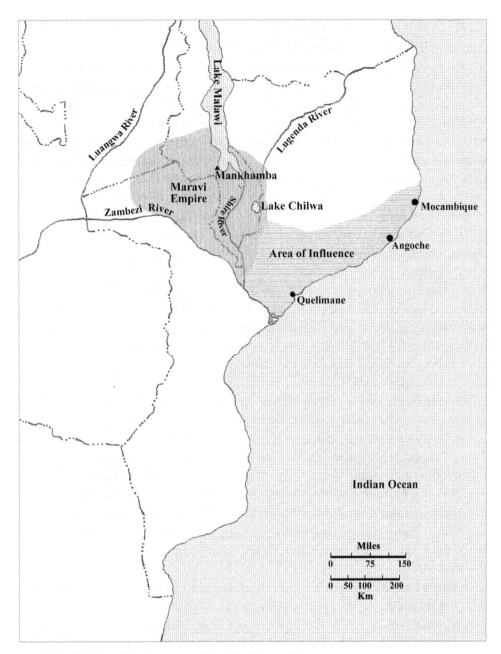

Map 12.2. The Maravi Empire as consolidated by Kalonga Muzura.
Source: Adapted from Alpers 1975

Muzura had simply returned to Mankhamba. Another scholar, Killick,[82] concluded that Muzura must have captured Mankhamba between 1616 and 1624 and deposed the Kalonga. That conclusion would, in the first instance, seem plausible in view of his military victory over Lundu during the same period. However, it is doubtful that such was the case because, first, the Portuguese were familiar with the area. A defeat of Kalonga at Mankhamba, particularly by someone as well known to them as Muzura, would have attracted their attention. Second, it is unlikely that after defeating Kalonga, Muzura would have chosen to occupy Mankhamba. For instance, there is no record that he occupied Lundu's headquarters after he defeated him in 1622. Moving to Kalonga's headquarters would probably have required a large military force to protect Muzura, as he would have been surrounded by an unfriendly people.

There is a simpler explanation for all this, and it is that the large size of the empire during the early seventeenth century made it necessary for Kalonga Muzura to operate from two centres. Mankhamba was simply too far away from the Zambezi River Valley trade route. The new centre cut the travel time to Tete in half.[83] It did not, however, diminish Mankhamba's status, which remained Muzura's seat of government where he was so powerful that at least some of the Portuguese who were familiar with the area and its politics felt that the lake might as well have been named after him.

So how did he find himself in the Zambezi Valley earlier on in his life? This had to do with his origins which, as we have noted earlier in this chapter, attracted some debate. It suffices to recall, however, that after Undi left Mankhamba, it became his responsibility to appoint Kalonga's successors. This means Muzura had been part of the royalty at Mano, Undi's headquarters, and not at Mankhamba. Mano was not far from the Zambezi Valley. Portuguese settlers and traders who used the Zambezi Valley trade route offered opportunities for gaining wealth through employment and trade. One can therefore speculate that Muzura went there to seek wealth. If successful, it would put him in a good position to influence Undi in his selection of the next Kalonga, and gain approval of Kalonga's counsellors at Mankhamba. The speculation ends there. What follows is not speculation, as the Portuguese, whom Newitt[84] and Schoffeleers[85] cited, recorded their observations.

Muzura could not have been a slave as stated by Newitt.[86] An escapee slave would hide and not go out hunting openly as Muzura did. If Schoffeleers[87] is correct, as *capataz*, Muzura must have been a leader or supervisor of an indigenous field work force on some Portuguese settler's plantation. It is not clear when exactly he became Kalonga, but

---

82   Killick 1990: 53.
83   Rangeley 1954: 19.
84   Newitt 1982.
85   Schoffeleers 1987.
86   Newitt 1982: 159.
87   Schoffeleers 1987: 345.

it had to have been before 1608, the year the Portuguese sought military support from him to fight against rivals of Mwene Mutapa Gatsi Rusere in Zimbabwe. Further, it is not possible to determine how long he ruled over the Maravi empire, but his name continued to appear in documents of the Portuguese until the late 1640s.[88] He had lived a very eventful long life.

The reason the scholarly debate was inconclusive is that it appeared to be based on the premise that long-distance trade was a critical factor in the establishment of the Maravi states. This may be true in relation to the state established by Lundu in the Lower Shire Valley in the sixteenth century. It does not apply to the original Maravi state, where control of land was central to its establishment. It will be recalled that Kalonga expanded his land area by allocating land to his relatives, a tradition that spread Chewa chiefs throughout much of central Malawi and the Upper Shire Valley. They became tributary chiefs who remitted to Kalonga part of the taxes and fees they collected from people and traders. The most important of the remittances was ivory.[89] The archaeological excavation at Mankhamba has amply proved that a great deal of ivory did indeed end up at Kalonga's capital. The growth of long-distance trade in the sixteenth and seventeenth centuries simply made an already existing Maravi state grow in wealth and size. Thus, contrary to Newitt's views, although the terms 'Maravi' and 'Kalonga' did not appear in the written documents of the Portuguese until the seventeenth century, this did not mean that the Maravi state never existed before that century. The Portuguese were describing a political entity that had been in place for a long time.

Finally, coming back to the question posed earlier, there are at least two reasons why the Portuguese mentioned Lundu earlier and more often than they mentioned Kalonga. The first is that before the rise of Muzura, the Lower Shire Valley and a section of the Zambezi River Valley were under Lundu's control. Commercially, this was a strategic area in view of the presence of trading stations of the Portuguese at Sena and Tete.[90] The Portuguese had frequent contacts with him. They bought ivory, *machila* cloth and other products from him.[91] Secondly, the Lower Shire Valley had plenty of water and fertile land. The words 'plenty of water' do not sound quite right considering that much of the Shire Valley floor has an annual rainfall of less than 820 millimetres.[92] However, the surrounding highlands represented by the Thyolo escarpment on the east and the Kirk Range on the west receive more rain than the Shire Valley. The result is that the valley floor, at an altitude of no more than 36 metres above sea level,[93] experiences annual flooding, the intensity of which is determined by the amount of rainfall on the

---

88   Alpers 1975: 68.
89   Schoffeleers 1987.
90   Ibid. 344.
91   Schoffeleers 1987.
92   Lineham 1972: 33.
93   Stobbs & Young 1972: 40.

highlands. While the floods do destroy crops, they provide sufficient moisture to facilitate both dryland and wetland cultivation in the flood plains or marshes, locally called *dambos*.[94] Wetland farming provided sufficient food to militate against the impact of drought. This has been the agricultural practice of the people of the Shire Valley for centuries.[95] In short, therefore, the Lower Shire Valley was always agriculturally productive all year round.

When inadequate rain in the Zambezi Valley led to crop scarcity, Portuguese settlers looked to the Shire Valley where food was always available.[96] Power to control food distribution made Lundu a ruler with whom the Portuguese needed to be on good terms and so they mentioned him at times when they wrote home. In contrast, Mankhamba-based rulers did not have regular contact with the Portuguese because the most important commodity at Mankhamba was ivory. Portuguese buyers of ivory rarely came to Mankhamba, often waiting for the local people to bring the ivory to them at Tete, a town with which the Chewa traded the most,[97] or at the coast.

Summary

Imported objects such as glass beads, cowrie shells and objects made of bronze began to appear in southern Zambezia before AD 900, but later in northern Zambezia where Mankhamba is located. Long-distance trade never became a prominent activity in the southern Lake Malawi area before the Chewa came to Mankhamba. Once they established themselves at that site, they began to import glass beads, ceramics, cowrie shells and metal, largely copper objects. They exchanged these for ivory, iron implements, cotton cloth, animal skins, salt and beeswax.

Not all scholars agreed with a date before the seventeenth century for the existence of indigenous states in the Malawi part of northern Zambezia. Newitt was one such scholar who believed that the Maravi state did not exist before the seventeenth century. Three scholars including Newitt himself debated that issue. The two others were Alpers, who believed there had been two Maravi states, and Schoffeleers, who said there were three states. The debate was apparently inconclusive because the scholars used the premise that long-distance trade played a role in the formation of the Maravi state(s). Perhaps that was true of later states such as the one Lundu established in the Lower Shire Valley in the sixteenth century. It was not true of Kalonga's state at Mankhamba, in which control of land was central to its establishment.

By the early seventeenth century, the Portuguese noted that there was a big empire in northern Zambezia ruled by an emperor, and a small political entity ruled by Rundo

---

94   Mandala 2005: 5.
95   Schoffeleers 1987: 344.
96   Ibid.
97   Langworthy 1969: 173.

(Lundu), whom they described as the number two person in the territory. That emperor was Muzura. He had worked for the Portuguese in the Zambezi River Valley for a while, and had been a hunter before he became Kalonga at Mankhamba. He conducted trade from a second settlement he had established in the Mwanza-Neno area. Trade made him powerful both economically and militarily. In 1622, he defeated Lundu with the help of the Portuguese, which made him the undisputed Kalonga of the Maravi Empire. His empire extended from Nkhotakota in the north to the Zambezi Valley, and his influence reached the Indian Ocean coastal area. Muzura remained in power until his death some time in the 1640s.

CHAPTER 13

The demise of the Maravi empire

The decline and fragmentation of the Maravi empire began in the eighteenth century,[1] reaching an irreversible point by the turn of the nineteenth century. Some of the reasons for this included the peculiar system of succession of Maravi kings,[2] conflict between them and some of their territorial chiefs, and the rise of the Yao as formidable long-distance traders.[3] The Maravi system of succession created conditions for instability in the absence of strong leadership.[4] As discussed in Chapter 4, the Maravi operated a decentralised political system. Because children could not succeed their father as Kalonga, they came up with an unusual way of choosing successors. They had to be members of the Phiri clan and descendants of Nyangu, Kalonga's sister or mother. This worked well until Undi and Nyangu's unilateral departure from Mankhamba. Since Nyangu was with Undi, it was his responsibility to nominate one of Nyangu's sons to succeed Kalonga. The nominee was, however, subject to the approval of Kalonga's counsellors at Mankhamba who were of the Banda clan, and he had to marry Mwali, also of the Banda clan. She would be his principal wife and therefore a powerful woman. Simply stated, the succession system gave the Banda clan the upper hand and the Phiri clan little or no say in issues pertaining to Kalonga's successor.[5] With time, the system isolated and weakened the Kalonga, who often had no dependable relations locally.

Sometime during the eighteenth century, perhaps due to the growing influence of the Banda clan, the requirement that Undi nominate Kalonga's successors was no longer enforced[6] which meant that counsellors of the Banda clan at Mankhamba assumed that responsibility. On the surface, it seemed sensible to appoint successors locally. After all, that was how they did it before Undi and Nyangu left. However, times had changed, and this time it did not work smoothly. Oral traditions recorded by Ntara[7] show that the system of succession had become open to all forms of manipulation and abuse by various powerful counsellors. Disturbances began to occur, as people who were not Phiris, such as Mchepera who was of the Mwale clan, began to aspire to become Kalonga.[8] For instance, Kampini, who preceded Sosola, the last Kalonga, was of the

---

1   Langworthy 1973: 133.
2   Langworthy 1973.
3   Alpers 1975.
4   Langworthy 1973.
5   Ibid: 133.
6   Ibid.
7   Ntara 1973.
8   Ntara 1973: 132; Langworthy 1973: 134.

Mbewe clan.[9] In addition to succession problems, Kalonga's success depended on the cooperation of his many territorial chiefs. It was through them that he managed the political and economic affairs of the state. Territorial chiefs were the leaders on the ground who controlled the masses. They remitted to Kalonga his portion of all taxes and fees they collected from traders, hunters and others. The territorial chiefs in turn expected fair treatment from Kalonga and his senior officials. This, however, was not what some of them received. For instance, although territorial chiefs remitted to Kalonga his ivory entitlement, he did not permit some of them to sell their portion of the ivory directly to foreign merchants.[10] In 1696, Portuguese merchants who could not get enough of this commodity complained that Kalonga and a select group of his territorial chiefs monopolised the ivory trade.[11] The affected territorial chiefs were as dissatisfied as the Portuguese merchants were. Controlling many dissatisfied territorial chiefs in such an over-extended empire was a difficult task.

Thus, throughout the eighteenth century, a growing state of instability characterised the political situation in the Maravi empire.[12] As territorial chiefs became increasingly independent, Kalonga's grip on power and trade became weak. Other ethnic groups were quick to notice that weakness and they took advantage of it. The best known of those ethnic groups were the Yao in northern Mozambique who developed their own trade routes in the region.[13] They became so successful that, by the 1740s, Portuguese merchants along the Indian Ocean coast recognised them as major traders[14] and some foreign merchants encouraged them to trade in slaves as well.[15] As discussed below, this trade involved slave raids and this had tragic consequences for the Chewa.

The archaeological evidence for the decline of the Maravi at Mankhamba is reflected in the paucity of Nkudzi pottery. This late eighteenth- to early nineteenth-century pottery was common at other sites in the southern Lake Malawi area, except at Mankhamba. Its decline there would not have meant much had Mankhamba not been the capital of the Maravi. In this case it did, because it shows that the pottery went into disuse at the site soon after its introduction, an indication that Kalonga and his people abandoned Mankhamba at about that time. Archaeological evidence shows that the site has remained unoccupied ever since.

Abandoning one's capital is a difficult decision for any leader, but Kalonga had no choice. The situation in which he found himself was the result of years of political instability. Ntara confirmed this when he stated, 'all the men who succeeded to the

---

9   Ntara 1973: 136.
10   Alpers 1975.
11   Ibid: 58.
12   Langworthy 1973.
13   Alpers 1975.
14   Ibid: 64.
15   Abdallah 1973: 30.

Kalonga House used to seize the chieftainship'.[16] In other words, they resorted to arms instead of following established succession procedures. There was a rapid turnover of Kalongas: Ntara[17] listed at least seven Kalongas, all of whom reigned probably from the late eighteenth to the first half of the nineteenth century. This shows that it was 'a violent period of near anarchy and very short reigns'.[18]

The slave trade, the Yao, the Maseko Ngoni and the British

Three groups of people, the Yao, the Maseko Ngoni and the British arrived in the southern Lake Malawi area after the Maravi had abandoned Mankhamba. Their arrival had an impact on local political dynamics. The Yao were already familiar with the Maravi, as their home in northern Mozambique was not far from the southern Lake Malawi area. Besides, they both participated in long-distance trade and it appears there was some economic cooperation between them.[19] In addition, Bleek[20] noted that they intermarried regularly. Although the Yao began to settle in the area peacefully probably from the 1820s,[21] the bulk of them came later as slave raiders and traders.

The Maseko Ngoni were one of the Ngoni groups that fled political upheavals in South Africa early in the nineteenth century, having left after Shaka's victory on the Mhlatuze River.[22] For a while, they settled at Domwe[23] in Mozambique, an area adjacent to Ntcheu and Dedza districts of Malawi. Around 1837, they abandoned Domwe and came down to the southern Lake Malawi area. They crossed the Shire River and proceeded north, a trip that took them to Songea in Tanzania.[24] A little over two decades later, they returned and settled again at Domwe[25] and some of them, led by Kachindamoto, settled later in the Mtakataka-Mua area.[26]

The British were the last group to arrive. They were encouraged by David Livingstone and the earliest of them made an unsuccessful attempt to settle in southern Malawi beginning from the early 1860s.[27] Success for them came later.

Of the three groups, the Yao had a lasting negative impact on the Chewa. They were efficient slave raiders and the only villages available to them were those of the Chewa and the Nyanja. They raided as far south as the Shire Highlands.[28] Their raids

---

16   Ntara 1973: 132.
17   Ibid: 131.
18   Langworthy 1973: 133.
19   Gamitto 1960; Livingstone & Livingstone 1866.
20   Bleek WHJ. 1856. *The languages of Mosambique.* London.
21   Gamitto 1960: 65; Cole-King 1982: 3
22   Omer-Cooper 1969: 57.
23   Pachai 1974: 37.
24   Ibid: 39; Omer-Cooper, 1969: 73.
25   Pachai, 1972b; 1974.
26   Pachai 1974.
27   Rowley 1969; White L.1990. *Magomero: Portrait of an African Village.* Cambridge: Cambridge University Press.
28   Rowley 1969; White 1990.

were successful many times because they attacked the Chewa with a single-minded purpose, often using guns.[29] They sold the slaves to Arab or Swahili traders.[30] Interestingly, some Chewa chiefs were quick to realise that the Yao made good profits from trading in slaves. They became slave raiders too, causing great harm to their own people.[31] Some of the foreign traders exacerbated the situation. Instead of waiting for slave caravans to come to their coastal trading centres, they went inland and dealt directly and indiscriminately with both territorial and lesser chiefs. As a result, some lesser chiefs became rich at the expense of territorial chiefs.[32] As they became economically empowered, the lesser chiefs began to feel politically independent.

The Ngoni also had the habit of raiding the Chewa, but their objectives were different from those of the Yao. Although they too were involved in some small-scale slave trading,[33] they attacked the Chewa mainly for food, to gain subjects,[34] and 'to fulfill the national pastime of warfare'.[35] The result was increased tension and instability in many villages. Eventually, the Chewa became a collection of mostly weakened independent villages that were often hostile to one another and militarily disorganised,[36] making it difficult for them to unite and resist external raids.[37]

Kalonga Sosola Kalimakudzulu

As stated earlier, the last Kalonga was Sosola Kalimakudzulu, commonly remembered as Sosola. Oral traditions about the life of this man, recorded sometime during the second half of the nineteenth century, came from first- or second-generation descendants of his contemporaries. Therefore, checking their reliability was probably easy. One such source was Che Stephen Mohammed, already mentioned in Chapter 6. He was at least 80 years old in the 1950s when he provided Rangeley with information about the Nkhudzi Bay burial site. He claimed he had a direct connection with Changamire and Sosola.[38] According to these sources, Sosola was the son of Nankumba, a Chewa chief of the Banda clan whose village was in the southern Lake Malawi area. His mother was referred to as Nyangu,[39] making him a person of royal heritage. This did not, however, entitle him to succeed Kalonga who at the time was a man called Kampini.[40] Even if he had been the heir apparent, political instability had done away with peaceful succession

---

29   Juwayeyi 1972–1973: 2.
30   Langworthy 1973: 144.
31   Langworthy 1973.
32   Ibid.
33   Omer-Cooper 1969: 84.
34   Langworthy 1973; Omer-Cooper 1969: 84.
35   Langworthy 1973: 145.
36   Pachai 1974: 37.
37   Langworthy 1973: 144.
38   Inskeep 1965: 1.
39   Langworthy 1973: 138.
40   Ntara 1973; Langworthy 1973.

by then. Individuals could now become Kalonga by any available means. With respect to Sosola, those means included his personality and shrewdness.[41] Sosola was the only member of the ruling clan who was quick to realise that unless the Chewa stopped the Yao from raiding their villages for slaves, there was a great likelihood that they would eventually overthrow the Kalonga and take over whatever was left of the Maravi state.

Perhaps it was the fear of that likely eventuality that led him to usurp the Kalongaship at the time he did. He moved quickly, convincing four chiefs jointly to attack and remove Kalonga Kampini from his position. These chiefs included the man who in the meantime had succeeded Sosola's father as chief, Nankumba. The other three were Yao chiefs: Mnanula, who later changed his name to Pemba, Liwewe and Ndindi.[42] The ostensible reason was that Kampini 'was not from the royal house of the Phiri. He was a Mbewe'.[43] The real reason, however, was that Sosola wanted to become Kalonga so he could deal with the Ngoni and the Yao from a position of strength. He believed that as Kalonga, the Yao and the Ngoni were likely to respect him and give him some attention. Langworthy[44] described Sosola as a warrior who also believed in using diplomacy to achieve his goals. In the end, he had mixed results. The attack was successful and he became Kalonga. However, even though he succeeded in usurping the position, those very 'friends' who had helped him eventually cut short his term of office.[45]

Sosola's efforts to contain the Yao and the Maseko Ngoni

Sosola's coming to power gave him no comfort as long as the militarily strong group of Mnanula and his fellow Yao chiefs were in the area and continued to raid Chewa villages with impunity. The Yao were a greater threat to his authority than the Ngoni because they meant to stay in the area. He knew he did not have the military capacity to expel them and so he resorted to what Langworthy referred to as 'diplomatic efforts'.[46] Just as he had convinced Mnanula and his fellow Yao chiefs to help him become Kalonga, he hoped to convince the Ngoni to help him chase the Yao from his area. At the time, the Ngoni were further south, either in Mulanje[47] or Matope at the Shire River.[48] Turning to them was easy for Sosola because he had dealt with them in the 1830s,[49] but the exact nature of the dealings remains vague. One story says that Sosola was the one who helped them cross the Shire River some time during that decade[50] when they were on the journey that took them to Songea.

41 Langworthy 1973: 138.
42 Ntara, 1973: 135.
43 Ntara 1973: 136.
44 Langworthy 1973: 138.
45 Ibid.
46 Langworthy 1973: 139.
47 Ntara 1973: 135; Langworthy 1973: 139.
48 Werner 1969: 181.
49 Pachai 1974: 37; Langworthy 1973: 139.
50 Langworthy 1973: 139.

In order to lure the Ngoni into following him, Sosola used cattle dung as his 'diplomatic tool'. He knew that the Ngoni loved and valued cattle greatly. As a patrilocal people, they preferred cattle to any other type of wealth in making bride-wealth payments. Sosola, therefore, showed the Ngoni a basket containing cattle dung and assured them that he would take them to a land ideal for raising cattle.[51] Apparently, the Ngoni were not impressed and refused to help him. According to Langworthy,[52] it seems that at about the same time, if not a little earlier, Sosola had turned to the Yao group led by Kawinga. He used the same 'diplomatic tool', but the Yao were interested in slaves and not cattle and so they did not help him.

The story about cattle dung sounds frivolous, but it has survived well in the oral traditions of the Chewa. With respect to the Ngoni, the only problem is that there is some disagreement regarding the place where Sosola showed them the dung. Ntara[53] and Langworthy,[54] citing Rangeley's sources, said it was somewhere in Mulanje. However, Werner,[55] who must have heard this story before 1906 when she first published it, and when some of the characters in the event may still have been alive, said it was at the Shire River at Matope. Apparently, the Ngoni had stopped there on their way from Songea. From Matope, they went back to Domwe.[56] Still not discouraged, Sosola approached another Yao group led by Msamala and his son Mponda.[57] Finally, he was successful. This group seems to have accepted Sosola's cry for help with no preconditions. There is no indication for instance that Sosola had tried to impress them with cattle dung. Msamala and Mponda fought the Yao group led by Mnanula and defeated them. They fled from the area and went north, settling around the mouth of the Linthipe River.[58] To Sosola's dismay, however, Msamala and Mponda did not leave him alone. They chose to stay in the area and began to mount slave raids on the Chewa. The devastation of Chewa villages was so severe that Sosola abandoned the Mangochi area. He went and settled near Mankhamba, which was within easy reach of Mnanula's settlement.[59]

With such close proximity, however, conflicts were likely to occur. One documented conflict reported by Ntara,[60] which started over the ownership of a bed, led to a war that resulted in Sosola's death. Information reached Sosola that Mnanula had made a bed on

---

51 Ntara 1973: 135; Werner 1969: 281; Langworthy 1973: 139.
52 Langworthy 1973: 139.
53 Ntara 1973: 135.
54 Langworthy 1973: 139.
55 Werner 1969: 281.
56 Pachai 1972b: 181
57 Langworthy 1973: 140.
58 Langworthy 1973.
59 Ibid: 140.
60 Ntara 1973: 137.

which he slept. This annoyed Sosola, who was of the view that Mnanula should have sent the bed to him as a tribute. He called for a meeting with the Yao chiefs to remind them that he was the Kalonga, that they occupied his land at his pleasure, and that he could take it back from them. The Yao apologised and promised to send the bed to him. When it arrived, however, Sosola's joy turned into rage when he noticed that the bed had been deliberately broken into pieces. Mnanula must have broken it deliberately as a challenge to Sosola. In the war that ensued, Mnanula himself shot and killed Sosola, capturing many slaves and taking the land. In Sosola's defeat, an ecstatic Mnanula changed his name to Pemba.[61] The bed story as narrated by Ntara sounds silly, but it helps to demonstrate the animosity that existed between the Chewa and the Yao in the area. The Chewa wanted the Yao simply to leave their land and go elsewhere, whereas the Yao wanted to stay because it was a lucrative area in terms of the slave trade. Regarding the death of Sosola, Ntara[62] observed that it marked the end of the house of Kalonga. In other words, this was how Kalonga and the Maravi state became extinct.

The Sosola-Mnanula (Pemba) war took place probably towards the end of the 1860s.[63] About a dozen years later, Robert Laws met Pemba. He described him as being 'tall, strongly built with a determined expression of countenance, who would not be likely to scruple about committing a cruel action to accomplish his ends'.[64] It is not clear if Laws was aware of the bed story and the killing of Sosola, but his description and impressions of Pemba put the episode involving the breaking of the bed in a better perspective. It is evident that Sosola grossly underestimated Pemba's military strength and capacity for cruelty.

The British, end of the slave trade and the disempowerment of indigenous chiefs

With the Ngoni gone and Sosola dead, the Yao were now in control and unchallenged in the southern Lake Malawi area for at least two decades. Although their slave raids took them to as far south as the Shire Highlands,[65] Chewa villages in the southern Lake Malawi area remained the most affected. This was because the Yao completely dominated the area.

When the British established their authority in the country a little over two decades after Sosola's death, they quickly noticed the devastation the slave trade had inflicted on the Chewa and the Nyanja. They therefore devoted a considerable number of resources to its eradication. Harry Johnston, the first commissioner and consul general, brought in a military force consisting of 71 Indian soldiers commanded by Captain Cecil

---

61 Ntara 1973: 138.
62 Ibid.
63 Langworthy 1973.
64 Laws 1879: 320.
65 Rowley 1969; White 1990.

Maguire.[66] He then proceeded to build three fortified centres in the southern Lake Malawi area staffed by the soldiers.[67] The goal was to fight the Yao slave raiders and to prevent slave caravans from travelling to the coast.

They built the first of the three forts on the west bank of the Shire River where the bridge across the Shire in Mangochi town is located. They named it Fort Johnston[68] which also became the name of the town and the district until after the country became independent, when the new government changed it to Mangochi. The soldiers stationed at Fort Johnston made it difficult or impossible for slave caravans to cross the Shire River. The second fort was located in Chief Makanjila's area at a spot opposite Salima where the main body of the lake is narrowest. They named it after Maguire who in the meantime had been killed in a war between the British and Makanjila.[69] Besides involving themselves in direct fights with slave raiders, the soldiers at Fort Maguire made it difficult for slave caravans to cross the lake from Salima. The British built the third fort on Mangochi Hill, an advantageous and concealed position with a good view of the surrounding land below,[70] which they called Fort Mangochi. During daytime, the soldiers could easily locate movements of slave caravans on the open land below.

By the turn of the twentieth century, the British had stopped the slave trade in Malawi. Peace and tranquility prevailed in the land. It was also a politically new landscape in which the authority of the Chewa had already broken down. No Chewa chief or leader of any other ethnic group had any real political power. Instead, the chiefs presided over the affairs of their respective people but under the overall authority of the colonial government, which until 1964 was run by British administrators. After Malawi became independent in that year, Malawians replaced British district administrators. The nature of the relationship between the central government and the chiefs remained unchanged.

Summary

Some of the reasons for the demise of the Maravi state were the peculiar system of succession of Maravi kings, the presence of some dissatisfied territorial chiefs and the rise of the Yao in long-distance trade. By the end of the eighteenth or the beginning of the nineteenth century, the authority of the Kalongas had declined to such an extent that the Maravi abandoned Mankhamba. The paucity of Nkudzi pottery at the site confirms the abandonment. What was left of the Maravi state became prone to Yao slave raids and to the raids of the recently arrived Ngoni, who raided the Chewa for food and subjects rather than slaves.

---

66   Kalinga & Crosby 2001: 222.
67   Johnston 1969; Cole-King 1982.
68   Johnston 1969: 100.
69   Cole-King 1982; Kalinga & Crosby 2001: 222.
70   Cole-King 1982.

The last Kalonga called Sosola Kalimakudzulu came to power in the midst of this instability. His 'diplomatic' efforts to get rid of both the Yao and the Ngoni from his land by pitting one against the other failed. In the fighting that ensued between him and Mnanula, a Yao chief, Mnanula killed Sosola which marked the demise of the Maravi state. About two decades after Sosola's death, the British established their authority in the country and made it their goal to end the slave trade. They concentrated their efforts on fighting the Yao. By the turn of the twentieth century, the British had stopped the slave trade. They took control of the country with the local chiefs operating under their authority.

CHAPTER 14

Conclusion

The early history of the Chewa is only a small part of the larger history of Malawi, which scholars must continue to investigate. The few published works that exist, such as those of Pachai[1] and McCracken,[2] are relatively incomplete, since they did not address specific ethnic groups in any detail. Moreover, their treatment of events before the colonial period was limited. The major topics they dealt with were the country's experiences with the slave trade, the arrival of immigrants such as the Yao, Ngoni and the British, and the colonial and postcolonial history. The authors had access to written records.

However, Malawi's history before the second half of the nineteenth century is part of the country's prehistory. Because there are no comprehensive written records for this period, writing this history requires information from oral traditions, ethnography and, most importantly, archaeology. Weaving the data from the three sources into one coherent account requires careful analysis, particularly of oral traditions. Sometimes informants of oral traditions narrated information that promoted their personal or ethnic interests and, in the process, altered or modified the traditions. Further, one cannot be entirely certain that recorders of oral traditions did not have their own interests too. Still, archaeologists whose research interests cover the last several centuries of the second millennium cannot afford to ignore oral traditions and ethnographic data. Equally important to the interpretation of the history is the physical environment. People made settlement choices based on the type of resources that the physical environment was likely to provide.

The Chewa-Luba connection

Oral traditions are clear regarding the home of origin of the Chewa. They came from Luba, located in the Shaba or Katanga area of the DRC. Evidence from ethnography, linguistics and archaeology also shows that there is a high probability that the Chewa came from there. The ethnographic evidence includes certain cultural practices of the Chewa that are traceable to the people of Luba, two of which stand out. The first is the use of masks by the Nyau secret society in Malawi. Apparently, the Bumbudye secret society of Luba make and use masks in some of their rituals.[3] In Malawi, only the Chewa in central Malawi and their breakaway relatives, the Mang'anja in the Lower Shire Valley,

---

1 Pachai 1972; 1974.
2 McCracken 2013.
3 Phiri 1977: 3.

use them. The second cultural practice is the use of the term 'Mwali,' which the Chewa adopted as the perpetual titular name for the principal wife of Kalonga. This term exists in Luba too.[4] Linguistics has also provided additional evidence linking the Chewa to Luba. From their Bantu homeland, Western Bantu speakers settled in the DRC/Angola border area, eventually spreading into central Africa and reaching Luba.[5] Scholars of Bantu languages have demonstrated that Chichewa is a Western Bantu language.[6] Even though this on its own may not be enough to conclude that the Chewa originated in Luba, it at least establishes the fact that the Chewa and the people of Luba have a common ancestry in relation to language.

Archaeology has provided more evidence. Unlike oral traditions and linguistics, archaeology has the distinct advantage of relying largely on material remains for various types of information. In studying the Iron Age, pottery is the most relied on of all material remains and archaeologists frequently use it to trace people to their area of origin. One example is that of the makers of Kwale and Nkope pottery traditions. Archaeologists traced both to the Great Lakes Region of East Africa and concluded that the Early Iron Age people who introduced those pottery traditions to southern Africa came from there.

There is some compelling pottery evidence that links the Chewa to Luba, which has to do with Naviundu pottery. Western Bantu speakers made Naviundu pottery and it was not part of the Chifumbaze complex.[7] Archaeologists found it at Naviundu near Lubumbashi in Katanga and at a site near Kinshasa.[8] Huffman[9] demonstrated that Naviundu pottery is related to Gundu pottery, which was found in southern Zambia, and to Luangwa pottery in eastern Zambia. Luangwa pottery has some affinity with Mawudzu pottery[10] which was recovered at Mankhamba and elsewhere in central and southern Malawi. It is not surprising that there is some relationship between Luangwa and Mawudzu pottery because central Malawi and eastern Zambia are one geographical and cultural region. British colonialists arbitrarily split it when they established a border between the two countries.

Thus, the archaeological evidence links Mawudzu pottery to Luangwa pottery which has links to Luba. In short, Luba is the place where evidence from oral traditions, ethnography, linguistics and archaeology appears to come together. Therefore, in the absence of any other data to the contrary, we must conclude that, indeed, the Chewa originated in the Luba area of the DRC.

---

4   Linden 1972: 15; Phiri 1977: 3.
5   Phillipson 1977 b.
6   Vansina 1984.
7   Huffman 1989.
8   Anciaux de Faveaux & De Maret 1984; De Maret 1985: 138.
9   Huffman 1989.
10 Phillipson 1976: 17.

Migrations

Oral traditions and archaeology have shed some light on the migrations of the Chewa from Luba to central Malawi. To recap the evidence from oral traditions, it was noted that the Chewa had clans and that the Banda and the Phiri (also referred to as the pre-Maravi and the Maravi respectively) were bigger and more influential than the other clans. Historians and other scholars believe that the pre-Maravi were the first to move out of Luba and that the Maravi followed later.[11] Mangadzi, a priestess whose title was Makewana, was the leader of the pre-Maravi. She led her people to Kaphirintiwa-Msinja and one of her responsibilities was to call rain. Societies characterised by rituals that involve calling rain tend to claim, among other things, to be the owners of the land.[12] The distribution of Luangwa pottery in eastern Zambia, and of Mawudzu pottery in central Malawi, contradicts oral traditions that suggest the pre-Maravi entered Malawi from a northerly direction.[13] The archaeology shows that from Luba they moved in a southeasterly direction and entered Malawi through eastern Zambia. They eventually arrived at Kaphirintiwa-Msinja, along the border of Malawi and Mozambique, located their primary rain-calling shrine there, and thus made it Makewana's centre of power. The site also housed *mbiriwiri*, the drum that the Chewa claim to have forcibly acquired from the Akafula. They still have the drum, which is venerated and kept in a shrine at Msinja.

The Maravi and their king, whose title was Kalonga, probably took the same route as the pre-Maravi. Events during their migration proved that they were expansionist invaders. When they arrived at Kaphirintiwa-Msinja, for instance, they attempted unsuccessfully to overthrow Makewana by force.[14] Invasions, though, need not necessarily be hostile or violent. They can be non-violent but still lead to the displacement or domination of original inhabitants. Later expansion of the Maravi appears to have been non-violent.

When their attempt to overthrow Makewana failed, Kalonga and the Maravi adapted to the ritual beliefs of the pre-Maravi, leading to Makewana and Kalonga recognising each other's societal responsibilities. Thus, all the Chewa recognised Makewana as their perpetual ritual leader and Kalonga as their perpetual secular leader. Such an arrangement ensured the success and prosperity of all the Chewa.

Although the dual leadership arrangement highlighted Makewana's ritual authority, it masked the fact that all along secular authority had been inherent in her role as a priestess. She had been a chiefly figure.[15] From her Kaphirintiwa-Msinja headquarters, she had the right to appoint 'spirit wives' to be in charge of major satellite

---

11 Langworthy 1969; Schoffeleers 1973; Phiri 1975.
12 Hamilton 1955.
13 Phiri 1977.
14 Ntara 1973; Schoffeleers 1973, 1992.
15 Schoffeleers 1979: 151.

shrines, such as Chirenje shrine near Nkhoma Mission. They in turn appointed 'spirit wives' at secondary shrines. It appears that the appointees also had inherent secular authority.[16] As such, the dual leadership arrangement was not exactly in Makewana's favour, as it rendered her secular authority dormant or even non-existent while at the same time it increased Kalonga's authority. Therefore, despite failing to dislodge Makewana at Kaphirintiwa, the arrangement gave Kalonga the upper hand and he did not hesitate to demonstrate it. For instance, he embarked on an expansion of his territory even before he arrived at Mankhamba. He needed to do this because the Maravi had been a 'state in exile' with no land that had clear boundaries. Kalonga began a policy of sending his relatives to establish new settlements in distant places. They became territorial chiefs and their distribution marked the boundary of the Maravi state, making Kalonga a powerful leader.

The Maravi empire

The Portuguese of the early seventeenth century had no qualms about acknowledging the existence of the Maravi state. They called it an empire owing to its size, military strength and perhaps to the charisma of Kalonga Muzura, its ruler. Luis Mariano, a Jesuit missionary resident at Tete, was the first Portuguese national who in 1624 let others know that the capital of the Maravi empire was located about three kilometres from the shores of Lake Malawi.[17] Long-distance trade was responsible for the growth of the Maravi state into an empire, beginning from the sixteenth century. The growth was gradual at first, which was probably why the Portuguese did not acknowledge its existence until the early seventeenth century. The other reason for their lack of acknowledgement was possibly due to Mankhamba's relative isolation in relation to the Zambezi River Valley trade route to southern Zambezia. The Portuguese and other foreign merchants plied this route more than they ventured into northern Zambezia. They wanted gold more than any other commodity and it was available only in southern Zambezia.

The major commodities at Mankhamba on the other hand were ivory, iron implements and probably cotton cloth. The problem Kalonga and the people of Mankhamba faced in trading in those commodities was that they had some competition. Lundu and his people in the Lower Shire Valley also traded in the same kinds of commodities and more. They sold food, too, to Portuguese settlers in the Zambezi Valley whenever drought hit them. Lundu and his people could do this because the environment of the Lower Shire Valley afforded them opportunities to engage in both dry- and wetland farming.[18] Therefore, the Portuguese had no need to venture as far north as Mankhamba. Instead, Kalonga and his people took their commodities to

---

16   Schoffeleers 1979.
17   Langworthy 1969: 169; Schoffeleers 1972: 93.
18   Mandala 2005.

Portuguese trading centres such as Tete. Thus, Lundu in relation to Kalonga was in a geographically and economically advantageous position.

It worked well for Lundu as long as the Kalongas at Mankhamba remained content with the status quo. The situation changed for him, however, when Kalonga Muzura ascended the throne. He was Undi's appointee who became Kalonga at Mankhamba. Unlike previous Kalongas, Muzura had lived and worked in the Zambezi Valley, eventually giving up his job to become a hunter. This gave him access to ivory and opportunities to trade with the Portuguese and other foreigners. It was probably the experience he gained when he worked there that made him appreciate how disadvantaged Mankhamba was in terms of trade. When he became Kalonga, he did two important things. First, he established a trading centre somewhere in the Mwanza-Neno area[19] in order to be near the Zambezi Valley trade route. Second, he engineered the defeat and overthrow of Lundu in 1622 with the help of the Portuguese.[20] With this military victory, Muzura became the undisputed ruler of two combined states of the Maravi, giving him tremendous political and economic power. The land under his control extended from central Malawi to the Zambezi Valley and his influence reached the Indian Ocean coastal area.[21] Such a big area gave credence to the claim made by the Portuguese that Muzura was the Emperor of the empire of the Maravi.[22] Empires rise and fall, though, and this one was no exception. It began to decline in the eighteenth century and changing trade dynamics was one of the reasons for this. Archaeological evidence shows that by the end of that century or the beginning of the nineteenth century, Kalonga and his people had abandoned Mankhamba and this marked the end of the Maravi empire.

The way forward

Archaeology may never provide enough data to enable scholars to make realistic conclusions regarding the nature and size of the Maravi empire. Currently, all that exists are the accounts of the early Portuguese and analyses of these accounts by individuals such as Alpers,[23] Newitt[24] and Schoffeleers.[25] The site of Mankhamba is the only excavated site directly linked to the Maravi. Therefore, the way forward should be more archaeological research. There is a need to locate and excavate sites at known Chewa settlements such as Kaphirintiwa-Msinja, Mawere a Nyangu and other settlements, as well as Mawudzu sites in Lilongwe, Dedza and Ntcheu districts. Further, Lundu's ancient headquarters in the Lower Shire Valley and the town that Muzura built in the Mwanza-

---

19 Rangeley 1954; Hamilton 1954.
20 Schoffeleers 1987.
21 Alpers 1975.
22 Barretto 1964: 480.
23 Alpers 1975.
24 Newitt 1982.
25 Schoffeleers 1987.

Neno area must be located and excavated. This will enable archaeologists to make meaningful conclusions regarding the nature and extent of the Maravi Empire.

Archaeologists must also investigate the archaeology of other ethnic groups in Malawi. This research should begin with those who settled in Malawi many centuries ago, such as the Tumbuka. This will eventually lead to the writing of a comprehensive history of Malawi.

Summary

Ethnography, linguistics and archaeology point to Luba as the place of origin of the Chewa. This evidence is in agreement with their oral traditions. The ethnographic evidence is about the use of masks in traditional rituals, used by both the Chewa and the Bumbudye of Luba. Linguistically, the Chewa and the people of Luba are Western Bantu speakers. The archaeological evidence is also compelling. Archaeologists recovered Naviundu pottery at a site by that name near Lubumbashi in the Luba area. It bears some relationship with Gundu pottery in southern Zambia and Luangwa pottery in eastern Zambia, which in turn has some affinity with Mawudzu pottery in Malawi. The Chewa were responsible for introducing this pottery in the country.

The pre-Maravi and their leader, Makewana, left Luba before the Maravi and their king, Kalonga, left. Although recognised as a priestess, Makewana's role had inherent secular authority: she was a chiefly figure. The archaeological evidence represented by Luangwa and Mawudzu pottery shows that the pre-Maravi moved in a south-easterly direction through eastern Zambia and established their centre at Kaphirintiwa-Msinja in central Malawi. Conflict between them and the Maravi when they arrived later was resolved by recognising each other's societal responsibilities. Makewana became the perpetual ritual leader and Kalonga the perpetual secular leader within a Maravi state. Eventually, Makewana's inherent secular authority became dormant.

Intensification of long-distance trade in the sixteenth and seventeenth centuries made the Maravi state prosper and grow into what the Portuguese referred to as the Maravi empire. The decline of the empire started in the eighteenth century, leading to its extinction by the end of that century or the early nineteenth century.

References

Harvard — University of Cape Town formatting by CitationMachine.net.

Abdallah YB. 1973. *The Yaos*. London: Frank Cass.

Achebe C. 1994. *Things Fall Apart*. New York: Anchor Books.

Agnew S. 1972a. Environment and history: the Malawian setting. In *The Early History of Malawi*. B. Pachai (ed). London: Longman: 28–48.

Agnew S. 1972b. Fishing. In *Malawi in Maps*. S Agnew & M Stubbs (eds). London: University of London Press: 94–95.

Alpers EA. 1969. The Mutapa and Malawi political systems to the time of the Ngoni invasions. In *Aspects of Central African history*. TO Ranger (ed). London: Heinemann: 1–28.

Alpers EA. 1973. Introduction to second edition. In *The Yaos*. Abdallah YB. London: Frank Cass: vii–xvi.

Alpers EA. 1975. *Ivory & Slaves in East-Central Africa*. London: Heinemann.

Amanze J. 2002. *African Traditional Religion in Malawi: the case of the Bimbi Cult*. Blantyre, Malawi: Christian Literature Association in Malawi.

Amblard S. 1996. Agricultural evidence and its interpretation on the Dhars Tichitt and Oualata, south-eastern Mauritania. In *Aspects of African Archaeology: Papers from the 10th Congress of the Pan-African Association for Prehistory and Related Studies*. G Pwiti & R Soper (eds). Harare: University of Zimbabwe Publications: 421–427.

Anati, E. 1986. Malawi cultural heritage with reference to rock art sites: evaluation of rock art and training of specialists. A report to UNESCO and to the Government of Malawi (unpublished).

Anciaux de Faveaux E & De Maret P. 1984. Premières datations pour la fonte du cuivre au Shaba (Zaire). *Bulletin de la Société Royale Belge d' Anthropologie et de Préhistoire*. 95: 5–21.

Arazi N 2017. Case study: heritage management in central Africa. In *Field Manual for African Archaeology*. AL Smith, E Cornelissen, OP Gosselain & S MacEachern (eds). Tervuren: Royal Museum for Central Africa: 37–41.

Arkell AJ. 1936. Cambay and the bead trade. *Antiquity* 10:292–305.

Axelson E. 1969. *Portuguese in South-East Africa: 1600–1700*. Johannesburg: Witwatersrand University Press.

Axelson E. 1973. *Portuguese in South-East Africa: 1488–1600*. Johannesburg: Struik.

Badenhorst S, Mitchell P & Driver JC (eds). 2008. *Animals and People: Archaeozoological Papers in Honour of Ina Plug*. Oxford: Archaeopress.

Baker CA. 1972. Administration: 1891–6 districts and government stations. In *Malawi in Maps*. S Agnew & M. Stubbs (eds). London: University of London Press: 44–45.

Barham L & Mitchell P. 2008. *The First Africans: African Archaeology from the Earliest Toolmakers to Most Recent Foragers*. Cambridge: Cambridge University Press.

Barham L & Jarman CL. 2005. New radiocarbon dates for the Early Iron Age in the Luangwa Valley, eastern Zambia. 'Azania' *Journal of the British Institute of Historical and Archaeology in East Africa*. 40(1): 114–121.

Barretto M. 1964. Report upon the State and Conquest of the Rivers of Cuama. In *Records of south-eastern Africa*. Vol. 3. GM Theal (ed). Cape Town: Struik: 463–495.

Bisson MS. 1975. Copper currency in central Africa: The archaeological evidence. *World Archaeology*. 6: 276–292.

Bleek WHJ. 1856. *The Languages of Mozambique*. London.

Blench R. 2012. Two Vanished African Maritime Traditions and a Parallel from South America. *African Archaeological Review*. 29: 273–292.

Bocarro A. 1964. Of the performance of the Portuguese in east Africa. In *Records of South-Eastern Africa*. Vol. 3. GM Theal (ed). Cape Town: Struik: 342–435.

Bostoen K. 2007. Pots, words and the Bantu problem: on lexical reconstruction and early African history. *The Journal of African History*. 48 (2):173–199.

Bostoen K. 2017. Historical Linguistics. In *Field Manual for African Archaeology*. AL Smith, E Cornelissen, OP Gosselain & S MacEachern (eds). Tervuren: Royal Museum for Central Africa: 257–260.

Bosquet D. 2017. From the field to the lab. In *Field Manual for African Archaeology*. AL Smith, E Cornelissen, OP Gosselain & S MacEachern (eds). Tervuren: Royal Museum for Central Africa: 152–156.

Brain CK 1974. Some suggested procedures in the analysis of bone accumulations from southern African Quaternary sites. *Annals of the Transvaal Museum*. 29:1–8.

Branch B. 1988. *Field guide to snakes and other reptiles of southern Africa*. Cape Town: Struik.

Bray W & Trump D. 1982. *The Penguin dictionary of archaeology*. Harmondsworth, England: Penguin Books.

Bruwer J. 1950. Note on Maravi origin and migration. *African Studies*. 9 (1):32–34.

Buchanan J. 1982. *The Shirè Highlands*. Blantyre, Malawi: Blantyre Printing and Publishing Co.

Burrett R. 2007. The Garonga ceramic assemblage. *Southern African Humanities*. 19: 153–166.

Burton RF. 1969. *The Lands of Cazembe: Lacerda's journey to Cazembe in 1798*. New York: Negro University Press.

Casalis E. 1861. *The Basutos*. London: James Nisbet.

Caton-Thompson G. 1931. *The Zimbabwe culture: ruins and reactions*. Oxford: Clarendon Press.

Chafulumira W. 1948. *Mbiri ya Amang'anja*. Zomba, Malawi: Nyasaland Education Department.

Chipeta MOJ. 1986. Labour in Colonial Malawi: A Study of the Malawian Working Class c.1890-1961. PhD thesis. Dalhousie University.

Chiphangwi SD. 1971-1972. The development of African participation in the Blantyre Mission. History seminar paper. Chancellor College, University of Malawi.

Chirikure S. 2014. Land and Sea Links: 1500 Years of Connectivity between Southern Africa and the Indian Ocean rim regions, AD 700 to 1700. *African Archaeological Review*. 31:705–724.

Chirwa WC. 1998. Democracy, ethnicity and regionalism: the Malawian experience, 1992–1996. In *Democratization in Malawi: A Stocktaking*. KM Phiri & KR Ross (eds). Blantyre, Malawi: CLAIM: 52–69.

Chittick HN. 1974. *Kilwa: an Islamic trading city on the East African coast*. Nairobi: British Institute in Eastern Africa.

Clark JD. 1956. Prehistory in Nyasaland. *The Nyasaland Journal*. 9: 92–119.

Clark JD. 1968. *Malawi antiquities programme*. Paris: UNESCO.

Clark, JD, Haynes CV, Mawby JE & Gautier A. 1970. Interim report on palaeoanthropological investigations in the Lake Malawi Rift. *Quaternaria*. 13: 305–354.

Clark JD & Haynes CV. 1970. An elephant butchery site at Mwanganda's Village, Karonga, Malawi, and its relevance for Palaeolithic archaeology. *World Archaeology*. 1(3): 390–411.

Clark JD. 1973. Archaeological investigations of a painted rock shelter at Mwana wa Chencherere, north of Dedza, central Malawi. *The Society of Malawi Journal*. 26:28–46.

Clist B. 1989. Archaeology in Gabon, 1886–1988. *African Archaeological Review*. 7:59–95.

Clist B. 1992. Interim report of the Oveng archaeological site 1991 excavations, Estuaire Province, Gabon. *Nsi*, 10/11: 28–35.

Cole-King PA. 1973. *Kukumba mbiri mu Malaŵi: a summary of archaeological research to March 1973*. (Department of Antiquities publication no 15). Zomba, Malawi: Government Press.

Cole-King PA. 1982. *Mangochi: the mountain, the people and the fort*. (Department of Antiquities publication no 12). Zomba, Malawi: Government Press.

Colson E & Gluckman M. 1951. *Seven tribes of British Central Africa*. London: Oxford University Press.

Connah G. 2009. *African Civilizations: An Archaeological Perspective*. Cambridge: Cambridge University Press.

Cooke CK. 1963. Report on excavations at Pomongwe and Tshangula Caves, Matopo Hills, Southern Rhodesia. *The South African Archaeological Bulletin*. 18:73–151.

Crader D. 1984a. *Hunters in Iron Age Malawi: the zooarchaeology of Chencherere rock shelter*. (Department of Antiquities publication no 21). Limbe, Malawi: Montfort Press.

Crader DC. 1984b. Faunal Remains from Chencherere II Rock Shelter, Malawi. *The South African Archaeological Bulletin*. 39:37–52.

Dalby D. 1975. The prehistorical implications of Guthrie's Comparative Bantu Part 1: problems of internal relationship. *The Journal of African History*.16: 481–501.

Daly P. 1969. Approaches to faunal analysis in archaeology. *American Antiquity*. 34 (2): 146–153.

Davison S. 1991. Namaso: a newly-defined cultural entity of the late first millennium AD, and its place in the Iron Age sequence of southern Malawi. *Azania: Archaeological Research in Africa*. 26:13–62.

Davison S. 1992. Namaso: a newly-discovered ceramic entity of the late first millennium AD, on the south-east arm of Lake Malawi. In *Occasional Papers of the Malawi Department of Antiquities* 1: 67–150.

De Couto, D. 1964. Asia: of the deeds which the Portuguese performed in the conquest and discovery of the lands and seas of the east. In *Records of South-Eastern Africa*, Vol. 6. GM Theal (ed). Cape Town: Struik. 357–410.

De Maret P. 1985. Recent archaeological research and dates from central Africa. *The Journal of African History*. 26: 129–148.

De Maret P. 2017. Radiocarbon dating. In *Field Manual for African Archaeology*. AL Smith, E Cornelissen, OP Gosselain & S MacEachern (eds). Tervuren: Royal Museum for Central Africa: 232–235.

Denbow J. & Campbell AC. 1980. National Museum of Botswana: archaeological research programme. *Nyame Akuma* November: 3–9.

Doke CW. 1931. *The Lambas of Northern Rhodesia: a study of their customs and beliefs.* London: George G. Harrap.

Dos Santos J. 1964. Eastern Ethiopia. In *Records of South-Eastern Africa*. Vol. 7. GM Theal (ed). Cape Town: Struik: 183–370.

Dos Santos JR Jnr & Ervedosa CMN. 1970. A estação arqueológica de Benfica (Luanda-Angola). *Ciencias Biologicas* (Luanda). 1 (1): 31–51.

Douglas M. 1968. The Lele of the Kalahari. In *African Worlds*. D Forde (ed). Oxford: Oxford University Press.

Drope J, Makoka D, Lencucha, R & Appau A. 2016. *Farm-level economics of tobacco production in Malawi*. Centre for Agricultural Research and Development (CARD). Lilongwe, Malawi: 1–54.

Dunnell RC. 1992. The notion site. In S*pace, time and archaeological landscapes.* J Rossignol & L Wandsnider (eds). New York: Plenum Press: 21–41.

Ebert JI. 1992. *Distributional Archaeology*. Albuquerque: University of New Mexico Press.

Eggert M. 1996. Pots, farming and analogy: early ceramics in the equatorial rainforest. In *The Growth of Farming Communities in Africa from the Equator Southward*. JEG Sutton (ed). Nairobi: The British Institute in Eastern Africa: 332–338.

Ehret C. 1982. Linguistic inferences about early Bantu history. In *The Archaeological and Linguistic Reconstruction of African History*. C Ehret & M Posnansky (eds). Berkeley, University of California Press: 57–65.

Ehret C. 2002. *The Civilizations of Africa: A History to 1800*. Charlottesville: University Press of Virginia.

Ellert H. 1986. *The Material Culture of Zimbabwe*. Harare: Longman.

Fagan BM. 1967. *Iron Age Cultures in Zambia*, Vol 1. London: Chatto & Windus.

Fagan BM. 2001. *People of the Earth: An Introduction to World Prehistory*. Prentice Hall: Upper Saddle River, New Jersey.

Feder KL. 2008. *Linking to the past: A Brief Introduction to Archaeology*. New York: Oxford University Press.

First impressions of African character. 1896. *The Central African planter*. 1 (8).

Fishes in Lake Malawi. nd. http://www.est.ryukoku.ac.jp/est/yuhma/FLM-pamph/ (accessed 21 October 2017).

Food and Agriculture Organisation (FAOa). nd. Tobacco in Malawi. http://www.fao.org/docrep/006/y4997e/y4997e0i.htm (accessed 30 November 2017).

Food and Agriculture Organisation (FAOb). 2005. Livestock sector brief. http://www.fao.org/ag/againfo/resources/en/publications/sector_briefs/lsb_MWI.pdf (accessed 2 December 2017).

Frank B. 1964. Der hund als opfertier und kulturheros in Afrika. In *Festschrift für Ad. E. Jensen*. E Haberland, MA Schuster & H Straube (eds). Munich: Klaus Renner Verlag: 135–153.

Freeman-Grenville GSP. 1962. *The East African Coast. Select documents from the first to the earlier nineteenth century*. Oxford: Clarendon Press.

Fuller C. 1923. Tsetse in the Transvaal and Surrounding Territories: An Historical Review. *Entomology Memoirs*. 1 (1): Department of Agriculture, Union of South Africa. Pretoria.

Gamitto ACP. 1960. *King Kazembe: being the diary of the Portuguese expedition to that potentate in the years 1831 and 1832*. Translated by I. Cunningson. Lisbon: Junta de Investigações do Ultramar.

Garlake PS. 1968. The value of imported ceramics in the dating and interpretation of the Rhodesian Iron Age. *The Journal of African History*. 9: 13–33.

Gelfand M, Mavi S, Drummond RB & Ndemera B. 1985. *The Traditional Medical Practitioner in Zimbabwe*. Gweru, Zimbabwe: Mambo Press.

Gérard I. 2017. Introduction to chapter 7. In *Field Manual for African Archaeology*. AL Smith, E Cornelissen, OP Gosselain & S. MacEachern (eds). Tervuren: Royal Museum for Central Africa. 302–303.

Gifford-Gonzalez D. 2000. Animal disease challenges to the emergence of pastoralism in sub-Saharan Africa. *African Archaeological Review*. 17:95–139. DOI: 10.1093/oxfordhb/9780199686476.013.27.

Gibb HAR. 1962. *The Travels of Ibn Battuta AD 1325–1354*. Vol II. Cambridge.

Gomani EM. 1999. Dinosaurs of the cretaceous sedimentary rocks of northern Malawi, Africa. PhD thesis. Southern Methodist University.

Gondwe N, Marcotty T, Vanwambeke SO, De Pus, C, Mulumba, M & Van den Bossche P. 2009. Distribution and density of tsetse flies (Glossinidae: Diptera) at the game/people/livestock interface of the Nkhotakota game reserve human sleeping sickness focus in Malawi. *EcoHealth*. 6 (2): 260–265. DOI: 10.1007/s10393-009-0252-y.

Greenberg JH. 1966. *The Languages of Africa*. Bloomington: Indiana University.

Grootes PM, Stuiver M, Farwell GW, Schaad TP & Schmidt FH. 1980. Enrichment of 14C and Sample Preparation for Beta and Ion Counting. *Radiocarbon*. 22 (02): 487–500.

Guthrie M 1967. *The Classification of the Bantu Languages*. London: International African Institute.

Hall M. 1977. Shakan pitfall traps: hunting technique in the Zulu kingdom. *Annals of the Natal Museum*. 23 (1): 1–12.

Hamilton RA. 1954. The route of Gasper Bocarro from Tete to Kilwa in 1616. *The Nyasaland Journal.* 7 (2): 7–14.

Hamilton RA. 1955. Oral tradition: central Africa. In *History and Archaeology in Africa.* RA Hamilton (ed). London: School of Oriental and African Studies. 19–23.

Harmand S, Lewis JE, Feibel CS, Lepre CJ, Prat S, Lenoble A, Boës X, Quinn RL et al. 2015. 3.3-million-year-old stone tools from Lomekwi 3, West Turkana, Kenya. *Nature.* 521: 310–315.

Haviland WE. 1955. The rise of the African tobacco industry in Nyasaland and its production problems. *South African Journal of Economics.* 23 (2): 141–152.

Hayes GD. nd. *A Guide to Malawi's National Parks and Game Reserves.* Limbe, Malawi: Montfort Press.

Herbert EW. 1984. *Red Gold of Africa: Copper in Precolonial History and Culture.* Madison: University of Wisconsin Press.

Huffman TN. 1971. A guide to the Iron Age of Mashonaland. *Occasional Papers of the National Museums of Rhodesia: Elizabeth Goodall 1891–1971 commemorative issue.* A4(1):20-44.

Huffman TN. 1982. Archaeology and ethnohistory of the African Iron Age. *Annual Review of Anthropology.* 11: 133–150.

Huffman TN. 1989. *Iron Age Migrations. The Ceramic Sequence in Southern Zambia: Excavation at Gundu and Ndonde.* Johannesburg: Witwatersrand University Press.

Huffman TN. 1994. Toteng pottery and the origins of Bambata. *Southern African Field Archaeology.* 3: 3–9.

Huffman TN. 1998. Presidential address: the antiquity of lobola. *The South African Archaeological Bulletin.* 53 (168): 57–62.

Huffman TN. 2005. The stylistic origin of Bambata and the spread of mixed farming in southern Africa. *Southern African Humanities.* 17: 57–79.

Huffman TN. 2007. *Handbook to the Iron Age: The Archaeology of Pre-colonial Farming Societies in Southern Africa.* Scottsville: University of KwaZulu-Natal Press.

Inskeep RR. 1965. *Preliminary investigation of a proto-historic cemetery at Nkudzi Bay, Malawi.* Livingstone, Zambia: The National Museums of Zambia.

Jackson JG. 1972. Vegetation. In *Malawi in Maps.* S Agnew & M Stubbs (eds). London: University of London Press: 38–39.

Jacobs L. 1993. *Quest for the African Dinosaurs; Ancient Roots of the Modern World.* New York: Villard Books.

Johnston H.H. 1969. *British Central Africa.* New York: Negro Universities Press.

Juwayeyi YM. 1972-1973. The Yao chieftainship of Nkanda, its origins and growth to 1914. History seminar paper. Chancellor College, University of Malawi.

Juwayeyi YM. 1981. The later prehistory of southern Malawi: a contribution to the study of technology and economy during the Later Stone Age and Iron Age periods. PhD thesis. University of California, Berkeley.

Juwayeyi YM. 1991. Late Iron Age burial practices in the Southern Lake Malawi Area. *The South African Archaeological Bulletin.* 46: 25–33.

Juwayeyi YM & Betzler C. 1995. Archaeology of the Malawi Rift: the search continues for Early Stone Age occurrences in the Chiwondo Beds, northern Malawi. *Journal of Human Evolution*. 28: 115–116.

Juwayeyi YM. 1997. Secrecy and Creativity: The Use of rockshelters by the Nyau Secret Society in Malawi. In *The human use of caves*. C Bonsall & C Tolan-Smith (eds). Oxford: Archaeopress: 185–192.

Juwayeyi YM. 2008. Human and animal interaction on the Shire highlands, Malawi: the evidence from Malowa rockshelter. In *Animals and People: Archaeozoological Papers in Honour of Ina Plug*. S Badenhorst, P Mitchell & JC Driver (eds). Oxford: Archaeopress: 83–93.

Juwayeyi YM. 2010a. Archaeological excavations at Mankhamba, Malawi: An early settlement site of the Maravi. *Azania: Archaeological Research in Africa*. 45 (2): 175–202.

Juwayeyi YM. 2010b. Culture heritage conservation programs in Malawi and public responses. In *Heritage 2010: Heritage and Sustainable Development*. R Amoeda, S Lira & C Pinheiro (eds). Barcelos, Portugal: Green Lines Institute: 133–139.

Juwayeyi YM. 2011a. Chewa migrations and the establishment of the Maravi State: a chronological perspective. *The Society of Malawi Journal*. 64 (3): 48–56.

Juwayeyi YM. 2011b. Excavating the History of Archaeology in Malawi. In *Comparative Archaeologies: A Sociological View of the Science of the Past*. L Lozny (ed). New York: Springer.

Kalinga OJM. 1974. The Ngonde kingdom of northern Malawi c.1600–1895. PhD thesis. University of London.

Kalinga OJM & Crosby CA. 2001. *Historical Dictionary of* Malawi. Lanham, MD: The Scarecrow Press.

Kalusa WT. 2010. *Kalonga Gawa Undi X: a biography of an African chief and nationalist*. Lusaka, Zambia: The Lembani Trust.

Karklins K. 1990. Analysis of the beads from a Late Iron Age site on Lake Malawi, Malawi. (Unpublished).

Kaufulu ZM. 1983. The geological context of some early archaeological sites in Kenya, Malawi and Tanzania: microstratigraphy, site formation and interpretation. PhD thesis. University of California, Berkeley.

Kaufulu ZM. & Stern N. 1987. The first stone artefacts to be found *in situ* within the Plio-Pleistocene Chiwondo Beds in northern Malawi. *Journal of Human Evolution*. 16: 729–740.

Kenyatta J. 1965. *Facing Mount Kenya: the tribal life of the Gikuyu*. New York: Vintage Books.

Killick D. 1987. European trade beads in southern Africa. *The Bead Forum, Newsletter of the Society of Bead Researchers*. 10: 3–9.

Killick DJ. 1990. Technology in its social setting: bloomery iron smelting at Kasungu, Malawi, 1860–1940. PhD thesis. Yale University.

Kirk J & Foskett R. 1965. *The Zambesi journal and letters of Dr. John Kirk, 1858–63*. London: Oliver & Boyd.

Kishindo PJ. 1994. The impact of a national language on minority languages. *Journal of Contemporary African Studies*. 12(2): 127–150.

Klapwijk M. 1974. A preliminary report on pottery from the north-eastern Transvaal, South Africa. *The South African Archaeological Bulletin.* 29 (113/114): 19–23.

Klapwijk M. & Huffman TN. 1996. Excavations at Silver Leaves: a final report. *The South African Archaeological Bulletin.* 51: 84–93.

Kottak CP. 2015. *Cultural Anthropology: Appreciating Cultural Diversity.* New York: McGraw Hill.

Kungoni Centre. 2012–2016. Kungoni Centre of Culture and Art, Mua Mission, Malawi. http://kungoni.org/page1.html (accessed 22 December 2018).

Lane PJ. 2017. Archaeological field survey and the recording and cataloguing of archaeological materials. In *Field Manual for African Archaeology.* AL Smith, E Cornelissen, OP Gosselain & S MacEachern (eds). Tervuren: Royal Museum for Central Africa. 79–83.

Langworthy HW. 1969. A history of Undi's kingdom to 1890: aspects of Chewa history in east central Africa. PhD thesis. Boston University.

Langworthy H. 1973. Introduction and chapter comments. In *The History of the Chewa (Mbiri ya Achewa).* SJ Ntara. Translated by WS Kamphandira Jere. Wiesbaden: Franz Steiner Verlag GMBH. ix–xvii.

Lavachery P. 2001. The Holocene Archaeological Sequence of Shum Laka Rock Shelter (Grassfields, Western Cameroon). *African Archaeological Review.* 18(4): 213–247.

Laws R. 1879. Journey along part of the western side of Lake Nyassa, in 1878. *Proceedings of the Royal Geographical Society and Monthly Record of Geography.* 1(5): 305–324.

Leakey MD, Owen WE & Leakey LSB. 1948. *Dimple-based Pottery from Central Kavirondo, Kenya Colony.* Nairobi.

Lee RB. 1980. *The !Kung San: Men, Women and Work in a Foraging Society.* Cambridge: Cambridge University Press.

Lee RB. 2003. The hunters: scarce resources in the Kalahari. In *Conformity and Conflict: Readings in Cultural Anthropology.* J Spradley & DW McCurdy (eds). Boston, MA: Allyn & Bacon. 109–123.

Linden I. 1972. 'Mwali' and the Luba origins of the Chewa: Some tentative suggestions. *The Society of Malawi Journal.* 25 (1): 1–13.

Lindgren NE & Schoffeleers JM. 1978. *Rock art and Nyau Symbolism in Malawi.* (Department of Antiquities publication no 18). Limbe, Malawi: Montfort Press.

Lineham S. 1972. Climate 4: rainfall. In *Malawi in Maps.* S Agnew & M Stubbs (eds). London: University of London Press: 32–33.

Livingstone D & Livingstone C. 1866. *Narrative of an Expedition to the Zambesi and its Tributaries: And of the Discovery of the Lakes Shirwa and Nyassa, 1858-1864.* New York: Harper & Brothers.

Macdonald D. 1882. *Africana; or, The Heart of Heathen Africa.* London: Simpkin Marshall & Co.

MacDonald K. 2017. Field Survey in the Sahel: an informal guide. In *Field Manual for African Archaeology.* AL Smith, E Cornelissen, OP Gosselain & S MacEachern (eds). Tervuren: Royal Museum for Central Africa: 65–68.

Maggs T. 1980. Mzonjani and the beginning of the Iron Age in Natal. *Annals of the Natal Museum.* 24: 71–96.

Maggs T. 1984 Ndondondwane: A preliminary report on an Early Iron Age site on the lower Tugela River. *Annals of the Natal Museum.* 26 (1): 71–93.

Maggs T & Ward V. 1980. Driel Shelter: rescue at a Late Stone Age site on the Tugela River. *Annals of the Natal Museum.* 24 (1): 35–70.

Malawi Department of Antiquities Report, 2013. Report on cultural heritage impact assessment along the new railway line from Moatize, Mozambique to Nkaya, Malawi. Malawi Department of Antiquities, Lilongwe. (Unpublished).

Malawi Department of Antiquities oral traditions collection, 1973–1974. Malawi Department of Antiquities, Lilongwe. (Unpublished).

Mandala EC. 2005. *The end of chidyerano: a history of food and everyday life in Malawi, 1860–2004.* Portsmouth, NH: Heinemann.

Marks SA. 1976. *Large Mammals and a Brave People: Subsistence Hunters in Zambia.* Seattle: University of Washington Press.

Marwick MG. 1963. History and Tradition in East-Central Africa through the Eyes of the Northern Rhodesian Ceŵa. *The Journal of African History.* 4: 375–390.

Marshall F & Hildebrand E. 2002. Cattle before crops: the beginnings of food production in Africa. *Journal of World Prehistory,* 16 (2): 99–143.

Mazel AD. 1986. Mbabane Shelter and eSinhlonhlweni Shelter: the last two thousand years of hunter-gatherer settlement in the central Thukela Basin, Natal, South Africa. *Annals of the Natal Museum.* 27 (2): 389–453.

McCracken J. 2013. *A History of Malawi, 1859–1966.* Woodbridge: James Currey.

McFarren WE. 1986. History in the land of flames: the Maravi states of pre-colonial Malawi. PhD thesis. University of California, Berkeley.

Mgomezulu GGY. 1978. Food production: the beginnings in the Linthipe/Changoni area of Dedza district, Malawi. PhD thesis. University of California, Berkeley.

Mitchell P. 2002. *The Archaeology of Southern Africa.* Cambridge: Cambridge University Press.

Mitchell P. 2017. Cultural heritage management in Africa. In *Field Manual for African Archaeology.* AL Smith, E Cornelissen, OP Gosselain & S MacEachern (eds). Tervuren: Royal Museum for Central Africa: 34–36.

Mitchell P & Whitelaw G. 2005. The archaeology of southernmost Africa from c. 2000 BP to the early 1800s: a review of recent research. *The Journal of African History.* 46 (2): 209–241.

Monuments Act 44 of 1965. 1965. *Laws of Malawi,* Zomba, Malawi: Government Printer.

Monuments and Relics Act, Chapter 29: 01 of 1991. 1991. *Laws of Malawi,* Zomba, Malawi: Government Printer.

Mortelmans G. 1962. Archéologie des Grottes Dimba et Ngovo (Région de Thysville, Bas-Congo). *Annales du Musée Royale de L'afrique centrale.* Sciences Humaines Pré- et Protohistoire. 40(III): 407–426.

Msamba F & Killick D. 1992. Kasungu and Kaluluma oral traditions. (Unpublished).

Musonda F. 1987. The significance of pottery in Zambian Later Stone Age contexts. *African Archaeological Review.* 5: 147–158.

National Statistical Office (NSO). 2018 Malawi population and housing census. www.nsomalawi.mw (accessed 31 May 2019).

Ndanga AJ. 2017. Archaeological exploration in an urban African context: the case of Bangui in the Central African Republic. In *Field Manual for African Archaeology*. AL Smith, E Cornelissen, OP Gosselain & S MacEachern (eds). Tervuren: Royal Museum for Central Africa: 56–59.

Nenquin J. 1959. Dimple-Based Pots from Kasai, Belgian Congo. *Man.* 59: 153–155.

Newitt MDD. 1972. The Early History of the Sultanate of Angoche. *The Journal of African History.* 13 (3): 397–406.

Newitt MDD. 1982. The Early History of the Maravi. *The Journal of African History.* 23: 145–162.

Ntara SJ. 1973. *The History of the Chewa (Mbiri ya Achewa)*. Translated by WS Kamphandira Jere. Wiesbaden: Franz Steiner Verlag GMBH.

Ogundiran A. & Agbaje-Williams B. 2017. Ancient polities: Archaeological survey in a metropolis and its colony. In *Field Manual for African Archaeology*. AL Smith, E Cornelissen, OP Gosselain & S MacEachern (eds). Tervuren: Royal Museum for Central Africa: 69–75.

Omer-Cooper JD. 1969. *The Zulu Aftermath: a Nineteenth-Century Revolution in Bantu Africa.* London: Longmans.

Oslisly R. 1996. The middle Ogooué Valley: cultural changes and palaeoclimatic implications of the last four millennia. In *The Growth of Farming Communities in Africa from the Equator Southwards*. JEG Sutton (ed). Nairobi: The British Institute in Eastern Africa. 324–331.

Oslisly R. 2017. Rescue and preventive archaeology: roads, thermal power stations and quarries. In *Field Manual for African Archaeology*. AL. Smith, E Cornelissen, OP Gosselain & S MacEachern (eds). Tervuren: Royal Museum for Central Africa: 42–44.

Owen RB, Crossley R, Johnson TC, Tweddle D, Kornfield I, Davison S, Eccles DH & Engstrom DE. 1990. Major low levels of Lake Malawi and their implications for speciation rates in cichlid fishes. *Proceedings of the Royal Society.* B 240: 519–553.

Pachai B. 1968. Samuel Josiah Ntara: writer and historian. *The Society of Malawi Journal.* 26 (2): 60–66.

Pachai B. 1972a. History and settlement. In *Malawi in Maps*. S Agnew & M Stubbs (eds). London: University of London Press: 42–43.

Pachai B. 1972b. Ngoni politics and diplomacy in Malawi: 1848–1904. In *The Early History of Malawi*. B Pachai (ed). London: Longman.179–214

Pachai B. 1974. *Malawi: the history of the nation.* London: Longman.

Passmore NI & Carruthers VC. 1979. *South African Frogs.* Johannesburg: University of Witwatersrand Press.

Phillipson DW. 1975. The chronology of the Iron Age in Bantu Africa. *The Journal of African History.* 16: 321–342.

Phillipson DW. 1976. *The Prehistory of Eastern Zambia.* Nairobi: British Institute in Eastern Africa.

Phillipson DW. 1977a. The Spread of the Bantu Language. *Scientific American*. 236 (4): 106–114.

Phillipson DW. 1977b. *The Later Prehistory of Eastern and Southern* Africa. London: Heinemann.

Phillipson DW. 2000. *African archaeology*. Cambridge: Cambridge University Press.

Phiri DD. 1999. *Let us die for Africa: an African perspective on the life and death of John Chilembwe of Nyasaland/Malawi*. Blantyre, Malawi: Central Africana Limited.

Phiri KM. 1975. Chewa history in central Malawi and the use of oral tradition, 1600–1920. PhD thesis. University of Wisconsin, Madison.

Phiri KM. 1977. The Maravi state system and Chewa political development to c. 1840. Proceedings of a teachers' conference. Chancellor College, Zomba. Malawi: 1–24.

Pike JG & Rimmington GT. 1965. *Malawi: A geographical study*. London: Oxford University Press.

Pike JG. 1972. Hydrology. In *Malawi in Maps*. S Agnew & M Stubbs (eds). London: University of London Press: 34–35.

Pikirayi I. 2001. *The Zimbabwe Culture: Origins and Decline of Southern Zambezian States*. Walnut Creek, CA. Altamira Press.

Plug I. 1996. Domestic animals during the Early Iron Age in southern Africa. In *Aspects of African Archaeology: Proceedings of the 10th congress of the Pan-African Association for Prehistory and Related Studies*. G Pwiti & R Soper (eds). Harare: University of Zimbabwe Publications: 515–520.

Plug I & Voigt EA. 1985. Archaeozoological studies of Iron Age communities in southern Africa. *Advances in World Archaeology*. 4: 189–238.

Plug I. Soper R. & Chirawu S. 1997. Pits, tunnels and cattle in Nyanga, Zimbabwe: new light on an old problem. *The South African Archaeological Bulletin* 52: 89–94.

Plug I & Badenhorst S. 2001. The distribution of macromammals in southern Africa over the past 30000 years as reflected in animal remains from archaeological sites. In *Transvaal Museum Monograph no 12*. Pretoria: Transvaal Museum.

Plug I & Badenhorst S. 2002. Appendix B: Bones from Muozi midden trench II. In *Nyanga. Ancient Fields, Settlements and Agricultural History in Zimbabwe*. R Soper (ed). London: British Institute in East Africa: 242–248.

Porter A. 1998. Review of 'Africa for the African': The Life of Joseph Booth by Harry Langworth. *The Journal of African History*. 39 (3): 497–498.

Punt WHJ. 1975. *The first Europeans in the Kruger National Park*. Pretoria: Simon van der Stel Foundation.

Quin PJ. 1959. *Foods and feeding habits of the Pedi*. Johannesburg: University of Witwatersrand Press.

Rangeley WHJ. 1952. Two Nyasaland rain shrines. *The Nyasaland Journal*. 5 (2): 31–50.

Rangeley WHJ. 1954. Bocarro's journey. *The Nyasaland Journal*. 7 (2): 15–23.

Rangeley WHJ. 1963. The earliest inhabitants of Nyasaland. *The Nyasaland Journal*. 16 (2): 35–42.

Rathje WL, Hughes WW, Wilson DC, Tani MK, Archer GH, Hunt RG & Jones TW. 1992. The archaeology of contemporary landfills. *American Antiquity*. 57 (3): 437–447.

Rathje WL & Murphy C. 1992. *Rubbish! The Archaeology of garbage.* Tucson, AZ: University of Arizona Press.

Reynolds B. 1968. *The Material Culture of the Peoples of the Gwembe Valley.* Manchester: Manchester University Press.

Renfrew C & Bahn P. 2004. *Archaeology: Theories, Methods, and Practice.* London: Thames & Hudson.

Roach J. nd. Emperor Qin's tomb. http://www.nationalgeographic.com/archaeology-and-history/archaeology/emperor-qin/ *National Geographic* (accessed 13 October 2017).

Robbins LH. 1985. The Manyana rockpaintings site. *Botswana notes and records* 17: 1–14.

Robinson KR. 1961a. An early Iron Age site from the Chibi District, Southern Rhodesia. *The South African Archaeological Bulletin.* 16 (63): 75–102.

Robinson KR. 1961b. Zimbabwe pottery. *Occasional Papers of the National Museums of Southern Rhodesia.* 3A: 159–92.

Robinson KR. 1963. Further excavations in the Iron Age deposits at the Tunnel site, Gokomere Hill, Southern Rhodesia. *The South African Archaeological Bulletin* 18: 155–171.

Robinson KR. 1966a. A preliminary report on the recent archaeology of Ngonde, northern Malawi. *The Journal of African History.* 7: 169–188.

Robinson KR. 1966b. Bambata ware: its position in the Rhodesian Iron Age in the light of recent evidence. *The South African Archaeological Bulletin.* 21 (82): 81–85.

Robinson KR. & Sandelowsky B. 1968. The Iron Age of northern Malawi: recent work. *Azania: Archaeological Research in Africa.* 3: 107–146.

Robinson KR. 1970. *The Iron Age of the southern lake area of Malawi.* (Department of Antiquities publication no 8). Zomba, Malawi: Government Press.

Robinson KR. 1973. *The Iron Age of the upper and lower Shire Malawi.* (Department of Antiquities publication no 13). Zomba, Malawi: Government Press.

Robinson KR. 1975. *Iron Age sites in the Dedza district of Malawi.* (Department of Antiquities publication no 16). Zomba, Malawi: Government Press.

Robinson KR. 1977. *Iron Age occupation north and east of the Mulanje plateau, Malawi.* (Department of Antiquities publication no 17). Limbe, Malawi: Montfort Press.

Robinson KR. 1979. *The Nkhotakota lakeshore and marginal areas, Malawi: an archaeological reconnaissance.* (Department of Antiquities publication no 19). Limbe, Malawi: Montfort Press.

Robinson KR. 1982. *Iron Age of northern Malawi: an archaeological reconnaissance.* (Department of Antiquities publication no 20). Limbe, Malawi: Montfort Press.

Roscoe J. 1966. *The Northern Bantu: An Account of some Central African tribes of the Uganda Protectorate.* London: Frank Cass & Co.

Ross AC. 1972. Scottish missionary concern 1874–1914: A golden era? *The Scottish Historical Review.* 60: 52–72.

Rowley H. 1969. *The Story of the Universities' mission to Central Africa; from its commencement under Bishop Mackenzie, to its withdrawal from the Zambesi.* New York: Negro Universities Press.

Ruspoli M. 1987. *The cave of Lascaux: the final photographs.* New York: Harry N. Abrams.

Russell T, Silva F & Steele J. 2014. Modelling the spread of farming in the Bantu-speaking regions of Africa: an archaeology-based phylogeography. *PLoS One.* 9(1): 1–9.

Sandelowsky BH. 1972. Later stone age lithic assemblages from Malawi and their technologies. PhD thesis. University of California, Berkeley.

Sandrock O, Dauphin Y, Kullmer O, Abel R, Schrenk F & Denys C. 1999. Malema: Preliminary taphonomic analysis of an African hominid locality. *Comptes Rendus de l' Académie des Sciences Paris.* 328(2):133–139.

Schneider HK. 1981. *The Africans: An Ethnological Account.* Upper Saddle River, New Jersey: Prentice Hall.

Schoenbrun D. 2017. Oral tradition. In *Field Manual for African Archaeology.* AL Smith, E Cornelissen, OP Gosselain & S MacEachern (eds). Tervuren: Royal Museum for Central Africa: 253–256.

Schoffeleers JM. 1972. The meaning and use of the name Malawi in oral traditions and precolonial documents. In *The Early History of Malawi.* B Pachai (ed). London: Longman: 92–114.

Schoffeleers JM. 1973. Towards the identification of a proto-Chewa culture: a preliminary contribution. *Journal of Social Science.* 2: 47–60.

Schoffeleers JM. 1976. The Nyau societies: our present understanding. *The Society of Malawi Journal.* 29 (1): 59–68.

Schoffeleers, JM. 1978. Nyau symbols in rock paintings. In *Rock Art and Nyau Symbolism in Malawi.* NE Lindgren & JM. Schoffeleers. (Department of Antiquities publication no 18) Limbe, Malawi: Montfort Press.

Schoffeleers JM. 1979. The Chisumphi and Mbona cults in Malawi: a comparative history. In *Guardians of the Land.* JM Schoffeleers (ed). Gwelo, Zimbabwe, Mambo Press: 147–186.

Schoffeleers JM. 1987. The Zimba and the Lundu state in the late sixteenth and early seventeenth centuries. *The Journal of African History.* 28: 337.

Schoffeleers JM. 1992. *River of Blood: The Genesis of a Martyr Cult in Southern Malawi, c. AD 1600.* Madison, WI: University of Wisconsin Press.

Schofield JF. 1938. A preliminary study of the prehistoric beads of the northern Transvaal and Natal. *Transactions of the Royal Society of South Africa.* 26: 341–371.

Schofield JF. 1958. Beads: Southern African beads and their relation to the beads of Inyanga. In *Inyanga: Prehistoric Settlements in Southern Rhodesia.* R Summers, (ed). Cambridge: Cambridge University Press: 180–229.

Schrenk F, Bromage TG, Betzler CG, Ring, U & Juwayeyi YM. 1993. Oldest Homo and Pliocene biogeography of the Malawi Rift. *Nature.* 365: 833–836.

Shroder JF. 1972. Geological history of rocks of post-basement complex, rift-faulting, and mineral occurrences. In *Malawi in Maps.* S Agnew & M Stubbs (eds). London: University of London Press: 22–23.

Scott K, Juwayeyi YM & Plug I. 2009. The faunal remains from Mankhamba, a Late Iron Age site of the Maravi in central Malawi. *Annals of the Transvaal Museum.* 46: 45–61.

Shepperson G & Price T. 1958. *Independent African: John Chilembwe and the origins, setting and significance of the Nyasaland native rising of 1915*. Edinburgh: Edinburgh University Press.

Shillington K. 1995. *History of Africa*. New York: St. Martin's Press.

Sinclair PJJ, Ekblom A & Wood M. 2012. Chibuene, understanding the dynamics between social complexity, long distance trade and state formation in southern Africa in the late first millennium AD. *Antiquity* 86: 723–737.

Skinner JD & Chimimba CT. 2005. *The Mammals of the Southern African Sub-region*. Cambridge: Cambridge University Press.

Skoglund P, Thompson JC, Prendergast ME, Mittnik A, Sirak K, Hajdinjak M, Salie T, Rohland, N et al. 2017. Reconstructing prehistoric African population structure. *Cell*. 171: 59–71.

Smith AB. 1992. *Pastoralism in Africa: origins and development ecology*. Johannesburg: Witwatersrand University Press.

Smith BW. 1995. Rock art in south-central Africa. A study based on the pictographs of Dedza district, Malawi and Kasama district, Zambia. PhD thesis. University of Cambridge.

Smith BW. 2001. Forbidden images: Rock paintings and the Nyau secret society of Central Malaŵi and Eastern Zambia. *African Archaeological Review*. 18 (4): 187–212.

Smith AL. 2017a. Introduction: Finding and describing archaeological sites. In *Field Manual for African Archaeology*. A Livingstone-Smith, E Cornelissen, OP Gosselain & S MacEachern (eds). Tervuren: Royal Museum for Central Africa: 54–55.

Smith AL. 2017b. Introduction: How to protect archaeological sites. In *Field Manual for African Archaeology*. A Livingstone-Smith, E Cornelissen, OP Gosselain & S MacEachern (eds). Tervuren: Royal Museum for Central Africa: 102–103.

Smith AL & de Francquen C. 2017. Pottery analysis. In *Field Manual for African Archaeology*. AL Smith, E Cornelissen, OP Gosselain & S MacEachern (eds). Tervuren: Royal Museum for Central Africa: 173–179.

Smithers RHN. 1966. *The Mammals of Rhodesia, Zambia and Malawi*. London: Collins.

Soapstone. nd. http://geology.com/rocks/soapstone.shtml (accessed 30 October 2017).

Soka LD. 1982. *Mbiri ya Alomwe*. London: Macmillan Education Limited.

Speed E. 1970. Specialist's report on the Nkope faunal remains. In *The Iron Age of the Southern Lake Area of Malawi*. KR Robinson. (Department of Antiquities publication no 8). Zomba, Malawi: Government Press: 104–115.

Stobbs AR & Young A. 1972. Natural regions. In *Malawi in Maps*. S Agnew & M Stubbs (eds). London: London University Press: 40–42.

Stubbs M. 1972a. Post and telecommunication services, 1969. In *Malawi in Maps*. S Agnew & M Stubbs (eds). London: University of London Press: 104–105.

Stubbs, M.1972b. Distribution of population, 1966. In *Malawi in Maps*. S Agnew & M Stubbs (eds). London: University of London Press.

Stuiver M & Suess H. 1966. On the relationship between radiocarbon dates and true sample ages. *Radiocarbon*. 8(1): 534-540.

Summers R. 1961. The southern Rhodesian Iron Age. *The Journal of African History*. 11:1–13.

Summers R. 1963. *Zimbabwe: A Rhodesian Mystery*. Johannesburg: Nelson.

Sutton MQ & Yohe RM II. 2003. *Archaeology: The Science of the Human Past*. Boston: Allyn & Bacon.

Taylor RE. 1985. The beginnings of radiocarbon dating in American antiquity. *American Antiquity*. 50 (2): 309–325.

Taylor RE. 1997. Radiocarbon dating. In *Chronometric Dating in Archaeology*. RE. Taylor & MJ. Aitken (eds). New York: Plenum Press: 65–96.

Theal GM. 1964. *Records of South-Eastern Africa*. Vol. 3. Cape Town: Struik.

Thomas DH & Kelly RL. 2006. *Archaeology*. Belmont, CA. Thomson Wadsworth.

Torrance JD. 1972. Climate 2: Temperature. In *Malawi in Maps*. S Agnew & M Stubbs (eds). London: University of London Press: 28–29.

Turnbull CM. 1961. *The Forest People*. New York: Simon & Schuster.

Van Binsbergen WMJ. 2011. In memoriam: Matthew Schoffeleers (1928–2011). *Journal of Religion in Africa*. 41 (4): 455–463.

Van der Merwe NJ & Avery DH. 1987. Science and magic in African technology: traditional iron smelting in Malawi. *Africa*. 57 (02): 143–172.

Van der Sleen WGN. 1956. Trade wind beads. *Man*. 56: 27–29.

Van der Sleen WGN. 1958. Ancient glass beads with special reference to the beads of east and central Africa and the Indian Ocean. *The Journal of the Royal Anthropological Institute of Great Britain and Ireland*. 88 (2): 203–216.

Vansina J. 1984. Western Bantu expansion. *The Journal of African History*. 25: 129–146.

Vansina J. 1985. *Oral Tradition as History*. Madison: University of Wisconsin Press.

Vansina J. 1989. Deep-down time: political tradition in central Africa. *History in Africa*. 16: 341–362.

Vansina J. 1990. *Paths in the Rainforests: Toward a History of Political Tradition in Equatorial Africa*. Madison, Wisconsin: University of Wisconsin Press.

Vansina J. 1995. New linguistic evidence and 'the Bantu Expansion'. *The Journal of African History*. 36 (2): 173–195.

Vogelsang R. 2017. The excavation of Stone Age sites. In *Field Manual for African Archaeology*. A Livingstone-Smith, E Cornelissen, OP Gosselain & S MacEachern (eds). Tervuren: Royal Museum for Central Africa: 104–108.

Voigt E. 1973. Faunal remains from the Iron Age sites of Matope, Namichimba and Chikumba, southern Malawi. In *The Iron Age of the Upper and Lower Shire, Malawi*. KR. Robinson. (Department of Antiquities publication no 13.) Zomba, Malawi: Government Press: 135–167.

Walker NJ. 1983. The significance of an early date for pottery and sheep in Zimbabwe. *The South African Archaeological Bulletin*. 38: 88–92.

Walker NJ. 1994. The Late Stone Age of Botswana: some recent excavations. *Botswana notes and records*. 26: 1–36.

Waller H. 1970. *The Last Journals of Livingstone in Central Africa*. Westport, Connecticut: Greenwood Press.

Wenner DB & Van der Merwe NJ. 1987. Mining for the lowest grade ore: traditional iron production in northern Malawi. *Geoarchaeology: an International Journal.* 2(3): 199–216.

Werner A. 1969. *Natives of British Central Africa.* New York: Negro Universities Press.

White L. 1990. *Magomero: Portrait of an African Village.* Cambridge: Cambridge University Press.

Williamson J. 1975. *Useful Plants of Malawi.* Limbe, Malawi: University of Malawi.

Wilmsen EN, Killick D, Rosenstein DD, Thebe PC, & Denbow JR. 2009. The social geography of pottery in Botswana as reconstructed by optical petrography. *Journal of African Archaeology.* 7(1): 3–39.

Wood M. 2000. Making connections: relationships between international trade and glass beads from the Shashe-Limpopo area. In *African Naissance: The Limpopo Valley 1000 years ago.* M Leslie & T Maggs (eds). Cape Town: South African Archaeological Society, Goodwin series. 78–90.

Wood M. 2009a. Report on Mankhamba glass beads. Unpublished.

Wood M. 2009b. The glass beads from Hlamba Mlonga, Zimbabwe: classification, context and interpretation. *Journal of African Archaeology.* 7 (2): 219–238.

Wotzka H. 2017. Village sites. In *Field Manual for African Archaeology.* A Livingstone-Smith, E Cornelissen, OP Gosselain & S MacEachern (eds). Tervuren: Royal Museum for Central Africa: 109–115.

Young TC. 1970. *Notes on the History of the Tumbuka-Kamanga Peoples.* London: Frank Cass.

Index

Entries in *italics* refer to diagrams, tables or plates.

CPSIA information can be obtained
at www.ICGtesting.com
Printed in the USA
BVHW010605020921
615736BV00003B/4